CAMBRIDGE

Engaging Language Learners in Contemporary Classrooms

Sarah Mercer
Zoltán Dörnyei

CAMBRIDGE
UNIVERSITY PRESS & ASSESSMENT

Shaftesbury Road, Cambridge CB2 8EA, United Kingdom

One Liberty Plaza, 20th Floor, New York, NY 10006, USA

477 Williamstown Road, Port Melbourne, VIC 3207, Australia

314–321, 3rd Floor, Plot 3, Splendor Forum, Jasola District Centre, New Delhi – 110025, India

103 Penang Road, #05–06/07, Visioncrest Commercial, Singapore 238467

Cambridge University Press & Assessment is a department of the University of Cambridge.

We share the University's mission to contribute to society through the pursuit of education, learning and research at the highest international levels of excellence.

www.cambridge.org
Information on this title: www.cambridge.org/9781108445924

First published 2020

20 19 18 17 16 15 14 13 12 11 10 9 8 7 6

Printed in Great Britain by Ashford Colour Ltd.

A catalogue record for this publication is available from the British Library

ISBN 978-1-108-44592-4 Paperback
ISBN 978-1-108-44596-2 Apple iBook
ISBN 978-1-108-44593-1 ebooks.com eBook
ISBN 978-1-108-44594-8 Google eBook
ISBN 978-1-108-44595-5 Kindle eBook

Contents

Acknowledgements

The authors and publishers acknowledge the following sources of copyright material and are grateful for the permissions granted. While every effort has been made, it has not always been possible to identify the sources of all the material used, or to trace all copyright holders. If any omissions are brought to our notice, we will be happy to include the appropriate acknowledgements on reprinting and in the next update to the digital edition, as applicable.

Photo:

Cover photography by Klaus Vedfelt/DigitalVision/Getty Images.

Text:

John Wiley & Sons Inc. for the text on p. 6 from *Student Engagement Techniques: A Handbook for College Faculty* by Elizabeth F. Barkley. Copyright © 2010 John Wiley & Sons Inc. Reproduced with permission of Copyright Clearance Center on behalf of John Wiley & Sons Inc.; Shelley Hill for the text on pp. 16–17. Copyright © Shelley Hill. Reproduced with kind permission; Ofsted for the text on p. 25 from 'Inspection report: Redhill Academy', https://reports.ofsted.gov.uk/provider/23/136361. Copyright © 2013 Crown Copyright and the Open Government Licence v3.0; The Redhill Academy for the text on pp. 25–26 from 'The Redhill Academy Pledge System'. Copyright © The Redhill Academy. Reproduced with kind permission; Crown House Publishing Limited for the text on p. 41 from *The Perfect Teacher Coach* by Jackie Beere and Terri Broughton. Copyright © 2013 Independent Thinking Press. Reproduced with kind permission of Crown House Publishing Limited on behalf of Independent Thinking Press; Prufrock Press for the text on p. 45 from *Mindsets in the Classroom: Building a Growth Mindset Learning Community (Updated ed.)* by M. C. Ricci. Copyright © 2017 Prufrock Press. Reproduced with kind permission; Oxford University Press for the text on p. 71 from *Classroom Dynamics* by Jill Hadfield. Copyright © 1992 Oxford University Press. Reproduced with permission; Roots of Empathy for the text on p. 79 from *Roots of Empathy: Changing the World Child by Child* by Mary Gordon. Copyright © 2009 Roots of Empathy. Reproduced with kind permission; John Wiley & Sons Inc. for the text on p. 100 from *Engaging Students: The Next Level of Working on the Work* by Phillip C. Schlechty. Copyright © 2011 John Wiley & Sons Inc. Reproduced with permission of Copyright Clearance Center on behalf of John Wiley & Sons Inc.; Taylor & Francis Group LLC Books for the text on p. 153–154 from *Motivational Currents in Language Learning: Frameworks for Focused Interventions* by Zoltán Dörnyei, Alastair Henry, and Christine Muir. Copyright © 2016 Taylor & Francis Group LLC Books. Reproduced with permission of Copyright Clearance Center on behalf of Taylor & Francis Group LLC Books; Getting Smart for the text on p 154–155 from *A Framework for High Quality Project Based Learning.* Copyright © Getting Smart. Reproduced with kind permission.

Thanks

We are both incredibly grateful to the wonderful team at Cambridge University Press who have supported the development of this book – a very special thanks goes to Karen Momber, Jo Timerick and Graham Skerritt. We also greatly appreciate the constructive and useful feedback given by the anonymous reviewers at all stages of the project. Our conversations and experiences with colleagues and learners from across the globe fill these pages directly and indirectly and we are grateful for the exchange and learning that characterises our communities.

Foreword

In our work with language teachers over the past years, as well as in our own teaching, we noticed that familiar notions of motivation were not meeting current teacher needs. While everyone recognised its continued importance for learning, there was also a sense that motivation alone was not enough to get learners on board and to ensure on-task engagement in the face of all the distractions students are exposed to in their twenty-first-century lives. We could sense a need for something 'extra'. And so the seed for this book was sown and our quest for this 'extra' began: trying to understand how best to engage learners in contemporary classrooms by building on existing motivational principles.

This meant taking a view of the big picture and bringing together insights from a range of fields and disciplines. As such, the journey of this book has sent us on a foray into a wide range of literatures and it has been a process of growth as we have been prompted to look at language learning and engagement from a diverse range of perspectives. We hope that we have been able to distil this broad base of literature into a manageable, relevant and accessible format. In particular, it has caused us to rethink our own practice in two fundamental ways: (a) recognising the teacher as a designer of learning experiences, and (b) highlighting the importance of putting learners and their learning at the centre of the design process.

The first shift in our thinking was to conceptualise teachers as *instructional designers*. This notion is not new. Gagné, Briggs and Wager (1974) already thought about principles that inform how we design learning experiences based on insights from psychology, and so began a whole movement concerned with instructional design. In light of technological developments, educators are currently revisiting this notion in the e-learning context; however, design principles are relevant in whatever context we teach and via whatever mode of learning we choose to work with learners. This being the case, in this book we do not dwell explicitly on the potential of technology for engagement, although it does doubtless fulfil many of the principles and actions we propose. Rather, we will suggest universal principles and actions to engage learners, applying diverse tools and resources whether digital or not.

The second and related shift in our thinking has been to alter our notion of *learner-centred teaching*. Learner-centredness has always been at the heart of communicative language teaching, but instead of placing learners at the centre of our *teaching*, we now propose to place them at the centre of their own *learning processes*. This means creating meaningful opportunities for learners to shape the way they learn, not just at home on their own but also in the classroom. Some may feel this is a mere matter of semantics, but for us it meant a small but critical shift of emphasis.

We have learnt a great deal in working on this book and we feel that it has made us more thoughtful and, hopefully, more effective educators. However, working on this book has also underlined the fact that our knowledge and thinking about learning is never finished. In fact, we strongly believe that it is this evolving understanding of teaching and learning that can give spice and joy to our profession. Our hope is that this book can become a valuable aid in your quest to maximise your students' language learning and to make their learning experiences as enjoyable, rewarding and effective as possible.

Introduction

Imagine your ideal language class. What would the students be like? How would they behave? We – Sarah and Zoltán – asked ourselves these same questions. We agreed that we would like our 'dream' classroom to be buzzing with activity; we would wish for students to be actively involved in language-related tasks, clearly focused on what they are doing, and finding their participation emotionally satisfying and academically beneficial. Such a state of active involvement has been described in educational psychology under the rubric of 'student engagement', described in the *Handbook of Research on Student Engagement* as 'effortful learning through interaction with the teacher and the classroom learning opportunities' (Christenson, Reschly and Wylie 2012: vi). Indeed, in a recent special issue of the journal *Educational Psychologist* dedicated to this subject, engagement was characterised as 'the holy grail of learning' (Sinatra, Heddy and Lombardi 2015: 1).

> *Engagement is one of the hottest research topics in the field of educational psychology. Research shows that multifarious benefits occur when students are engaged in their own learning, including increased motivation and achievement.*
>
> (Sinatra et al. 2015: 1)

Sometimes the dream scenario of having an entire class of engaged learners who pursue learning proactively, with focus and passion, does come true, making these periods some of the most memorable and fulfilling times in a teacher's career. At other times, however, classroom reality turns out to be less rosy, with students remaining distant, distracted and disengaged. Rather worryingly, Pekrun, Goetz, Daniels, Stupnisky and Perry (2010) report that boredom is one of the most frequently experienced emotions by pupils in schools. Shernoff, Csikszentmihalyi, Schneider and Shernoff (2003: 159) explain that:

> *research has found high rates of boredom, alienation, and disconnection with schooling. Studies have characterized high school students, in particular, as bored, staring out classroom windows, counting the seconds for the bell to ring, and pervasively disengaged from the learning process.*

Such less-than-ideal states of student involvement are alarmingly common. Shernoff et al. (2003), for example, report that in one study, 50% of students evaluated their classes as boring, and this estimate has been confirmed by a recent Gallup (2015) survey in the US, involving over 900,000 public school students from over 3,300 schools. The results revealed that only half of the students were engaged in school, while 29% of them were not engaged and 21% were actively disengaged. Furthermore, when the data was broken down to specific grades, a consistent trend of decline emerged: while in the fifth grade (ages 10–11) only about a quarter of the students reported being disengaged, this proportion increased to two-thirds by Grade 11 (ages 16–17).

What's happening? Why are so many schools failing to engage such a high percentage of their learners? Why are some learners not engaged, while some of their classmates are? How can the situation be improved to ensure more, if not all, learners are engaged? What can we as teachers do to strive towards realising our ideal language classroom? Finding answers to these questions has been the main motivation for us behind writing this book. In order to set the scene, this introduction will address four main issues: (a) What is 'engagement' and what is it not? (b) Why is student engagement particularly important in language classes? (c) What are the benefits of focussing on engagement rather than other related concepts such as motivation or self-regulation? (d) And, finally, what is this book intended to offer and how?

What is 'Student Engagement'?

The most telling answer to the question of what 'student engagement' is has probably been given by Barkley (2010: 4) who said, 'Well, the answer is that it means different things to different people.' This variability is partly caused by the fact that the word *engage* and its derivatives (e.g. *engagement*, *engaging*) are used both in everyday language and as technical terms, which means there are a wide range of acceptable meanings. The essence of the notion is seemingly straightforward: it concerns *active participation* and *involvement* in certain behaviours – in the case of student engagement, in school-related activities and academic tasks.

What complicates things is the fact that this student involvement has both external and internal dimensions, with the former concerning the amount of actual learning behaviours a student displays through their observable actions, and the latter relating to internal aspects, such as a learner's cognitive and emotional engagement. In the ideal scenario, the two dimensions go hand in hand. However, it is well known that it is possible for someone to merely 'go through the motions', that is, to exhibit seemingly active participation in a task without involving themselves at the level of thought or affect. Indeed, some students can become very good at merely keeping up a pretence, complying with expected norms without engaging in active learning in a meaningful manner. In such 'shallow' engagement, the external dimension is not augmented by the internal dimension, and this imbalance considerably reduces the learning potential of the activity.

The realisation that engagement can have different dimensions that do not always align with each other has led scholars to define the notion as a multifaceted concept. A number of different taxonomies have been proposed over the past two decades, typically distinguishing between behavioural, cognitive, affective and social aspects (see e.g. Finn and Zimmer 2012). However, while it is clear that there are different levels and dimensions of engagement, we have chosen to agree with Skinner, Furrer, Marchand and Kindermann (2008: 778) in that the 'core construct, most prototypical of engagement, is behavioural participation in the classroom'. This active, participatory aspect of the concept is the most attractive characteristic for us, especially for the language classroom, and, in our view, this is indeed one of the features that commends considering this construct over other related concepts such as motivation and self-regulation (which refers to learners' managing and directing their thoughts, feelings and actions around learning). Thus, in this book, we perceive 'engagement' to be always associated with *action*, ideally combined with internal dimensions of cognitive and affective involvement.

> *Behavioural engagement draws on the idea of participation; it includes involvement in academic and social or extracurricular activities and is considered crucial for achieving positive academic outcomes and preventing dropping out.*
>
> (Fredricks, Blumenfeld and Paris 2004: 60)

Why is Student Engagement Particularly Important in Language Classes?

It is easy to understand why the notion of engagement has made such an impact in educational psychology over the past two decades: it promises meaningful learning accompanied by active participation in classrooms and school life. The emphasis on active task engagement is equally important in the second language (L2) classroom – in fact, one might argue that in language education the significance of student involvement is even greater than in pursuing other subject matters. This is because the automatisation of L2 skills requires an extended practice period, not unlike learner drivers having to go through a lot of hands-on practice on the road in order to reach mastery.

Most language teaching professionals would agree that mastering communicative language skills simply will not take place without participating in extensive communicative practice, and this requires the learners' willing engagement: students have to 'stick their necks out' and actively take part in what is a rather face-threatening and stressful activity (i.e. communicating in a foreign language with limited language resources). Accordingly, one of the key principles of communicative language teaching – and of task-based language learning in particular – has been the 'learning-through-doing' tenet, which foregrounds the learners' participatory experience in meaningful L2 interaction within communicative tasks. No method of language teaching can deliver results without ensuring that students are actively engaged in the process.

The term *engagement* is appearing with increasing frequency in the literature on Second Language Acquisition (SLA) and language teaching methodology. In her article on 'Engagement with language', Svalberg (2009) offered the first systematic discussion of the concept in our field. However, as the title of her paper indicates, she adopted a language awareness perspective (i.e., engaging with the 'language'), whereas the current conceptualisation concerns the motivational dimension (i.e., engaging with 'language learning'). In her recent overview, Svalberg (2018) reaffirms her use of the term as 'Engagement with Language' and acknowledges how this differs from the meaning adopted by us in this book. However, engagement with learning is also gradually gaining increased scholarly attention within SLA (e.g. Philp and Duchesne 2016; Quint Oga-Baldwin and Nakata 2017; Stroud 2017; Snyder and Alperer-Tatli 2007).

> *Saying 'I taught students something, they just didn't learn it' is akin to saying 'I sold them the car, they just didn't buy it.'*
> (Barkley 2010: 16)

What are the Benefits of Focusing on Engagement in Contemporary L2 Classrooms?

Most teachers would agree on the significance of engagement. However, is this the best thing to focus on when trying to improve instructional practices in the language classroom? After all, teaching methodologists and educational psychologists have been successfully examining a range of other factors related to classroom performance and student achievement; for example, in our own work, we have focused on issues such as motivation, metacognition, self-regulation, self-concept, learner beliefs, mindsets and group dynamics amongst others (e.g. Dörnyei 2009; Dörnyei and Ryan 2015; Mercer 2011; Mercer, Ryan and Williams 2012; Williams, Mercer and Ryan 2015), and we hope that these efforts have generated useful insights for scholars and practitioners.

Discussions of engagement, on the other hand, have been largely absent from the literature of L2 learning and teaching. This is not because language teachers do not want to see active and involved students in their classes; in fact, as we have argued above, student involvement is arguably even more important for the purpose of effective communicative language teaching than for many other subject matters. Instead, the reason behind this neglect has more to do with the fact that most language specialists focusing on the psychological dimension of instructed SLA have traditionally turned to another term, *motivation*, when discussing the students' overall academic commitment and their attitudes towards the process and the contexts of language learning.

The study of L2 motivation has a history of five decades, producing considerable theoretical and practical insights (see e.g. Dörnyei and Ushioda 2011). Because it has been a highly fruitful direction in explaining student success and failure, motivation research has become a success story in applied linguistics (see e.g. Boo, Dörnyei and Ryan 2015). As a result, one could almost say that the high level of interest in motivation has 'stolen the show' and diverted attention away from engagement. In addition, there has also been a great deal of work in SLA on certain cognitive and behavioural factors that are also connected to 'engagement' in psychology – most notably learning strategies and self-regulation (e.g. Cohen 2011; Cohen and Macaro 2007; Griffiths 2013; Oxford 2011). In this way, the field of SLA has already included strong and constructive lines of inquiry to examine student performance. This, then, begs the question of why we propose in this book to digress from these established avenues and open up yet another pathway, this time centred around *engagement*. What are the specific benefits of focusing on engagement, and in what way does this line of thinking promise to be more useful than other factors examined in the past?

Our answer to these questions concerns three key features of engagement: its inherently *active, holistic* and *practical* nature. We would like to propose that: (a) the term's emphasis on active involvement suits well the changing nature of contemporary classrooms; (b) the term is fully compatible with recent calls in the field of SLA for a more dynamic and holistic consideration of the multiple factors that contribute to language learning success; and (c) the term suggests an intuitively appealing, teacher-friendly and practical approach to involving students in their learning. Let us look at these three points in a bit more detail.

Engagement Includes Active Involvement That Suits Contemporary Classrooms

The notion of 'engagement' offers a crucial advantage over motivation and other relevant learner characteristics, one we believe is critical for effective teaching practice in the fast-paced reality of the twenty-first century: its direct link to concrete classroom behaviours. Most learner characteristics are not manifest directly in the students' actions, but only *indirectly*; they only indicate a student's *potential* for successful learning, rather than how this potential is actually realised. Let us consider motivation, which is the concept most closely related to engagement; it is clear that although a motivated student is likely to do well at school, this cannot be taken for granted, because various distractions can cancel out, or put on hold, even relatively strong motivational commitments. In today's globalised, digital age, young people are continuously bombarded with information and communications through multiple channels, all intended to captivate their attention, and the pace of social life has been intensified by social media in an unprecedented manner. Consequently, there are simply too many competing influences on a student's mind at any time, and this creates a whole new situation for educators and psychologists to consider.

> *Teachers in institutions across the country tell me that teaching today can be tough. The "twitchspeed" pace and multi-layered delivery of modern media can make a lecture feel incredibly slow and boring ... Globalization and open door access have filled our classrooms with learners reflecting such a dizzying array of backgrounds and academic preparedness that teachers are often hard-pressed to find a collective starting point or the commonalities that create a sense of community. ... For many of us teaching today, competing for the attention of our students and engaging them in meaningful learning is a profound and ongoing challenge.*
>
> (Barkley 2010: xi-xii)

It appears, therefore, that in the changing educational and social landscape of the contemporary classroom, it may not be enough to merely create a facilitative learning environment for students to take advantage of (as has traditionally been recommended); we need to also ensure that the students' positive disposition is *realised in action,* without being hijacked by the plethora of other pressing and ever-salient distractions. To be sure, motivation is undoubtedly necessary for 'preparing the deal', but engagement is indispensable for *sealing the deal.* As Jang, Reeve and Deci (2010: 588) conclude, 'In classroom settings, engagement is particularly important because it functions as a behavioural pathway through which students' motivational processes contribute to their subsequent learning and development, including the skills they develop and the grades they make.'

On the basis of these considerations, we propose that the main benefit of exploring the notion of engagement over motivation is that it allows us to address both the motive and its activation *together*, in a *unified* concept: when students are engaged, they are inevitably fuelled by some motivation that gives direction to their action, but the fact that they are engaged also means that this motivational drive has succeeded in cutting through the surrounding multitude of distractions, temptations and alternatives. One could almost say that focusing on engagement is like killing two birds with one stone: by engaging students we motivate them *and* ensure that their motivation is realised.

Engagement Suits a Holistic Consideration of Factors Contributing to Successful Language Learning

The integrative nature of the notion of 'engagement' described above offers a second, and perhaps somewhat unexpected, bonus: it makes the concept compatible with the recent focus in the field of SLA on complex dynamic systems. A complex dynamic system is a system which comprises multiple components which all interact together. Such a system has emergent characteristics, which means that the characteristics of the whole system are more than merely the sum of its component parts. In other words, the system as a whole develops its own unique characteristics through the interaction of the component parts.

L2 scholars and teachers have long known that language learning success requires the combined and interactive operation of a number of different elements and conditions that are relevant to specific learning situations. Over the past two decades, there has been a paradigm shift in several areas of applied linguistics towards adopting the principles of complex dynamic systems theory in order to better account for such a dynamic and holistic perspective (see e.g. Larsen-Freeman 2012; Verspoor, de Bot and Lowie 2011). This approach has been prominent in the study of language learning psychology and of L2 motivation in particular (see Dörnyei, MacIntyre and Henry 2015).

As part of an attempt to reconceptualise learner characteristics in a holistic and dynamic vein, Dörnyei (2009) has proposed that we should focus on the interaction of three fundamental ingredients of the human mind – cognition (i.e. thoughts), motivation and affect (i.e. emotions) – and that we should see every learner characteristic as emerging from their dynamic relationship with each other. We can appreciate the special value of the notion of engagement against this backdrop: in line with the above proposal, engagement does indeed emerge from the interaction of cognition, motivation and affect while also involving corresponding *behaviours* and actions. In this sense, Fredricks et al. (2004: 60) are right to conclude that, 'engagement can be thought of as a "meta" construct'. In other words, it is more than the sum of its dynamically interacting parts.

> *The fusion of behaviour, emotion, and cognition under the idea of engagement is valuable because … these factors are dynamically interrelated within the individual; they are not isolated processes. Robust bodies of work address each of the components separately, but considering engagement as a multidimensional construct argues for examining antecedents and consequences of behaviour, emotion, and cognition simultaneously and dynamically, to test for additive or interactive effects.*
>
> (Fredricks et al. 2004: 61)

Engagement Offers a Practical Approach to Involving Students in Their Learning

We have argued above that teachers often face challenges - perhaps more so than ever before - when trying to involve students in contemporary classrooms, and, for this reason, the dynamic, action-oriented nature of the notion of engagement is appealing to educators across disciplines and contexts. Two further key characteristics make engagement especially attractive in practical terms: it is *teacher-friendly* and *malleable*.

- *Teacher-friendliness.* An observation that initially prompted us to start considering writing this book was the fact that whenever the phrase 'engaging students' came up in discussions with teachers, they seemed to respond to the concept keenly, showing great interest in it - more even than in the popular term 'motivation'. Yes, they agreed, motivation *is* relevant and important, but their immediate classroom concern was more than merely motivating learners; they wanted to *engage* them in the various tasks and activities. The fact that engagement resonated with classroom practitioners so readily is fully consistent with the arguments cited earlier about the educational immediacy of the notion.
- *Malleable quality.* Teachers not only find the notion of 'engaging students' relevant and important, but also applicable. A traditional teacher role is to involve students as much as possible in the classes, and therefore an approach that foregrounds how to work with this is intuitively appealing to classroom practitioners. While a more abstract notion such as 'motivating learners' might raise the question of whose responsibility this task should be, engagement is more straightforward in this respect, as it emphasises actions and strategies that teachers can execute. Learner engagement is something teachers can proactively affect and develop, although, naturally, there remain a number of reasons beyond the teacher's control why sometimes learners just do not engage. However, as Jang et al. (2010: 588) rightly point out, when students do engage in classroom learning, 'there is almost always some aspect of the teacher's behaviour that plays a role in the initiation and regulation of the engagement'. Pham (2019) used the wonderful metaphor that will be familiar to many, but with a twist. She explained that indeed teachers can take a horse to water but they can't make it drink; however, they can make it thirsty! Focusing on engagement thus underlines the fact that who teachers are and what they do matter.

> *Another reason for the growing interest in engagement is that it is presumed to be malleable. ... Routes to student engagement may be social or academic and may stem from opportunities in the school or classroom for participation, interpersonal relationships, and intellectual endeavours. Currently, many interventions, such as improving the school climate or changing curriculum and standards, explicitly or implicitly focus on engagement as a route to increased learning or decreased dropping out.*
>
> (Fredricks et al. 2004: 61)

What is This Book Intended to Offer and How?

As we have outlined, engagement emerges from the interaction of a number of factors and is best appreciated from a holistic perspective. To that end, in Chapter 1 we look at how learner engagement is affected by contextual factors at various levels, including the level of the language and society, school as an institution, and learners' family settings. The following chapters are concerned with the aspects of learner engagement that the teacher can affect more directly. In Chapters 2, 3 and 4, we consider how the teacher can create the foundations for learners to engage. We focus in particular on learner mindsets, teacher-student rapport, and classroom dynamics and culture. Then in Chapters 5 and 6, we focus on classroom tasks and look at how teachers can design tasks which trigger and maintain learner engagement.

Chapters 2 to 6 are organised into a series of principles and action points. Our logic behind this structure was to begin with the ideas and thinking that can be distilled into a number of principles. We then draw on all these principles to differing degrees to suggest concrete actions that teachers could take in their classrooms to enact the principles. The principles do not match one-to-one with the action points, but rather multiple principles can be reflected in a single action point. We hope this structure will enable teachers to reflect on the rationale behind the principles and then take away some concrete actions to try out in the classroom - as well as allowing them to use the principles to think of their own action points.

Our intention is to be highly practical, focusing on strategies and approaches that we believe can work in a range of L2 classrooms without being too prescriptive; while we will draw on a solid theoretical foundation of existing research in psychology and language education, we will take a deliberately applied approach in discussing the various ideas in terms of classroom practices, illustrated by quotes and reflection tasks. However, we would like to stress that this book is not intended to be a 'recipe-style' teaching resource. We are sensitive to the diversity of language learners and teaching contexts across the globe and agree that one size does not fit all; therefore, what we intend to offer is a guiding set of ideas and principles for an age where teachers must work with learners who have ever shorter attention spans and for whom visual stimuli and digital teaching are no longer a novelty or motivating per se.

As such, we do not advocate a specific set of tools to use or not use but rather propose a series of actions that teachers can select from to implement in ways which suit them, their learners, their available resources, and their intended teaching aims. We believe that introducing language educators to the whole breadth of the construct of 'engagement' may help many of them to reflect on how they can ensure that their teaching practice is engaging for their learners as well as for themselves. As we have mentioned earlier, our focus on 'engagement' has been motivated by actual (and reported) teacher needs, and we feel that this new agenda for the field is not only highly promising but also overdue.

1 The contexts of learner engagement

No man is an island.
(John Donne)

In this book, our main focus is on the language classroom and on factors that teachers can directly influence in order to promote learner engagement. However, language classrooms do not exist in isolation. All classrooms are situated within broader contexts and cultures that impact on what the teacher does and can achieve. This has two important implications for student engagement. The first is that the teacher can potentially draw on support and strength from other sources in the wider contexts to boost and promote the involvement of the learners. Yet, the existence of contextual interference also means that if a teacher's attempts to foster learner engagement in their classroom fail, this may be partly due to causes and events beyond their control which are thwarting their efforts towards learner engagement. These serious implications for instructional practice warrant a brief initial overview of contextual matters, in order to raise awareness of the dynamics of the wider social environment made up of interacting sociocultural, linguistic and educational landscapes and how this relates to learner engagement.

Principles Related to the Wider Social Context

In an ideal scenario, there is system-wide commitment to supporting learner engagement accompanied by interventions across the ecological system surrounding the learners and the school – all geared at promoting learner engagement and involving all stakeholders, including parents, school managers and educational policy makers. Such a broad consensus is necessary because learner engagement emerges from the interaction of every aspect of the learner's life and not only from what happens in the language classroom. Such an ideal, integrated, engagement-centred scenario, however, may often be only wishful thinking rather than the reality that we experience.

In this chapter, we consider five principles that can prompt a deeper consideration of the contexts of learner engagement, as well as ways in which these contexts can affect learner behaviour. Unlike the chapters that follow, here we will not suggest concrete actions for teachers to pursue, as we recognise that the principles often lie beyond the individual teacher's locus of control. Instead, our hope is that highlighting some pertinent issues will be helpful for language teachers to further reflect on the implications of the specific layers of the broad educational context they are part of, and that such reflection will have benefits (direct or indirect) for creating a more engaging environment for L2 learning. Identifying key issues may also act as an inspiration for collective and wider systemic action to address learner engagement at various local, regional and perhaps even national levels.

REFLECTION TASK 1

Take a moment to reflect on the contexts of your work. Think how your teaching is affected by the institution and its policies, your local community, your culture(s), your language(s), national policy, international policy and broader sociopolitical factors surrounding the language you teach. Which has the greatest impact in your case?

Principle 1: Recognise That Individual Languages Have Sociocultural Status and Social Capital

The languages we teach are subject to influences that come from beyond the walls of our L2 classrooms. Languages are socially encumbered with meaning and associations that are subject to the vagaries of global politics and economics. That is, when students think of an L2, what will be decisive for their overall impression is usually not merely how this L2 is being taught at school but also the various messages they have picked up regarding this L2 and its users from the media or from family and friends. Thus, languages are far from being neutral but have definite sociopolitical status within a country, and this standing will affect their learning and their use. In fact, it was precisely this recognition which inspired Robert Gardner's pioneering approach to understanding language learning motivation in the late 1950s, because he realised that it was simply impossible to understand the nature of language education in the bilingual Francophone/Anglophone environment of Montreal, where he conducted his research, without an awareness of these social issues.

The fundamental social issues underlying the learning of the language of another community are, of course, not limited to Canada. For example, in a British Council report on languages needed in the UK for the future following Brexit, the withdrawal of the United Kingdom from the European Union, (Tinsley and Board 2017), the authors consider the top ten most important modern languages in the UK - which include the same top five since 2013: Spanish, Mandarin, French, Arabic and German - and note a change since their earlier report whereby Russian, Portuguese and Turkish have declined in importance. They explain this by stating, 'These movements are caused by economic and political circumstances in Russia, Turkey and Brazil and are not related to Brexit' (Tinsley and Board 2017: 4). In a similar vein, Lanvers, Doughty and Thompson (2018) argue that because language learning has inevitable political undertones, teachers need to reflect on how the L2 they teach is being politicised so that they may counter any negative discourse that might exist. We agree that the various global forces do trickle down into our classrooms and into learner behaviours and attitudes, and thus teachers benefit from an awareness of and sensitivity to these issues.

> *The motivation to learn another community's language is not merely an individualistic affair but is strongly related to various social attitudes prevailing in the learner's community concerning the target language group and towards the sociocultural 'baggage' the L2 carries.*
>
> (Dörnyei, Csizér and Németh 2006: xi)

The socially prompted associations about a language are not related only to its prestige or usefulness but can take on more intriguing characteristics. For example, in a fascinating study by Williams, Burden and Lanvers (2002), entitled 'French is the language of love and stuff', secondary schools students in the UK reported distinctive perceptions about different languages that affected their overall willingness to engage with these languages. In particular, the researchers found that boys were more motivated to learn German than French, as they associated the French language with more feminine things, whereas they perceived German to have a more masculine character. This suggests that our students possibly come to our classes with certain preconceived L2-related ideas which may be helping or hindering their engagement with the language. For this reason, research on L2 motivation has traditionally offered strategies to foster positive language attitudes and to address counterproductive learner beliefs (see panel below). It has indeed been evidenced many times that exploring the 'L2-related baggage' that our learners bring to class may be highly beneficial in dispelling any unhelpful myths they may hold. Also, focused work on the image and associations of the L2 can help to create in our learners a more fertile basis on which to teach the language (for a detailed discussion of how to create such positive language images, see Dörnyei and Kubanyiova 2014).

STRATEGIES TO PROMOTE LEARNERS' LANGUAGE-RELATED VALUES

Promote 'integrative' values by encouraging a positive and open-minded disposition toward the L2 and its speakers, and toward foreignness in general.

- Include a sociocultural component in your language curriculum.
- Quote positive views about language learning by influential public figures.
- Encourage learners to conduct their own exploration of the L2 community (e.g. on the internet).
- Promote contact with L2 speakers and L2 cultural products.

Promote the students' awareness of the instrumental values associated with the knowledge of an L2.

- Regularly remind students that the successful mastery of the L2 is instrumental to the accomplishment of their valued goals.
- Reiterate the role the L2 plays in the world, highlighting its potential usefulness both for themselves and their community.
- Encourage the learners to apply their L2 proficiency in real-life situations.

(Dörnyei 2001: 139–140)

Some learners of a language may find themselves 'forced' to learn the specific L2 because of global influences that have caused them to be displaced or migrate. They may have their own particular mixed attitudes towards the language they are having to acquire, intermingled with their personal histories. It is also quite possible that for some of these learners, learning the language will have considerable impact on their social, economic and personal status within their new society. As Erling (2017: 11) states, 'ultimately it is knowledge of the host country language that supports integration and economic stability', but she also shows that other languages, most often English, can act as a bridge 'to make human connections across linguistic and national borders'. Languages having this capacity are often referred to as *lingua francas*, but we should remember that such a status is a double-edged sword in the sense that English, for example, has a complex past connected to issues of colonialism as well as globalisation and the threat it poses to other languages (e.g. Pennycook 2017).

In sum, whatever language we teach, it is important to recognise that its learning and use is connected to wider global and social issues. As educators, we can seek to develop sensitivity among our learners and a healthy critical attitude to the social status, politics, power and inequalities underlying language use, policy and education. It is known that teaching learners higher-order critical thinking through the language is an especially engaging methodological approach (see Chapter 6). When treated with care and respect, this topic is perhaps one of the most real and relevant aspects of learning any language that we can explicitly address and bring into class – after all, many have strong views about the positive or negative effects of English-speaking films and TV programmes on diverse cultures and languages, about the number of English loan words in any language, or about the status of minority or heritage languages.

> *The social context of language learning and teaching is greatly impacted by a nation's political decision to give special status to a particular language or languages. This status can be achieved either by making the language an official language of a country or by giving special priority to the language by requiring its study as a foreign language.*
>
> (McKay and Rubdy 2009: 10)

Principle 2: Connect Language Learning in Class to Life Beyond the Classroom

During the past twenty years, learners have witnessed an explosion in term of opportunities for language use and access to artefacts in the target language beyond the classroom. When we started our language teaching career, obtaining authentic materials in an L2 could be a real challenge, whereas nowadays the internet offers virtually inexhaustible language resources. In Sweden, for example, as Henry, Sundqvist and Thorsen (2019: 28–29) explain, the role of English has taken on a brand new character, signifying a more universal trend:

> *The intensification of globalization over the last two decades, and in particular the spread of high-speed mobile networked communication, has meant that the landscape of English language acquisition processes and English language teaching has undergone radical transformations. ... For young people who spend substantial periods of their free-time in online environments, English has become integrated into their lives, and implicated in their identities to an extent that its influences have moved beyond those normally associated with a second language.*

However, the consequences of this new reality are not always as positive as one would anticipate. As Illustration 1 below demonstrates, the divide between language learning inside and outside of the classroom can become uncomfortably salient. Of course, the advent of communicative language teaching highlighted the importance of using the L2 beyond the classroom (Nunan 2014), but bridging the gap between the curricular and extracurricular spheres may not always be straightforward: while language teachers may view the extracurricular digital world as a rich bounty to explore, some learners may simply not associate language use in their personal lives with the language classes in school. They may even resent a teacher's perceived intrusion into a space that they consider private and personal. It may, therefore, be a real challenge to create a connection between the two spheres. However, if it can be done, for the majority of learners, this will be a considerable boost that helps them to see the real-world relevance of the language and to make its use personally relevant.

ILLUSTRATION 1: THE CHANGING ENGLISH LANGUAGE LEARNING LANDSCAPE IN SWEDEN

Describing the emerging language-learning landscape in Sweden, Henry et al. (2019: 28–32) highlight a growing divide between 'the English of free-time activities (as a *lingua emotiva*), and the English encountered in school (as a *lingua academica* and a *lingua cultura*)'. They point out that the extensive interaction with digital media that can take up a significant proportion of young people's leisure time is highly enticing for many learners. Particularly for those who are engaged in online activities such as digital gaming and fanfiction writing – which involve high levels of creativity – 'encounters with English take place in contexts that are highly identity-congruent.' This, however, as the researchers point out, constitutes a formidable challenge, because 'students who perceive that English encountered in school is somehow not as "real" as English encountered outside school would experience that things done in the classroom lacked authenticity, and ... this too could negatively influence their motivation.' In other words, the exposure to English in the classroom is often no match to the quality of experience students may be having using English in the globalised digital world, and this imbalance can have the potential to demotivate in class.

For language teachers who wish to connect their teaching to the space beyond the classroom, one idea that has been put forward to help to achieve this aim is 'contact assignments', that is, assignments whose stated purpose is to establish authentic interaction with people outside the school via the L2 (Nunan 2014). These assignments can vary in form and scope, from interviewing someone local to study abroad trips, tandem e-learning partnerships, study villages (e.g. camps within a country creating a language community of use for a short time) or other projects designed to foster contact with L2 speakers. In particular, study abroad trips and exchange schemes can have long-lasting effects on learners which they will remember many years later (Mercer 2011) and which will act as notable 'milestones' (Steinwidder 2016: 18) not only in their linguistic but also in their social, cultural and personal development.

> *Many students who show signs of disengagement in school show more positive emotion and stronger behavioural engagement in out-of-school contexts ... The differences in engagement across these two contexts raise important questions. Why are schools such disengaging places for these students? Why do these same students show higher engagement in other settings?*
>
> (Fredricks 2014: 65)

When language learning takes place within the host environment (e.g. learning French in Paris), opportunities for L2 contact are seemingly abundant, but this does not necessarily mean that learners will be able to take advantage of the various openings without some explicit guidance. For example, there is evidence that some international students studying in the UK fail to experience any real engagement with the local L2-speaking community, and thus their exposure to the L2 largely remains restricted to what they learn in the classroom (see e.g. Zahran 2005). Illustration 2 from Canada indicates that this problem is not limited to the UK, but on the positive side, Shelley Hill's account of an intriguing project in Vancouver shows that engagement with the local community can be substantially enhanced through focused teacher intervention.

ILLUSTRATION 2: A CASE STUDY OF A CONTACT ASSIGNMENT IN CANADA

Shelley Hill teaches in an English for Academic Purposes programme in Vancouver, Canada. The learners typically come from diverse countries in Asia and South America. She noticed that after attending class from 8:30 to 12:30 every day, many of her students would go home and spend the rest of the day playing video games, despite being in a vibrant English-speaking environment. That is, they were not engaging with their classmates, the college or their local communities. Shelley decided to change this situation by giving them a contact assignment in each of these three categories (i.e. classmates, college, community). Students received a worksheet which explained the assignments and which also offered suggestions for possible engagement. They were asked to carry out one activity every two weeks, until they completed all three categories. As Shelley explains, she tried to make the task fairly simple because the students' workload in the course was heavy, so they only had to write a few sentences about their experiences and then post it on an online bulletin board, along with an illustrative photo or video. Here is what she found:

> *The response was amazing! Students were trying new places, joining workshops at the college and helping each other with homework. Also, by sharing their experiences on our class [website], they were able to see what their classmates were doing and get ideas of new things to do from there. They wrote about how useful the college workshops were and that they would be attending more in the future. They also tried community events and met new people. And they started to explore Vancouver. It was very exciting! At the end of the project, I gave them a reflection worksheet and asked about their experience in the project. 95% gave positive feedback and thanked me for helping them try new things. The only negative comments were that it was too much work. My students are certainly more engaged than ever!* (Personal communication, 14th February, 2019)

Community-service projects also offer particular potential for getting involved in the local community in a way that also benefits that community. Language-related examples of such projects could be reading aloud to the visually impaired, organising a charity fundraising event (see e.g. Muir, in press), tutoring younger children in school, performing a play in the target language for senior citizens, or interviewing and writing the stories of the 'invisible' or 'unsung heroes' in the local community. It may be even more effective in engagement terms when learners are the ones to identify the service need and establish the steps of the project in their local community. From a language teaching point of view, it is, of course, easier to devise projects when the context is an L2 setting, but the same notion can also work online and at a distance with communities globally that use the language you are teaching. For example, students could write letters or greeting cards to those in need (see UNHCR n.d.), create an online magazine, join international social initiatives to support the needy and champion worthwhile causes, or offer (perhaps online) services to L2 visitors to their country – in short, in our globalised age, if one looks more closely, there are many potential openings, and once your students realise this, they might well feel able and willing to seek out something appropriate for themselves. Setting the right tone for any projects like these is of crucial importance. Illustration 3 offers a telling example in this respect, as it shows that the same learners can display very different attitudes and action towards two different languages they are studying.

ILLUSTRATION 3: FINNISH LEARNERS' DIFFERENT ENGAGEMENT WITH ENGLISH AND SWEDISH

Kalaja, Alanen, Palviainen and Dufva (2011) report on a study which examined the ways in which Finnish learners, who all spoke the same L1, engaged with the languages they were learning – English and Swedish – beyond the classroom. The researchers show how, despite easy access to resources and media, the learners were more proactive in seeking out language use opportunities for English than for Swedish. They reflect on possible reasons for these differences in learner agency and conclude that the learners' attitudes and beliefs about the perceived popularity and usefulness of English impacted on how engaged and active they were in seeking out ways to use the language beyond the classroom. They conclude by noting that social discourses about the respective languages – including Swedish being 'obligatory' – will influence learner beliefs and subsequent behaviours. That is, how and why learners engage with language beyond the classroom is not just about availability and access but also about beliefs and attitudes.

Principle 3: Families Are a Valuable Resource for Learner Engagement

As Hattie (2009: 61) states, 'home can be a nurturing place for the achievement of students, or it can be a place of low expectations and lack of encouragement in learning'. There are various aspects of a learner's *home life* that can affect their engagement in class including: the attitudes they pick up at home towards learning, towards languages and towards screen time in general; the kinds of literacy practices that are present in home life; and the degree of autonomy and academic support the learner receives (Arzubiaga, Rueda and Monzó 2002; Fan and Williams 2010; Mo and Singh 2008). It has also been shown that parental/family practices and role modelling play a decisive role in shaping children's academic motivation (Pomerantz, Grolnick and Price 2007), and for this reason, L2 motivation research has traditionally included measures of parental encouragement / family influence, either as a separate variable or as part of a broader dimension (e.g. the ought-to L2 self) (see Dörnyei and Ushioda 2011: 276–277). It is important to note that we are using the term 'parents' here to refer to whoever looks after a child outside of school (see e.g. Cowley 2009). Naturally, the family environment of adults learning a language can also be important for the degree of support and encouragement they receive (see Castles 2004; Flynn and Harris 2016; Park and Choi 2009).

> *... one high-impact form of parental involvement did not actually involve kids or schools at all: If parents simply read for pleasure at home on their own, their children were more likely to enjoy reading too. That pattern held fast across very different countries and different levels of family income. Kids could see what parents valued, and it mattered more than what parents said.*
>
> (Ripley 2013: 111)

An important parent-related factor affecting student engagement is *parental involvement in school life* (Fan and Chen 2001; Hill and Tyson 2009; Jeynes 2007). This refers to attending parents' evenings, parent–teacher conferences and school events, as well as volunteering in school contexts such as in parent groups. Goodall and Montgomery (2014) explain that there is a difference between parental involvement in school and parental engagement in their child's learning. They recommend that the focus be less on parents supporting the school but rather for the child's learning to be at the centre of the school relationship, by involving parents and promoting their active interest in and appreciation of their child's engagement and progress in school. However, there is a word of caution that involvement by parents should not be perceived by the child as controlling or as a form of surveillance but should be conducted in an autonomy-supportive manner, otherwise the child risks demotivation and damage to their self-concept (Fan and Williams 2010; Hattie 2009).

In this way, student engagement can be enhanced by means of explicitly seeking to build partnerships between the school and parents through greater community connections and deliberately opening up pathways of communication between school and family. To maximise parental involvement, schools are encouraged to broaden the range of options and access points for parents. For example, they recommend accommodating scheduling diversity for working parents and offering multiple channels of connecting with schools and children's learning that do not always involve the parents having to physically come to the school, including digitally by sharing school life in closed online groups (Gonzalez-DeHass, Willems and Holbein 2005).

A final point is that schools and teachers should also contact parents to tell them *positive* stories about their child's actions and activities, and not only when things are not going well. In the same spirit, parents should be invited to attend student performances at school (or online), and they could even be recruited as partners in seeking ideas on how best to improve the school space or help the children in extracurricular activities. In short, the above points reflect the same principle that if the school treats the parents with respect and in a spirit of partnership, this can also pay off in terms of student engagement with the school.

> *When parents show an interest in their child's education by getting involved, students adopt a mastery goal orientation to learning where they are more likely to seek challenging tasks, persist through academic challenges, and experience satisfaction in their school work.*
>
> (Gonzalez-DeHass et al. 2005: 117–118)

Principle 4: School Priorities, Curricular Relevance and Testing Policies Have a Bearing on Engagement

In schools and universities, students receive important indirect messages about the social status of the L2 they are learning through the way the national curriculum and the institution prioritise it as a subject matter. Unfortunately, teachers rarely have any meaningful say in these matters, despite the fact that factors related to institutional and curricular policies can undermine their work and weaken student engagement. Indeed, research has shown that the overall curricular status of L2 learning, whether it is compulsory or voluntary, as well as the number of teaching hours assigned to it, will affect how seriously a learner (and their parents) will take the subject (McKay and Rubdy 2009).

These macro-factors are, however, not the sole determinants of relevant student perceptions, as the latter can also be modified by more subtle micro-variables. In the UK, for example, some secondary schools have been officially designated as 'specialist language academies', and although this was largely a ceremonial title that merely recognised the school's interest in promoting language studies, it could make a psychological difference. When a school we personally knew had dropped the title from its official name, and even though the change was not accompanied by any immediate curricular modifications, it took only a few years before the school began treating modern languages as less important subjects.

So, what can the institution do to boost the status and value of language teaching? The scope of possible measures is wide, including examples such as the following: the institution can communicate explicitly and indirectly to students, parents and the local community that languages are taken seriously and linguistic diversity is respected and embraced; it can support excursions, exchanges and language-related projects; it can provide time and resources to support activities such as students performing a play in the L2; it can hold events where members of various L2 communities are welcomed into the school or university to share aspects of their languages and cultures in a 'languages day'; and it can stock the library with sufficient L2 books and films. In Austria, one school strategy is to have a 'language week', where the pupils and their teacher, along with guests from outside the school, come together to enjoy a full immersive week of only language classes and project work. This usually takes place outside of the curriculum and pupils are exempt from other lessons for that one week.

REFLECTION TASK 2

Reflect on your institution's language policy. How explicitly do they support linguistic diversity generally? What kinds of institution-supported extracurricular options are available for foreign language learning? Have you ever conducted a language week at your institution? Do you think this would work in your context? Why / Why not?

A second pertinent curricular aspect is that the learners' perceptions of the usefulness, relevance and importance of the *content* of their classes has considerable implications for their engagement (Shernoff 2013). This means that it is not just *how* we teach that engages learners but also *what* we are teaching. A study by Orthner, Jones-Sanpei, Akos and Rose (2013) found, for example, that when the curriculum was reformed at the school level to make instruction more career-relevant, students' levels of engagement rose significantly, as did the value they placed on their schooling generally.

Probably the best example of a curricular innovation that has had a measurable impact on student motivation and engagement has been the European Union's initiative of introducing Content and Language Integrated Learning (CLIL) to revitalise language education in Europe (see e.g. Genesee and Hamayan 2016; Lasagabaster 2011). Although CLIL has had a somewhat chequered history, working well in some environments and not realising the hopes attached to it in others, the fact that it involves the teaching of ordinary school subjects in the L2 has made language learning more broadly relevant and real-life applicable. This greater relevance undoubtedly serves as a booster for student engagement - and we will come back to the significance of relevance with regard to the content of learning tasks in Chapters 5 and 6 - but, arguably, part of CLIL's impact has also been due to the fact that it tends to carry the seal of government and school approval. This creates excitement around it that teachers can capitalise on in various ways (for a sensitive overview, see Hüttner, Dalton-Puffer and Smit 2013).

For adult learners, CLIL can help to make explicit the ways in which the language can be relevant and useful for their professional and/or personal lives, depending on their motives for learning the language.

> *One of the many teaching strategies highlighted in school reform efforts involves augmenting the relevance of the curriculum so students can establish a link between the content they are learning and either their environment or their expectations for their future.*
>
> (Orthner et al. 2013: 27)

Finally, curricular impacts on student engagement cannot be fully discussed without mentioning *national high-stakes tests*. The controversial role of testing in education is of course a much-discussed topic with a robust literature, and summarising the various views would go beyond the scope of this section. Here we would merely like to draw attention to some key issues that relate to engagement. As Au (2007) found in his metasynthesis of multiple studies, high-stakes tests, on the whole, narrow the content focus of teaching, lead to the fragmentation of content to meet test norms, and increase teacher-led pedagogies - factors that are known to be damaging to learner engagement (Shernoff 2013). Indeed, in a case study in the US, Mora

(2011) found that the testing culture and focus on tests led to increased boredom among learners, as teachers resorted to more lecture-style teaching and practice exams, with fewer opportunities for group work and projects.

One especially damaging consequence for engagement is when the focus of teaching turns to test performance - that is, 'teaching to the test' - rather than to the mastery of learning the content (see Chapter 2). It is noteworthy, however, that there is some research evidence that schools which adopt a mastery approach to learning (e.g. differentiated approaches, scaffolded learning, chances to repeat content in personalised time frames, formative assessment; see Chapters 2, 5 and 6) find that their learners then meet the standardised test requirements anyway (Guskey 2010; Zimmerman and Dibenedetto 2008).

> *Everybody is a genius. But if you judge a fish by its ability to climb a tree, it will live its whole life believing that it is stupid.*
> (often attributed to Albert Einstein)

Principle 5: Whole-School Culture Can Cultivate or Kill Learner Engagement

Our final principle is related to the obvious fact that every classroom is situated within a school culture that can be defining for how the students and teachers feel about their work. The common observation is that many students' general disposition to learning is to a large extent determined when they enter the school gate, even before they reach the language classroom. School culture emerges from the structures, policies, norms and physical spaces of the school, as well as from informal and invisible dimensions of school life, such as beliefs and emotional climate. These create an ethos that pervades the whole school and influences the collective behaviour of staff. In schools with a healthy, supportive climate, students are more likely to feel a positive attitude towards the school - a *sense of belonging* - and, subsequently, will be more inclined to be engaged in school work (Cemalcilar 2010; Osterman 2000). Baumeister and Leary (1995: 497) define a need to belong as 'the need to form and maintain strong, stable interpersonal relationships'; accordingly, the sense of belonging to a school is dependent on how much the particular school is able to foster a perception of a community that learners feel connected to and safe within. This applies equally to schools that adults may join for language learning, as well as state institutions.

There are a number of steps that schools as institutions can take to nurture a community spirit and learner engagement. One way is to increase the democratic participation of learners in school. A core life-skill being promoted across the curriculum in most countries is that of citizenship and social responsibility. The best way to have students practise this skill is to encourage them to participate actively in democratic structures and decision-making. School offers the perfect context for learning those skills and enacting those competencies (Hoskins, Janmaat and Villalba 2012). There are various degrees of democratic participation that a school can offer, ranging from smaller-scale opportunities to school-wide structures, as in the most notable example of A. S. Neill's Summerhill School (Summerhill School website). Typically, a school can have a policy of involving students in various policy decisions, hosting elections for positions of student representatives on various committees and ensuring maximum student participation throughout levels of school activity, including encouraging student-led events. Such democratic structures and participatory options communicate a vital message to students about how they are respected, their voices heard and their opinions valued (see Chapters 4 and 5).

Another factor known to affect school climate is the whole-school policy regarding behaviour management. This goes beyond micro-level interventions that teachers deal with in their classes daily, as it also concerns a whole-school strategy and structures to promote respect, safety and positive behaviour among learners. The aims are to reduce bullying, strengthen community, promote positive relationships and help learners take ownership of their behaviour, while maintaining a focus on educational concerns. Having such a structure in place not only helps learners to have consistent, clear expectations, but it is also known to help reduce levels of stress among teachers, who can rely on collegial support and a clear school-wide policy for managing behaviour (Rogers 2007). When the whole school focuses on supporting positive behaviour and creating a safe climate for all learners, their engagement increases, as do overall levels of achievement, and there is a decrease in disciplinary problems (e.g. Luiselli, Putnam, Handler and Feinberg 2005).

SOME CHARACTERISTICS OF A WHOLE-SCHOOL APPROACH TO BEHAVIOUR MANAGEMENT

- Staff, students and parents understand the policies, the rationale behind them and the values underpinning them
- Students are aware of their rights, responsibilities, expectations and rules, as well as consequences of their behaviour
- Ideally, students and parents can be involved in shaping the policy
- Staff share good practices and create a collaborative knowledge base; they act more consistently across the school
- Positive behaviours are actively promoted and supported
- Staff feel more confident and experience less stress

(adapted from Rogers 2007)

Another whole-school policy that impacts on learner engagement and school climate is how the school supports staff well-being. Not surprisingly, when teachers experience higher levels of well-being, they are better able to teach more creatively and effectively, and, subsequently and not unexpectedly, student achievement levels also increase (Bajorek, Gulliford and Taskila 2014; Day and Gu 2009; Klusmann, Kunter, Trautwein, Lüdtke and Baumert 2008). An interesting aspect of dialogue with teachers as part of various projects investigating language teacher well-being in Austria has been their mention of small things that could make a big difference by implying that they are valued and cared for, such as a decent coffee machine in the staffroom, clean staff toilets and personal desk space.

> *Teachers who enjoy high levels of well-being are likely to be successful teachers, more engaged with their language teaching practice, and better able to face challenges that occur along the way. It is time we understood more fully what resources, psychological and otherwise, best promote language teacher flourishing across settings and time.*
>
> (Talbot and Mercer 2018: 427)

Finally, a key determinant of school engagement is the amount of participation in out-of-school, extracurricular activities learners take part in. Research has shown that participating in extracurricular activities leads to higher achievement, more engagement, improved self-esteem and well-being, as well as a greater likelihood of the students continuing on to higher education (Feldman and Matjasko 2005; Kort-Butler and Hagewen 2011). For example, Dotterer, McHale and Crouter (2007: 399) studied the connection of out-of-school activities and engagement with 140 African American adolescents and concluded, 'The results of this study highlight the importance of structured extracurricular activities for school engagement, particularly school self-esteem and school bonding'. As we shall see in Chapter 4, extracurricular activities can play a highly positive role in classroom dynamics by promoting cohesiveness amongst the students, but the point to be made here is that school trips and excursions can also have a positive impact at the whole-school level.

> *Some educators assume that activities such as sports and the arts are just 'extras' and are only useful for fun and recreation. Another common assumption is that participating in extra-curricular activities competes for students' time and attention and can take away from time that they can spend on homework. This is a myth ... The reality is that for some students, the opportunity to participate in organised non-academic contexts such as sports and the arts is the only reason they come to school, stay in school, and do their school work. Cuts to extracurricular programming are devastating for these youths.*
>
> (Fredricks 2014: 62)

A positive example: the pledge system of Redhill Academy, Nottingham

Let us conclude the discussion of the significance of a whole-school culture by offering a case study of a British school, Redhill Academy, not far from where Zoltán lives and works, which managed to reach excellence through transforming the school climate and ethos, thereby increasing student engagement. What is particularly relevant for the current discussion is the Pledge System they introduced as a tool to promote these changes.

Redhill Academy is a secondary school located in North Nottingham. In 2013, the Local Education Authority (LEA) of Nottingham was ranked the 144th of 151 LEAs in the UK. Despite this, Redhill Academy was the first secondary school in Nottinghamshire to gain the highest UK rating for the quality of teaching (in 2008) and has maintained this qualification ever since. Here are three relevant extracts from the last official government appraisal of the school (Ofsted 2013):

> *'Teaching is outstanding. Teachers plan lessons that engage and challenge students. Work is matched well to the needs of students.'* (p. 1)
>
> *'During the inspection ... the teaching observed was consistently effective in capturing students' interest and engagement.'* (p. 5)
>
> *'All students sign a pledge to commit to a range of spiritual, moral, social and cultural activities throughout their time in the academy.'* (p. 7)

As highlighted in the Ofsted report, the Redhill Academy Pledge System (see below) has played an important part in the revitalisation of the school. As the school's official description states:

> *In order to further develop this [the school's] ethos and raise expectations around the importance of engagement from everyone, we have in place an exciting programme called 'Pledges'. This sees students awarded Pledges for their wider contribution to academy life. The theme of our Pledges are displayed throughout the academy and staff dedicate time to focus on helping students in identifying opportunities to achieve their Pledges and the importance of doing so. ... Our Pledges will further engage students in opportunities and events that take place in the Academy.* (Redhill Academy website)

The Redhill Academy's Ten Pledges

1. *To successfully participate in residential trips, representing the academy's ethos, values and code of conduct at all times.*
2. *To represent the academy in sports or to contribute to Academy Performing Arts events.*
3. *To read a range of novels every year and complete a book review for at least one per term.*
4. *To participate in at least three different assemblies or contribute to organising a Tutor activity or event.*
5. *To organise or actively participate in at least three fundraising events.*
6. *To represent the academy in ten different events; tutors to record events in Passport.*

7. To take part in community projects.
8. To participate in activities that support others within the academy, e.g. mentoring, coaching, induction, options or paired reading.
9. To attend cultural or sports events outside of school.
10. Individual Pledge; to be set by the Tutor with student.

(https://www.theredhillacademy.org.uk/mod/resource/view.php?id=13781)

From the perspective of this book, four aspects of the Pledge System are particularly noteworthy: (a) staff dedicate time to convey the importance of the Pledges and to help students in identifying opportunities to achieve their Pledges; (b) each student has their own individual Pledge Passport; (c) the Pledges are displayed on posters throughout the school; (d) students' Pledge achievements are regularly celebrated at school events. That is, the school goes beyond merely superficial acknowledgement; by introducing a concrete set of pledges that students are asked to subscribe to, students are actively brought on board. The school has demonstrated its commitment to the Pledges by officially endorsing them through public displays and by spending precious staff time focusing on them.

The reality of the Pledges is further underlined for the students by getting them to set personalised Pledge goals, keeping Pledge records in the students' own Pledge Passports and regularly celebrating Pledge achievements. What is perhaps the most remarkable aspect of Redhill Academy's initiative is that the Pledges do not directly concern academic achievement as such, but rather are aimed at strengthening the foundation of such achievement by promoting a climate of school-wide student engagement. By producing a well thought-through and creatively executed pledge system to formalise their engagement programme, the school has managed to build up sufficient socio-educational capital to transform an unremarkable, non-selective secondary school into a model institution in just over a decade.

Summary

This chapter has reflected briefly on the contexts beyond the language classroom that can also affect learner engagement. No student is an island. As teachers, it can be useful to reflect on the multiple contexts and layers of learners' lives and the messages, values, attitudes and expectations they bring with them. This helps us to understand and be sensitive to the ways learners invest in their academic lives generally, and how they engage or approach language learning specifically. Structures in society and the school specifically can impact on the value and status assigned to language learning, as well as on the sense of belonging that a learner forms to their school. To further strengthen learners' identification with language learning specifically, there is a multitude of opportunities for L2 use globally, and in most cases also locally. Consciously building a bridge from the classroom to these out-of-school contexts can make a notable positive contribution to enhancing learner autonomy, confidence and engagement (Nunan and Richards 2015).

In the rest of the book, we turn our attention to life inside the language classroom and the range of options open to language teachers to design and create engaging language learning opportunities. However, this chapter has been intended to serve as a reminder that our language classrooms are embedded in a wider ecology, and much of what is communicated to learners there about their autonomy, relatedness and competence, as well as the value of languages, will impact on what happens within actual L2 classes.

CHAPTER IN A NUTSHELL

Learner engagement in class is connected to attitudes and beliefs stemming from a host of contextual factors that affect both the learner and the school.

IF YOU WANT TO FIND OUT MORE

Benson, P. and Reinders, H. (eds.). (2011). *Beyond the Language Classroom.* Basingstoke: Palgrave Macmillan. (A rich collection of investigations into how language use can be fostered beyond the classroom.)

Crehan, L. (2016). *Cleverlands.* London: Unbound. (A frustrated teacher visits world-leading education systems to critically examine their positive and negative components.)

Ripley, A. (2013). *The Smartest Kids in the World: And How They Got That Way.* New York, NY: Simon and Schuster. (A thought-provoking, popular science book that challenges us to think critically about diverse education systems across the globe.)

Sahlberg, P. (2015). *Finnish Lessons 2.0.* New York, NY: Teachers College Press. (Takes a holistic view in looking at the Finnish education system and how all the parts of the system contribute to its success. An interesting insight into the world's leading education system.)

2 The facilitative learner mindset

REFLECTION TASK 1

Think about your learners. What are the characteristics of those who you would refer to as proactive? What do they do? How do they think about themselves and their learning? In what ways do they differ from learners who are more passive and less self-directed?

Whether a learner engages with the language learning opportunities available depends not only on the nature of those opportunities (e.g. whether they are seen as interesting or useful) but also on several other factors that are either *internal* to the learner (such as personal characteristics, often labelled as intrapersonal factors) or which concern their *social relationships* with others (interpersonal factors). Such internal and social factors can make a real difference in facilitating learner engagement, in the sense that they can either constitute fertile conditions for initiating a learner's willingness to engage in language learning within and beyond the classroom, or, alternatively, they can cancel out even our best efforts to create an engaging learning environment.

> *We are creatures of both brains and hearts, and when both are engaged, compelling learning erupts.*
> (VanDeWeghe 2009: 24)

Chapters 2–4 of this book address these intrapersonal and interpersonal factors in terms of three main pillars that can be seen to support engaged learner behaviour: the learner's *psychological state*, their *relationship to the teacher* and their *relationship with their peers*. In this chapter, we start with the learners themselves and reflect on the kinds of beliefs and feelings – both regarding themselves as human beings in general and language learners in particular – which may give them the sense that taking engaged action is worthwhile. For example, if a learner does not think that they are very good at learning a language, it is going to be an uphill struggle to get them engaged with the classroom tasks and materials. From their point of view, why should they bother? Obviously, such a negative frame of mind needs to be challenged: we need our students to believe that it *is* possible to improve, that they *have* the means to do so and that their sustained perseverance over time *will* reap rewards and lead them towards personally meaningful goals.

Rationale

'Whether you think you can or think you can't, you're right'. This famous saying has been quoted hundreds of time, with good reason. It speaks to a truth about the significance of what we believe when facing a task: essentially, that our belief in our own abilities in respect to an activity will facilitate or inhibit engagement. In other words, this sense of competence - and more generally, of self-image - is *defining* for engagement. This explains why the notion of 'I can' is at the heart of a multitude of motivational theories, most notably in Deci and Ryan's (1985; Ryan and Deci 2017) famous Self-Determination Theory (represented by the key component 'need for competence'), Bandura's (1997) Self-Efficacy Theory and Dweck's (2006) Theory of Mindsets. In order to be willing to engage, learners first need to feel they can cope with whatever tasks they face, that they can affect the outcomes and that they can successfully achieve goals. These facets make up a crucial dimension of an overall *facilitative mindset* - which is the term we have chosen to refer to the sum of all the relevant learner-internal factors - and they need to be complemented by strategies of how to seek support and how to manage upcoming challenges.

The second central dimension of a facilitative mindset is related to what Deci and Ryan (1985) call the 'need for autonomy', which refers to the learners' sense that they are in charge, that is, that they can affect their own learning and hold a degree of responsibility for its outcomes. Accordingly, educational psychologists agree on the principle that for optimal effectiveness, learners need to be convinced that they are not just passive recipients of teacher input but that they have 'agency' and can proactively shape their learning opportunities and processes (e.g. Reeve and Tseng 2011). Indeed, while we can do our best to encourage learners to become engaged, the final decision whether to act or not will always rest with the individual.

REFLECTION TASK 2

Think of an aspect of your job or a hobby where you feel very confident. Reflect on where that sense of competence comes from. What contributes to your feeling that you can do something? How does feeling confident affect your behaviour? Think also about how much freedom you have in your work and how that affects your motivation.

> *Believing we are capable of doing something or achieving a certain objective is a vital element of being willing and able to take control of and responsibility for our actions.*
>
> (Williams et al. 2015: 45)

Principles for a Facilitative Mindset

We have argued above that in order to get learners into a facilitative state of mind, we need to help them to develop a broad sense of competence and autonomy. Also, we need to prepare them for the long haul, developing sufficient learning stamina and persistence in their engagement, given that language learning is a marathon, not a sprint. How can we accomplish these goals in actual practice? In the following, we first explore five principles that facilitate learners' readiness and willingness to engage, and then we move on to suggest five concrete teacher actions which can support the enacting of these principles. As will become clear, the five principles - promoting a sense of competence, a growth mindset, ownership, proactiveness and grit in the learners - are related to each other, representing various facets of a positive, facilitative frame of mind.

Principle 1: Promote a Sense of Competence

'Yes, you can!' and 'I can do it!' are phrases that have become frequently used in all kinds of contexts, as they capture well the motivational power of believing that one can succeed. This sense of positive self-belief is exactly what we would like to engender in our learners: we want them to feel able to manage a task - be that a specific classroom activity or more broadly defined, the mastery of a foreign language. We have already emphasised the general significance of this principle on the previous pages, so let us here specifically highlight what is arguably the most useful concept in this respect: *self-efficacy*. This has been defined as an individual's beliefs about whether they feel that they can successfully complete a specific task in a specific context (Bandura 1997); that is, it is how learners would respond to the question, 'Do I feel as if I could manage this task in this particular situation and under this set of conditions?' Research over the past three decades has produced ample evidence that self-efficacy is likely to determine what tasks learners select to engage with, as well as their ongoing commitment to persisting and completing the task.

> *Self-efficacy can lead to more engagement and, subsequently, to more learning and better achievement; however, the relations also flow back to self-efficacy over time. Accordingly, the more a student is engaged, and especially the more they learn and the better they perform, the higher their self-efficacy.*
>
> (Linnenbrink and Pintrich 2003: 123)

Broadly speaking, there are four important ways through which learners can increase their self-efficacy: (a) having experiences of success themselves; (b) getting positive, constructive and encouraging feedback from significant others; (c) observing others succeed who are similar in competences to themselves; and (d) evaluating their own emotional states and their responses to experiences (see Bandura 1977).

Success: Perhaps one of the most effective ways for learners to develop a sense of competence is for them to experience success. We all know the expression 'success breeds success' but the point to stress here is that in order to boost confidence, success needs to be *genuine* and needs to be *earned.* There are no gains to a person's sense of competence from easy success that requires little effort; however, having to work for something and then witnessing the rewards of one's efforts is perhaps the most valuable experience learners can have.

> *The feeling of competence results when a person takes on and, in his or her own view, meets optimal challenges. Being able to do something that is trivially easy does not lead to perceived competence, for the feeling of being effective occurs only when one has worked towards accomplishment ... One does not have to be best or first, or to get an 'A', to feel competent: one need only take on a meaningful personal challenge and give it one's best.*
>
> (Deci and Flaste 1995: 66)

Feedback and scaffolding: Feedback is a well-known educational tool with both motivational and instructional power. It can emphasise two different aspects of someone's performance: what has *already* been achieved and what is *yet* to be achieved. From an engagement perspective, the first type particularly – usually termed *'progress feedback'* – is relevant: positive progress feedback (affirmative formative feedback) makes progress toward the target feel real and achievable and thus fuels subsequent efforts. Self-efficacy is particularly enhanced if this kind of feedback is also combined with conscious 'scaffolding' efforts by the teacher, including breaking down tasks into more manageable sub-segments, providing structure which is gradually removed, demonstrating ways of completing tasks, offering detailed instructions and guidance, getting learners to work together in collaborative support groups, and generally being available and approachable to turn to if guidance or encouragement is needed.

Role modelling and 'vicarious learning': Bandura (1997) has emphasised that *role models* are able to exert considerable positive motivational influence on one's learning: 'seeing or visualizing people similar to oneself perform successfully typically raises efficacy beliefs in observers that they themselves possess the capabilities to master comparable activities' (p. 87). Indeed, observing others and learning through their experiences – which is usually termed *'vicarious learning'* – is a well-known form of indirect learning that has the capacity to strengthen one's belief that a task is doable. Within the context of SLA, *'near peer role models'* – that is, role models similar to the learner in terms of age, profession, status, etc. – have been demonstrated to have particular motivational potential (Dörnyei and Murphey 2003; Murphey and Arao 2001), as their success is more easily transferable to the learner's own situation when there are perceived similarities between themselves and the role model.

Emotional regulation: Another important source of information for learners about their sense of competence is their emotions. If learners are happy on task, feel energised and experience a sense of enjoyment and pride while working, they are likely to translate this into a sense of efficacy. These positive feelings can naturally stem from many of the instructional design features discussed in later chapters, as well as from enabling a sense of autonomy in learners. In contrast, a learner's sense of competence can – obviously – be shaken by feeling anxious, worried or embarrassed in class. This suggests that the facilitative state of mind is not just a thinking state but also a *feeling* state.

> *Educating the mind without educating the heart is no education at all.*
>
> (often attributed to Aristotle)

Principle 2: Foster a Growth Mindset

REFLECTION TASK 3

Do you believe that all of your learners can improve their language learning skills? Are there some learners who you view really as 'hopeless cases'? Is language learning ability something that only language-talented people can succeed at? The beliefs underlying your answers represent your mindset about language learning and will affect how you teach and your expectations of learners.

American psychologist Carol Dweck (2006) has made an intriguing proposal concerning one's core perception of abilities: she suggests that people can be placed on a continuum between two extremes, one involving the belief that a person is born with fixed amounts of abilities such as intelligence, and that these amounts cannot be changed (i.e. the 'fixed mindset'), with the other extreme representing the view that everyone can develop their potential further and 'grow' their intelligences or change their personal traits (i.e. the 'growth mindset'). This dichotomy plays a vital role in all aspects of education and, accordingly, Dweck's theory of mindsets has become prominent in educational psychology.

> *If we were to carry on assuming that some children are born 'intelligent', while others simply do not have the 'brain-power' required to master difficult ideas in physics or history, say, then the options for change, no matter how pressing that change is felt to be, will be limited. If, on the other hand, intelligence is seen itself as learnable, then a whole different set of educational possibilities become thinkable.*
>
> (Lucas and Claxton 2010: 8)

Applying the mindset theory to language learning, holding a fixed mindset means that someone believes that one's ability to learn a language is by and large fixed – it is something you either have or you do not. This can be seen, for example, in the way people talk about individuals having a 'natural talent' for languages or someone not being a 'languages person'. In contrast, a person with a growth mindset would believe that language learning abilities can always be enhanced through strategic efforts and that everyone can improve on their base level of abilities. This is not to say everyone will reach the same ultimate level of proficiency, but it is to say that everyone can improve on their current levels, given the will, opportunities and right kinds of strategic approaches. It should be immediately apparent how important it is for our learners to hold a growth mindset and to believe in their potential to improve, and the good news is that past research has shown that it is possible to retrain unproductive mindsets: there is a way to move learners from fixed to growth!

> *A fixed mindset may impede learning but a growth mindset can function as a powerful resource, influencing learner motivation, the setting of goals, and how learners respond to setbacks and 'failures' that are an essential part of language learning.*
>
> (Williams et al. 2015: 71)

METHODS THAT CAN PROMOTE A GROWTH MINDSET

Gershon (2016) provides a series of activities and tasks which can be used to promote a growth mindset with learners. Adapting his overarching framework, below is an outline of key areas and ways we can focus on developing a growth mindset in our learners:

- Getting the language right – thinking about how we talk about abilities, mistakes, talent, and effort.
- Changing how students perceive mistakes – welcoming mistakes.
- Targeted student effort – effort with direction and purpose.
- Giving the right kind of feedback.
- Thinking about thinking – discussing strategies and how learners think about language learning.
- Creating a challenge culture – challenge is not risk but a chance for growth.
- Focusing on processes of learning, not products of learning.

Principle 3: Promote Learners' Sense of Ownership and Control

The well-known 'theory of planned behaviour' in social psychology (Ajzen 1988) contains the concept of *perceived behavioural control*, which concerns the individual's beliefs about the presence of primarily external factors that may support or hinder their performance. If a sense of control is perceived to be low, this will hinder engagement, because people will feel that the outcome is not completely under their control (e.g. in a business venture because of corruption in the system, or in an exam because of hot weather making it hard to concentrate). In this sense, perceived behavioural control is similar to self-efficacy, in that both refer to the presence or absence of constraints to perform an activity in a given situation, with self-efficacy referring to internal capabilities, whereas perceived behavioural control concerning primarily external ones (although see Ajzen (2002), which suggests that in reality the two types of factor often overlap).

In accordance with Ajzen's theory, engagement will only take place if students feel some degree of control and ownership of their learning. Of course, the notion of 'ownership' can be conceptually rather slippery, yet we believe it is intuitively recognisable to most teachers. Ownership is typically thought of in relation to a person and an object; however, people can also feel ownership towards non-material things, such as ideas, topics or hobbies. When we 'own' something, we tend to have strong emotions about it and this can exert a potentially powerful effect on how we behave and respond towards the object of our ownership. In language education, we want learners to feel ownership towards their learning and the language itself. In other words, we want learners to step up and 'own' their language learning.

Having a growth mindset and a sense of competence are key components contributing to learners having a sense of control, and so is a third established notion in motivation research: *learner attributions* (Weiner 1992). Attributions concern the various explanations that learners give to explain their past successes and especially their past failures. Such explanations are highly subjective: what one person perceives of as a failure for themselves might be seen by another learner as a great achievement. It has been found that future willingness to engage with tasks is improved by a learner making 'healthy' attributions, that is, concentrating on factors contributing to their failures that they can influence and change. That is, future engagement will occur if students feel they have some control over their learning outcomes, which is not the case if they attribute their failures to fixed or unchangeable factors such as insufficient ability. For example, after failing a test, one can offer the healthy attribution of 'I didn't work hard enough' (which can be changed) or unhealthy ones, such as 'The test was too difficult' or 'I'm no good at it'.

REFLECTION TASK 4

Think about your own attributions. If a class does not go well, what are some of the reasons you give for why this is the case? Which of the reasons are something you can change? How does this motivate you to approach teaching in the future? How do you feel when things out of your control derail your teaching?

> *Students with low perceived control believe that academic outcomes are beyond their control, attributing performance to uncontrollable factors such as course difficulty, unfair professors, bad luck, etc. For these low-perceived-control students, a psychological profile emerges involving low expectations, negative affect, de-motivation, and poor performance, despite the presence of highly effective instruction. Simply put, vulnerable, failure-prone students are most 'at risk' and in need of enriched educational opportunities such as effective instruction, but are unlikely to derive the academic benefits that normally accrue in such learning conditions.*
>
> (Haynes, Perry, Stupnisky and Daniels 2009: 230)

Principle 4: Develop Proactive Learners

Proactive personalities are increasingly becoming the focus of a body of research in organisational psychology, as they are seen as critical assets in the contemporary world of work: proactive people can make the most of resources, take the initiative, seek out opportunities for action and are usually more willing to make changes to their environments in order to create better working or study conditions (e.g. Fuller and Marler 2009). In a similar vein, it has been found that proactive learners tend to be more engaged, more open to learning, more willing to speak up and connect with others; all of which in turn lead to more positive outcomes (Wang, Zhang, Thomas, Lu and Spitzmueller 2017). They self-initiate action, take control and make things happen.

The point we would like to make here is that being proactive is not simply a personality feature. Although some people may appear to be more naturally enterprising and dynamic than others, it is also dependent on the environment. In order to be proactive, people need to feel safe and supported so that their self-initiated actions are not seen as risks. This means that in a classroom setting where teachers are open to and appreciative of learners speaking up and taking action, learners can become more proactive in taking ownership and control of their learning (Parker and Wu 2014). In other words, proactive personalities are not something people either are or are not, as learners can feel more empowered and consequently become more proactive, given the right supportive conditions. Chapters 3 and 4 will focus on such conditions in terms of teacher–student relations and the peer group climate.

REFLECTION TASK 5

Can you think of somebody who you would describe as a proactive personality? What is it that characterises them as proactive? Do you recognise any of your learners as proactive? What kind of situations do they flourish in? What kind of support do they need from you as their teacher?

The issue of proactiveness is sometimes discussed under the rubric of 'agency' in the literature, referring to an individual's will and capacity to act (Gao 2010). This body of literature has produced suggestions not unlike the ones presented earlier: for learners to feel agentic, they need to perceive that they have a sense of influence to be able to actively shape their learning experiences and to manage their affective responses (Bown 2009). Cleary and Zimmerman (2012) argue that in order for agentic engagement to happen, learners need to possess both the 'will' and the 'skill' to engage, both of which can be developed through self-regulated learning approaches. Self-regulated learning is typically defined as 'self-generated thoughts, feelings, and actions that are planned and cyclically adapted to the attainment of personal goals' (Zimmerman and Cleary 2009: 247). It involves being aware of one's own strengths and weaknesses, being able to set appropriate goals, having a knowledge of strategies to direct and affect learning, and being able to evaluate one's own sense of progress through feedback loops based on one's own performance. The emphasis is on learners feeling able to control, direct and regulate their own learning.

> *Student involvement in self-regulated learning is closely tied to students' efficacy beliefs about their capability to perform classroom tasks and to their beliefs that these classroom tasks are interesting and worth learning. At the same time, these motivational beliefs are not sufficient for successful academic performance; self-regulated learning components seem to be more directly implicated in performance. Students need to have both the 'will' and the 'skill' to be successful in classrooms.*
>
> (Pintrich and De Groot 1990: 38)

Principle 5: Develop Gritty Learners

> *To be gritty is to keep putting one foot in front of the other. To be gritty is to hold fast to an interesting and purposeful goal. To be gritty is to invest, day after week after year, in challenging practice. To be gritty is to fall down seven times, and rise eight.*
>
> (Duckworth 2016: 275)

Many people compare the long-term endeavour of learning a foreign language to running a marathon. In such an extended process, actual gains and progress can be hard to detect and there are plenty of opportunities for knock-backs along the way. There is no short cut or express route to the mastery of a foreign language, and it is not hard to see why learners can get disheartened along the way. This being the case, we need to prepare students for the long haul mentally: we need them to develop language learning *grit*. Duckworth (2016) has made popular the notion of 'grit' and its value in education. It is a combination of passion, perseverance, resilience and optimism in pursuing long-term goals. It does not merely concern working hard, as it is also about having the stamina and determination to stick the course all the way to the end, even in the face of adversity.

> *Many of us, it seems, quit what we start far too early and far too often. Even more than the effort a gritty person puts in on a single day, what matters is that they wake up the next day, and the next, ready to get on that treadmill and keep going.*
>
> (Duckworth 2016: 50)

Thankfully, grit can be learnt and developed. Many of the factors that we have already discussed above contribute to grit, but a key component that has not been highlighted yet is the learner's *self-control*. This factor is particularly vital in the current age of multiple digital, online and other forms of distractions, because it involves the capability to effectively manage one's attention, emotions and behaviours in order to keep on task when faced with diverting temptations. Many will be familiar with the famous marshmallow study in which children were offered one marshmallow now or two marshmallows if they could wait 15 minutes (Baumeister and Tierney 2011; Mischel 2014). Perhaps unsurprisingly, the children who could delay gratification and use strategies to resist the temptation of the immediate reward were more academically successful in the long term.

Self-control can be effectively enhanced by developing positive behavioural patterns and habits which reduce the need for effortful control. In this way we do not deplete our limited stock of willpower (Baumeister and Tierney 2011), and the same purpose is achieved if temptation is simply removed from the learners' immediate environment so that no effort is required to resist them. Learners can also be encouraged to develop 'if-then' plans in their minds (Hattie and Yates 2014), which are specific statements in which the learner gives themselves a strategy such as, 'if my phone rings, then I will tell whoever it is that I have to work until 5 pm and that they should call me back after that'. Formulating such concrete, clear plans to deal with possible distracting scenarios has proved to be an extremely effective tool in managing distractions (see e.g. Gollwitzer and Oettingen 2012).

> *Self-control is crucial for the successful pursuit of long-term goals. It is equally essential for developing the self-restraint and empathy needed to build caring and mutually supportive relationships. It can help people avoid becoming entrapped early in life, dropping out of school, becoming impervious to consequences, or getting stuck in jobs they hate.*
>
> (Mischel 2014: 6)

Teacher Actions

The principles outlined above summarise the 'big picture' that we wish to aim for in order to generate an optimal mindset in our learners that will facilitate their engagement with learning opportunities within and beyond the classroom. Although the previous discussions have already presented a few practical considerations, the emphasis was on describing the general nature of the different concepts involved. Now we shall turn to five specific action areas that are intended to support the development of these principles in our learners.

Action 1: Think and Act Like a Coach

This first action point - *thinking and acting like a coach* - underlies many of the other actions proposed throughout the book, so let us try to explain what we mean by this in some detail. To start with, what do we mean by 'coaching' and in what way is it relevant to language education? The contemporary use of 'coaching' goes beyond the traditional practice of a sports coach, as it has been extended to apply to a specific way of facilitating learning and development in general. However, because it is related to the promotion of individual performance - that is, coaches are concerned with helping learners/trainees to *do* rather than *know* something - the term still retains a flavour of its traditional association with skill-based activities such as sports and music (Barber and Foord 2014). Such a skill-centred perspective is not alien to language education in the sense that the primary aim for most learners is to be able to communicate in, rather than know about, the target language.

Emphasising a coaching mindset in education, including SLA, usually means that we see learners as *active architects* of their own learning rather than passive recipients of teaching; as Beere and Broughton (2013: 228/1738) concisely sum up the essence of coaching, 'It is the powerful process of *supporting* someone to move forward towards their goal' (our emphasis). The support, as these authors emphasise, is a highly solution-focused process and is in many ways more performance-specific than the related notions of mentoring or counselling.

It needs to be underlined that adopting a coaching mindset and thus placing the onus of learning onto the learner does *not* mean abdicating our teaching role; quite the opposite: in a coaching situation learners need the crucial support of their teachers but in ways which foster their *own* capacity and ability to self-direct their learning efforts. As already discussed in Chapter 1, the available opportunities to engage with the L2 are ubiquitous nowadays and stretch well beyond the classroom or educational institution. If learners wish to make notable progress, they need to be able to recognise such wider L2 learning opportunities, and to know how to self-regulate their learning in these contexts - a good language coach enables them to achieve just that. Of course, for many teachers, such a coaching mindset may simply be part of good instructional practice; however, we have found in our own teaching that it can be useful to actively remind ourselves of what it means to think like a coach, in order to ensure that we really *are* seeking to help learners take ownership of their learning and be their own agents directing their learning.

DIFFERENCES BETWEEN A TEACHING AND A COACHING FOCUS

Traditional teaching focus	**A coaching focus**
Responsibility for learning rests with teacher	Responsibility for learning rests with learner
Talking *to* the learners	Dialogue *with* learners
Learners depend wholly on teacher for learning direction	Learners know in what ways the teacher can help them to learn
Teacher tells learner what to do	Teacher guides and challenges learners to set their own direction
Emphasis on what teacher does for learners	Emphasis on actions learners take themselves
Teacher asks questions to evaluate knowledge	Teacher asks question to prompt thinking
Focus on linguistic gains	Focus on the development of a facilitative L2 learning mindset

(based on Barber and Foord 2014)

An important dimension of coaching is that coaches reflect not only on the learners' linguistic performance but also on their psychological state of mind (Barber and Foord 2014), which is key to this chapter centred around a facilitative mindset. Indeed, coaches strive to empower learners with the skills to promote their own linguistic performance by establishing effective self-regulatory practices, setting personally meaningful and realistic goals and fostering the optimal mental state for successful engagement. It is worth reiterating this central maxim in a slightly different way: thinking and acting as a coach means working with learners not only towards their desired language-related outcomes, but also towards generating the kinds of facilitative psychological states that have been outlined in the five principles above. It means therefore thinking of the learner as a person with psychological needs and drives that can be supported through teaching and interaction.

This is a major departure from the traditional teacher role, which tends to be confined to finding effective ways of providing knowledge input and facilitating its intake. For example, teachers often question whether developing more motivated learners in general is part of their job description or whether they should only focus on achieving short-term performance targets; in contrast, coaches *know* that generating motivation is a central aspect of their job, and, indeed, some form of 'visionary training' is a natural part of the coaching plan of virtually all Olympic athletes. In terms of a sporting analogy, a traditional trainer would focus on polishing the technique of the athlete, whereas a coach offers a broader service by also developing the winning mindset in the athlete.

To summarise, thinking like a coach means putting learners in the director's chair. It emphasises that learners should be doing the thinking and the role of the coaches is only to prompt and guide them by asking thoughtful and open questions, listening actively to their responses, respecting their reflections and, as a result, adapting the teaching approach to the uniqueness of the learners' values and goals (see e.g. Downey 2014). There is no single way to coach well, given that much depends on the individuals involved and the context of the particular coach–learner partnership.

> *In practice, coaching is a discussion, or series of discussions or structured conversations, which:*
> - *Are highly motivating for the coachee.*
> - *Use skilful questioning to identify issues.*
> - *Facilitate learning and commitment from the coachee.*
> - *Encourage the coachee to take responsibility for their actions and outcomes.*
> - *Give choice about the content and direction of the discussion.*
> - *Allow creative solutions to problems to emerge.*
> - *Lead to clear targets and definite commitment by the coachee to agreed courses of action.*
> - *Promote personal and professional development.*
>
> (Beere and Broughton 2013: 236/1738)

The most popular contemporary model in coaching is arguably the GROW model (Whitmore 2017): learners need to be supported by the coach in setting their goals (G); reflecting on what the current reality (R) looks like; exploring the options (O) for achieving the goals and desired future outcomes; and then planning what learners will (W) do in concrete terms to keep moving forward towards their goal. (See the panel below for a summary of these four aspects as four simple questions.) GROW involves learners setting their own immediate and long-term goals and developing a metacognitive awareness of their own strengths and weaknesses, as well as gaining an understanding of the nature of tasks they face and the contexts they are in, in order to know how to evaluate their options. They need to know how to learn and have to be familiar with possible strategies and pathways forward, and they need to repeatedly evaluate their effectiveness along the way and adjust as required. Of course, all these elements are reminiscent of characteristics of self-regulatory learning in general, but we find that the coaching metaphor adds coherence and a certain amount of tangibility to them.

THE GROW MODEL SUMMARISED IN FOUR QUESTIONS

1. What are your **G**oals?
2. What is the **R**eality?
3. What are your **O**ptions?
4. What **W**ill you do?

REFLECTION TASK 6

In the light of the previous discussion, to what extent do you feel you already think like a coach in how you interact with and guide your learners? Are there any areas where you could further improve? (Of course, a coach's answer to this last question would always be yes...) Do you have opportunities to use questions more to guide learners? Do you feel there are limitations to a coaching mindset for your practice?

Action 2: Make Learning Progress Visible

One of the most practical things we can do to empower and motivate our learners to engage is to help them *see progress*. Language learning is a slow, incremental process, and gains can be hard to detect for both teachers and learners. In order to develop a sense of competence, learners need to be able to see that they are improving and that their efforts are worthwhile. One way of achieving this is to set measureable objectives, which learners can easily identify for themselves when they have accomplished them. Some L2 teaching textbooks have done this through the use of 'can do' statements at the end of each unit, and, indeed, some version of this approach can even be adopted in every lesson, such as through exit tickets, which are quick informal student responses collected at the end of a class.

On a longer timescale, learners can also be encouraged to keep *portfolios of work* throughout the year. Some coursebooks now come with a language portfolio for students to record their progress and keep examples of their work. However, a portfolio can simply be a collection of pieces of work from the student over an extended period of time to create documentation and an archive of the student's work. It can be done physically or digitally. Through conscious reviewing of the portfolio and guided reflection on their achievements, learners can be made aware of the gains they have made throughout the year, noticing how their language work has improved in complexity, creativity, fluency and accuracy. Portfolios can also visually display just how much work learners have done.

A further effective visualisation technique for a sense of progress can be provided by the *coursebooks* themselves. At the beginning of the school year, it can be interesting to ask learners to look at the very last page or unit of the book and see how much they understand or recognise in a specific section. Assuring them that the whole class will manage to work on the final unit eventually, you can then return to this at the end of the year and it can serve as the ultimate evidence for learners that what before seemed impossible is now manageable.

A frequently used formative assessment technique is the use of *correction logs*, where learners categorise and keep track of things they need to work on still. Each time they get a piece of work back, they revisit the log and add corrected mistakes from their work to the relevant category in their log. It is used as a way of drawing attention to problem areas and ensuring learners engage actively with feedback. As the name suggests, correction logs typically focus on mistakes and the things going wrong in language production; however, it is important to also actively support learners in spotting strengths and building on them. In this vein, the correction log can also be used as a strengths log in which learners are encouraged to make note of things they did especially well. Having both corrections and strengths in the 'learning log' not only gives learners a more balanced view of their own competences, but it also raises their awareness of what a competence in a specific skill area is comprised of. For example, they can note their correct use of linking words to create cohesion in a text, or the appropriate use of discourse markers in an oral presentation.

Finally, another popular technique is the use of *exit tickets* (see e.g. Lemov 2015). These are a very short, quick set of written questions that invite learners to show to what extent they have managed the learning objectives for a session. Exit tickets can ask specific questions or follow a general open format, with learners being anonymous or named depending on the purpose and format. They are not a test and should not be perceived as such. Ideally, they should ensure there is at least one positive aspect or response for every learner to achieve or respond to. Essentially, exit tickets can serve a dual purpose: (1) they can help learners take stock of what they can and cannot yet do; and (2) they can provide teachers with vital information about what aspects may need more time spending on and what aspects learners enjoy / did not enjoy. They need not necessarily serve all these functions at the same time. Wilden (2017) suggests that exit tickets are especially well suited to being done digitally through online surveys or chat groups to quickly and immediately provide feedback on the learners' response to a class.

SAMPLE EXIT TICKET

- What I learnt today: ______________________
- How confident I feel about being able to do this:
  Not at all / Not very / Somewhat / Very / Completely
- What I still feel unsure about: ______________________
- What I especially enjoyed: ______________________

REFLECTION TASK 7

How consciously do you draw your learners' attention to their strengths? How visible do you think the sense of progress is for learners in all your classes? How could you make both immediate and long-term progress / learning gains more visible?

Action 3: Discuss Beliefs Explicitly

When it comes to mindsets, there are many strategies you can use (as shown in other sections of this chapter) but sometimes the most direct route – that is, explicitly discussing learner mindset beliefs – can be the most effective. When we talk about 'beliefs', the first obvious question to ask is 'beliefs about what?' In this respect, Schommer's (1990) pioneering research is informative, as she linked 'belief' as a scientific term to the individual's views held about the *nature of knowledge* and *knowledge acquisition*. Within this paradigm, it is useful to make a further distinction between *explicit* and *implicit* beliefs (for a discussion, see e.g. Dörnyei and Ryan 2015). Explicit beliefs are those that we are aware of and that we can articulate reasonably effectively, and there has been a great deal written about how harmful beliefs can be changed and constructive beliefs generated through explicit and critical discussion about them and about their consequences (see e.g. Chapter 4 in Williams et al. 2015). However, for the current discussion, implicit beliefs are particularly relevant, because mindset beliefs fall under this rubric.

Being largely implicit, that is, not necessarily part of conscious awareness, mindset beliefs are usually deeply held and this makes them difficult to change. However, it is possible to help learners adopt a growth mindset little by little, and we are convinced that it is possible for everyone in the class to develop 'growth thinking'. One of the core approaches for building a growth mindset has been to move mindset beliefs from the implicit into the explicit domain. One way to do this is to teach learners about the malleability of the brain, which is a way of challenging any fixed beliefs about ability or intelligence. Dweck and colleagues (Blackwell Trzesniewski and Dweck 2007) have developed a programme, in which children are taught about how the brain is like a muscle which can be stretched, trained and strengthened. Seeing this and understanding the mechanics of why a growth mindset is justified acts as a great motivator for learners and helps them be willing to try harder and engage with tasks. Their beliefs are challenged as they can see that their brains are not fixed but have a potential to become stronger through certain types of practice and learning. In terms of resources, there are numerous videos and worksheets available online that teachers can use to introduce brain malleability, or 'neuroplasticity' as it can also be known. As Claxton, Chambers, Powell and Lucas (2011: 31) explain, we want learners to see classroom work and activities as 'being like a mind gym, with each lesson making use of the content and activities to create a pleasurably taxing mental 'workout'.

> *Teach students about the brain ... This is not just about teaching a few lessons. It is an area that must be revisited and built upon over time. It is about introducing and explicitly teaching students, then routinely revisiting the concept of malleable intelligence so that students realize that intelligence is not about a fixed number, a grade on a paper, or a report card. Students must understand that intelligence is constantly changing based on effort, persistence, and motivation. They will soon realize that intelligence is something that grows as you use it and languishes if you don't.*
>
> (Ricci 2017: 22)

Learners can also be prompted to discuss mindset beliefs through the use of texts, quotes, films and literature, identifying and examining role models who exemplify growth mindsets. They can look for examples of growth mindsets online or in the community, they can analyse language which reflects mindset beliefs, and they can even keep their own mindset logs (see, e.g. Ricci 2017; Williams, Puchta and Mercer in press). In these logs, they can complete statements, agree/disagree with responses in questionnaires to identify their own mindsets, and then discuss how that may be affecting their approaches to learning. It is important to note at this stage, though, that learners with a fixed mindset must not be criticised for thinking that way; rather, they should be helped to question their beliefs and look for evidence that challenges the idea that their abilities as a language learner cannot be changed.

REFLECTION TASK 8

Think about your beliefs about teaching. Here are some possible questions to think about: How much control do you feel you have over learner motivation? How do you think learners learn to write best? What do you think is the most effective way to encourage learners to speak in class? What do you believe has the strongest impact on learner attitudes to homework? What evidence do you have for the veracity of these beliefs? How could you challenge yourself about these beliefs?

> *Mindset change is not about picking up a few pointers here and there. It's about seeing things in a new way. When people ... change to a growth mindset, they change from a judge-and-be-judged framework to a learn-and-help-learn framework. Their commitment is to growth, and growth takes plenty of time, effort and mutual support.*
>
> (Dweck 2006: 238)

Action 4: Build in Choice and Voice

A key factor in promoting learners' sense of agency is enabling them to have choice and to express their voice where possible. The degree to which this can be achieved depends partly on contextual constraints, partly on the nature of the course and partly on how comfortable we, the teachers, feel with this. There are all kinds of small and non-intrusive ways we can bring in choice and allow learners to contribute. The easiest ones tend to concern the 'how' of their learning; for example, choosing between two tasks, selecting who to work with or deciding how big the group size should be. We can also ask learners how long they think they will need for a task, or we can let them choose between different output modes or formats. We can even give them a choice of tasks to do in class or at home. Essentially, any form of genuine dialogue or negotiation opens the avenue for learners to feel empowered to influence their own learning conditions, even if this is only to a small degree.

> *In principle, any practice that encourages and enables learners to take greater control of any aspect of their learning can be considered a means of promoting autonomy.*
>
> (Benson 2001: 109)

The aspect of 'what' students learn is often not readily open to discussion, as this is regulated by the curriculum. However, sometimes there may be some opportunities even in this area, for example, choosing between different texts to read or films to watch. We can also tweak tasks to enable learners to relate the content to personal interests, and in some settings, it is possible to offer them choice by doing *project work*. Projects involve concentrated work by groups of students on a particular topic or task, and, at the core, a project is all about letting learners make the decisions and putting them in an active role. Partly as a result, projects can be some of the most engaging work formats in teaching and are often the things students remember about school many years later (see e.g. Chapter 9 in Dörnyei, Henry and Muir 2016).

ESSENTIAL PROJECT DESIGN ELEMENTS

Larmer, Mergendoller and Boss (2015: 34) describe the conditions that lead to 'gold standard project-based learning', referring to seven key elements:

1. Challenging problem or question
2. Sustained inquiry
3. Authenticity
4. Student voice and choice
5. Reflection
6. Critique and revision
7. Public product

An intriguing approach worth mentioning is what is known as the 'genius hour' (see also Chapter 6). This stems from an idea introduced at Google Inc. which allows employees to spend 20% of their time working on any project they like. The idea behind the initiative is that giving people the freedom to work on something they are passionate about and deeply interested in will increase their overall productivity. In the language classroom, such a scheme would of course only work if the learner group is sufficiently mature and cohesive (see Chapter 4), because we would in effect leave students to their own devices to use productively a certain number of teaching hours (the original idea was a 20/80 time split, but there is no reason why this time frame could not be altered). Working in groups or individually, learners select a specific question they wish to answer, set a concrete deadline for completing the exploration and then create an output to be shared in a format of their choice. As teachers, we can set class time aside for making ourselves available to guide and keep learners on track if need be, but learners are the drivers, the designers and the directors of their project.

> *If you want to prepare students for life after school, 20% Time and inquiry-driven learning is a must. Students don't need to fill in answer sheets or bubbles on a piece of paper. They need to be given time to produce something of value, to themselves and the world.*
>
> (Juliani 2015: 19)

REFLECTION TASK 9

What opportunities do you have within your setting for giving learners choice and voice in respect to how they learn and what they learn? What kind of projects could you do that will still also cover curriculum requirements?

Action 5: Teach How to Learn

We have argued earlier that the 'will' and 'skill' to engage are interconnected in a learner: if they are confident that they know *how* to learn effectively, they are more likely to actively engage with the actual process of learning. Teaching to learn is a rather broad area, involving at least three types of knowledge that are beneficial for learners in developing the necessary 'skill': knowledge about (a) themselves as learners, (b) the tasks presented and (c) how to learn (Flavell 1979).

The *knowledge about oneself as a learner* requires developing skills of self-reflection and self-assessment. This is often easier said than done; one of us, Sarah, has found her tertiary-level learners resistant to the notion, and even the term, 'reflection'. However, when she applied a more structured approach with guiding questions and frameworks, and switched from using the term 'reflection' to 'critical evaluation' (with no sense of 'critical' being negative), the process seemed more acceptable to the students and more effective. Some scholars suggest setting up 'intentional reflective dialogues' between the learner and the teacher or learning advisor (Kato and Mynard 2016: 6), and a tool that is frequently recommended involves students keeping a learning diary or journal, which can be supported through a probing question-framework and which can be discussed with teachers and/or peers, depending on content and levels of disclosure.

> *There is a danger in students relying solely on their teacher for the evaluation of their performance. If they are never trusted to evaluate their own experience, they will not acquire the habits and skills of reflecting on their performance, and so they will not develop the ability to improve themselves. The aim must surely be to produce a student who has the confidence and skill to reflect and evaluate independently of the teacher. Give students the confidence in their ability to learn from their own experience, and when your teaching finishes, their learning continues. The student becomes a 'reflective practitioner'.*
>
> (Petty 2014: 315)

The second type of knowledge concerns the *learning tasks*. Here the main objective is to help learners to see the 'why', that is, to bring them on board about the purpose of the specific activities they are asked to participate in. For some learners, attending class is like being in the military, in that they are often told to do things without receiving any rationale or justification for the instruction. However, having clear guidelines and transparent learning objectives, accompanied by an outline of possible steps to be taken to complete the task, can notably facilitate the learning process and learner engagement.

The third type of knowledge is *how to learn* and is typically taught in classroom settings through the use of *language learning strategies*. Strategies refer to conscious actions that learners can employ to help them when learning; when we organised 'sharing sessions' amongst the learners in the past - for example, before having to prepare for an exam - they always displayed admirable creativity about the techniques they developed to make the learning process more personalised or doable. The typical approach to 'teaching' learning strategies is to take an experiential approach (see e.g. Gregersen and MacIntyre 2014; Griffiths 2013; Mercer 2005; Oxford 2017), in which students are first presented with a wide repertoire of strategies, either by the teacher or through a questionnaire (or even through the sharing sessions mentioned above). It is emphasised at this stage that there are no inherently 'good' or 'bad' strategies, but rather that every individual has to find the strategies that suit their particular needs, goals and style. Next, learners are encouraged to try out new strategies over a period of time, keeping records and evaluating how they felt about using them and how effective they were. Learners can then decide whether they want to adopt the strategy, or make any changes for future tasks, or try a different strategy.

> *If learners believe they have the capacity to learn the language, and assuming they are motivated and willing to take an active role in learning, then they need to know what action to take to learn that language.*
>
> (Williams et al. 2015: 121)

Summary

We started out this chapter by arguing that in order for learners to respond to our efforts of engaging them in various L2 learning opportunities within and beyond the classroom, they need to possess an optimal facilitative psychological frame of mind. In five principles, we highlighted what we see as the main facets of such a frame of mind: a sense of competence, a growth mindset, a sense of ownership and control over the learning process, confidence/willingness to be proactive and, finally, grit. We then discussed five specific action areas that can be pursued to support these principles:

- Thinking and acting like a coach, in the sense of treating the learners as partners who have the chief responsibility for accomplishing their own performance goals.
- Making the learning progress visible, so that improvement can be perceived and satisfaction and sense of competence gained.
- Discussing beliefs explicitly, in order to develop in the students healthy rather than counterproductive ways of thinking about learning.
- Building choice and learner voice into the learning process, to foster a more autonomous and active involvement on the part of the students.
- Teaching learners how to learn by raising awareness about their own learning characteristics, the nature of the learning tasks and a repertoire of effective strategies that they can choose from.

CHAPTER IN A NUTSHELL

Learners are more likely to engage with language learning if they feel competent to do so and have some ownership and control over their development and experiences.

IF YOU WANT TO FIND OUT MORE

Beere, J. and Broughton, T. (2013). *The Perfect Teacher Coach.* Carmarthen: Independent Thinking Press. (An introduction and overview of how coaching can be incorporated in practical ways into teaching.)

Dweck, C. S. (2006). *Mindset: The New Psychology of Success.* New York, NY: Ballantine Books. (This is the book which made Dweck's mindset theories popular and is a must-read for all educators to get a core understanding of the power of a growth mindset for learning.)

McCombs, B. L. and Miller, L. (2007). *Learner-Centered Classroom Practices and Assessments: Maximizing Student Motivation, Learning, and Achievement.* Thousand Oaks, CA: Corwin Press. (This book presents a series of core principles based on research which can support learner growth and development, providing cornerstones for engagement.)

Williams, M., Mercer, S. and Ryan, S. (2015). *Exploring Psychology in Language Learning and Teaching.* Oxford: Oxford University Press. (This book outlines many of the aspects touched on in this chapter in language learning contexts, such as beliefs, the self, agency, strategies and self-regulation.)

3 Teacher–student rapport

REFLECTION TASK 1

Reflect on your own time in school or in teacher training. Can you think back to a favourite teacher in whose class you 'blossomed'? Or perhaps a fictional teacher who you find inspiring? How would you describe the relationship such a teacher has with their students? What do they do that fosters learning and engagement in their classrooms?

The key figure in any learner's educational life is the teacher. Like us, you are likely to be able to remember some teachers who were able to engage you, using little in the way of props or fancy techniques, and yet others who seemingly ticked all the boxes in terms of activity design and use of resources, but who just could not get you to engage with them as individuals or the subject they were trying to teach. In fact, how learners engage with the teacher is critical to all other forms of engagement. If learners feel cared for and supported by their teachers, then they are much more likely to be willing to engage with them and, consequently, also with other aspects of the educational experience. The focus of this chapter is this critical engagement and its foundation, the teacher–student relationship. We will explore the nature of this engagement and we will reflect on the main principles and behaviours underlying quality teacher-student rapport.

> *An extensive body of research suggests the importance of close, caring teacher–student relationships and high-quality peer relationships for students' academic self-perceptions, school engagement, motivation, learning, and performance.*
>
> (Furrer, Skinner and Pitzer 2014: 102)

Rationale

Education is inherently relational. The reason we go to school or any kind of educational institution is to be with, and learn together with, other people. For language learning, the need for fellow interlocutors means that learning is deeply social, possibly more so than for other academic subjects. How well we get on with the people in our educational settings - peers, colleagues, and teachers - can make or break our learning, or our teaching, experience. For both teachers and learners, the central relationship in schools is that between teacher and learner.

REFLECTION TASK 2

Take a moment to think of a relationship that is important to you, such as with a friend, a colleague, or a partner. What are the characteristics that you look for in such a relationship?

Whoever we are, most people want similar things from their relationships. Roffey (2011: 100) lists the following relational qualities:

- Mutual respect
- Trust and honesty
- Reciprocity - give and take
- Acceptance of you as a whole person
- Open communication
- Equality
- Warmth
- Reliability - being there in good and bad
- Feeling comfortable and enjoying being together

As teachers, we often get caught up in the mechanics of teaching, thinking about which resources to use or which language forms to focus on, and continuously considering test formats and administrative pragmatics. These are important, unavoidable aspects of our profession, but it is equally important to plan and teach with the quality of our relationship with our students at the forefront of our minds.

> *One teacher can help a child love school; another can make a child hate school. It all depends on our relationships with the children.*
>
> (Bahman and Maffini 2008: 13)

A positive teacher-learner relationship is defined by characteristics such as *pedagogical caring* (Wentzel 1997), *trust* (Bryk and Schneider 2002; Tschannen-Moran 2014), *teacher involvement* (Skinner and Belmont 1993), *respect* (Tomlinson 2011) and *empathy* (Cooper 2011; Gkonou and Mercer 2017). There are also two theoretical frameworks which help us to better appreciate what learners need from their relationships with us, *self-determination theory* and *attachment theory*:

- Self-determination theory (SDT) (Ryan and Deci 2000) has been a popular perspective for understanding engagement (Reeve 2012), and we draw on it specifically in respect to relational engagement. The SDT framework suggests that the quality of one's well-being is influenced by whether the person feels that three basic core needs are being met: the need for *relatedness*, *competence* and *autonomy* (Patrick, Knee, Canevello and Lonsbary 2007).

- *Relatedness* refers to our 'need to belong' (Baumeister and Leary 1995) and describes how we are driven to seek out supportive, strong interpersonal relationships. In Chapter 4, we shall see the significance of positive group dynamics and peer relations for determining a sense of belonging in the classroom, and here we add that the learners' relationships with their teachers are also a key contributory factor to this feeling of belonging.
- *Competence* concerns learners' need to believe in their capabilities to cope with and complete tasks. The teacher's input and subsequent scaffolding of learning is a vital ingredient in this respect.
- *Autonomy* is the feeling that learners have some control and direction over what they do. It does not mean independence and is thus not in any way at odds with the need for relatedness. Indeed, autonomy can be highly social (Murray 2014), as long as learners feel an active sense of control over aspects of their learning lives. Of course, this sense of volitional control greatly depends on the teacher's approach (an issue we will come back to later).

- Attachment theory (Bowlby 1969) describes the characteristics and functions of a child's attachment to a key caregiver, typically the mother. Ideally, when the caregiver - or in this case, the teacher - responds to the learner in predictable, sensitive and caring ways, then the relationship is characterised by a sense of stability and security. In turn, this enables the learner to explore, take risks, be creative and develop a sense of self-worth and trust in others. Regarding learners, on the one hand, they need to develop a sense of trust and care with their teacher, knowing that they can rely on us for support if needed; on the other hand, they also need the confidence to become autonomous in their actions. Although attachment theory has typically been employed to understand the relationships between teachers and young learners (Wentzel 2009), the core relational qualities are relevant for any type of relationship including between adults (Hazan and Shaver 1994).

Principles for Learner Engagement With Teachers

In order to promote deep learner engagement with teachers in relational terms, learners need to connect with them on all four engagement dimensions described in the introduction: social, affective, cognitive and behavioural. We will begin by considering the kinds of principles that facilitate the more *social* and *affective* aspects of engagement, and then move on to teacher actions which also support the more *cognitive* and *behavioural* dimensions.

Principle 1: Be Approachable

To engage with us, learners have to feel that we are open to being engaged with: that is, we need to be *approachable*. This can be communicated on two levels. First and most obviously, it is conveyed in terms of whether we are actually *physically present* and available to talk to. Often institutions will have opportunities, such as 'office hours', where learners (and parents) can come and talk to teachers about their concerns, but less formal opportunities of contact are perhaps even more welcome, such as a regular time slot spent in, say, the school canteen. More recently, some teachers have started to use social media (e.g. WhatsApp, Facebook) and online platforms (e.g. Moodle, Blackboard) to make themselves more accessible to learners, which is an important practical step towards ensuring we are approachable in the digital age. However, teachers might wish to draw up a basic 'code of conduct' to create boundaries and to protect personal time when they are not available, such as agreeing that nobody may contact the group via social media after 5 pm on weekdays or at all at weekends.

The second level of approachability concerns our *general disposition* as teachers. There are many direct and indirect ways in which we can convey our approachability, with *self-disclosure* being a particularly effective tool. As language teachers, we are continually asking our learners to share many personal details in terms of their likes, dislikes, hopes and fears, etc. as part of the communicative interaction. In building rapport, it can make a considerable difference if we also offer some degree of self-disclosure in return. Research has shown that college instructors who engaged in more self-disclosure were more positively evaluated by their students (Lannutti and Strauman 2006), which in turn is connected to learner motivation and interest (Cayanus, Martin, and Goodboy 2009). However, a word of caution is needed here: everything in moderation – over-sharing is not professional or indeed appropriate.

> *A degree of self-disclosure shows a desirable openness towards others and an honesty and lack of defensiveness about ourselves. It also shows a readiness to trust others, and is an essential ingredient in social intimacy.*
>
> (Fontana 1988: 294–295)

Humour can be another way to lower the affective filter and generate positive affect, revealing to learners our 'human' side. Perhaps it is obvious, but it still needs to be stressed that this, too, must be used with care. Wanzer, Frymier and Irwin (2010) explain that learners need to recognise a statement or comment as being humorous, and only when the content is relevant and the form of humour appropriate will it lead to deeper cognitive processing, better relationships and more effective learning.

> *[According to communication expert Melissa Wanzer,] 'Students don't necessarily want Jerry Seinfeld [a US comedian] as their instructor. They want appropriate humour that is relevant, lightens the mood and makes the information memorable.'*
>
> (Stambor 2006)

Principle 2: Be Empathetic

Learners need to feel understood and appreciated. In any relationship, *empathy* is the key ingredient. Empathy has been defined as getting 'into' somebody else's feelings and thoughts, attempting to understand them, and seeking to convey that understanding to others (Howe 2013: 9). In other words, it means being able to step into somebody else's shoes and see the world from their perspective. Empathy does not mean agreement but is about trying to *understand* others. To do this, we make inferences and interpretations based on other people's behaviours, as well as on their verbal and non-verbal communications. We can continually improve our skills in these areas through conscious effort at learning to read body language and gestures, by reading literature written about our learner age group or population (e.g. young adult literature if we work in schools, or migrant stories if we work with migrant populations) or by learning to improve our communication skills by listening without judgement (see Action Point 3 below). We can also act as valuable role models in displaying empathy in our interactions with learners, promoting such skills consciously in our learners and helping them to work more empathetically with each other (see also Chapter 3).

> *There must be no misapprehension about the nature of empathy or emotion in learning. It does not represent a sentimental or woolly approach, but is fundamental to every aspect of how human beings relate to and learn from each other.*
>
> (Cooper 2011: 3)

Principle 3: Be Responsive to Learner Individuality

Related to our empathic skills is our sensitivity to the diversity among our learners. All our learners like to know that you really *know* who they are and that they are valued as individuals. Learner-centredness has been one important approach that has drawn attention to what learners as individuals bring to the classroom and their learning (see e.g. Brandes and Ginnis 1986; Nunan 1988). A useful definition is offered by McCombs and Whisler (1997: 9):

> *'Learner-centred' is the perspective that combines a focus on individual learners – their heredity, experiences, perspectives,*

> *backgrounds, talents, interests, capacities, and needs – with a focus on the best available knowledge about learning and how it occurs and about teaching practices that promote the highest levels of motivation, learning, and achievement for* all *learners.* (our emphasis)

There are two facets to this definition worth highlighting: the focus on learner uniqueness and the intention to ensure that *all* students learn. The first implies the importance of getting to know the learners as people with lives beyond the classroom and as students with prior knowledge and experiences. You cannot plan your teaching effectively if you do not know what they already know, what you can connect to and build upon, or what would be personally interesting, meaningful or relevant for them.

> *Understanding the students' current identity concerns ... implies more than merely doing a needs analysis in order to try and make language tasks relevant to the particular characteristics of the learners. What is really involved is a conscious effort to gain an understanding of the persons that the students in the classrooms are and of the range of unique life experiences, dreams and worries that they bring into the learning environment with them.*
>
> (Dörnyei and Kubanyiova 2014: 39)

In terms of getting to know our learners, there are many steps we can take to personalise our interactions and strengthen our rapport. The most basic is to *remember student names*. As Bonwell and Eison (1991: 22) state, 'perhaps the single most important act that faculty can do to improve the climate in the classroom is to learn students' names'. This also means that teachers need to make an effort to learn how to pronounce students' names properly when they come from a different linguistic background to the teacher. This small effort on the part of the teacher can mean a lot for the learner in terms of a sense of belonging and feeling respected. As language educators, we are in the ideal position to connect with learners personally when they share their stories and personalities as part of communicative tasks. We can also build in opportunities for learners to share their histories or stories of their language encounters beyond the classroom (see Mercer 2013). As Rubie-Davies (2015: 174) explains, 'Taking the time to get to know students, enjoy them, and appreciate their abilities can go a long way to building strong interpersonal relationships'. Although we may find relationships easier to build with some learners than others, all learners have individual strengths and characters which we can learn to appreciate.

BUILDING RAPPORT WITH STUDENTS

Dörnyei (2001) lists a variety of small gestures that do not take up much time yet which can convey personal attention, including:

- Greet students and remember their names.
- Learn something unique about each student and occasionally mention it to them.
- Ask them about their hobbies and lives outside school.
- Recognise birthdays.
- Include personal topics and examples about students in discussing content matters.
- Send notes/homework to absent students.

The second part of the definition of learner-centredness offered by McCombs and Whisler (1997) stresses that *all* learners need to be supported. This reflects a tension of balancing individual learner needs with whole group needs (Williams et al. 2015). One current popular approach is to *differentiate* our teaching (see also Chapter 6), which ideally means designing lessons so that all learners achieve the same goals and aims, but in different possible ways. We can differentiate in terms of the task itself, the process of working on it, the form of output required from the learners or the working set-up, such as alone, in pairs or groups (see Petty 2014). Reasons for differentiating can include different preferred ways of working, different interests and also different abilities and degrees of readiness. However, there is a word of caution needed here regarding differentiating for perceived ability: it may lead educators to create overly low challenges and low expectations for some learners perceived as being of weaker ability. This can result in teachers accepting poorer performance from them and may also mean teachers offering less informative feedback about learning progress and future steps to such learners (Rubie-Davies 2015). Instead, the aim is to differentiate but in ways which challenge and engage *all* learners.

> *High expectations do not mean having the same expectations for all students: high expectations are relative to each individual student. High expectations are beliefs that all students will make accelerated progress, beyond what they have previously achieved. That is, in this classroom, the learning trajectory of* all *students will be augmented.*
>
> (Rubie-Davies 2015: 218; our emphasis)

Principle 4: Believe in All Your Learners

Central to having high expectations of all our learners is the fundamental belief in the potential of all our learners to improve. This means teachers need a *growth mindset* about learners' language learning abilities. In language education, we must resist the myth of the existence of the 'natural-born linguist' (Mercer 2012); it may well be that some learners find it easier to learn a language than others, but there is a potential for improvement in *all* learners. The learners also need to share our beliefs in growth mindsets, and this can be promoted not only through explicit discussion, but also through other actions that can send important growth mindset signals to them. For example, we need to encourage learners to embrace making mistakes and to see them as a non-threatening part of the learning process (see Action Point 2). Gershon (2016) goes so far as to suggest allocating a 'mistake quota' in a lesson and prompting learners if they do not make any mistakes, explaining to them that they are not learning or pushing themselves enough if there are no mistakes. In addition, if a learner does experience a setback, we have to help them have optimism to believe they can still achieve their goals, but maybe need to reflect on things within their control, such as time expended, effort invested and strategic pathways used. Fundamentally, learners need to see that a talent is not something that people are born with, but something they develop with practice (Subotnik, Olszewski-Kubilius and Worrell 2012).

Another way of showing learners that we believe in their potential is through how we *care* for them. In an educational setting, caring involves showing emotional support and investment in the relationship with students, but it is also about what we do and say in our behaviours and interactions about their learning (Davis, Summers and Miller 2012). Students need to feel that their learning and progress is important to us, that we 'care' about their learning. Our investment in our teaching materials, preparation and organisation are all important markers for learners about how seriously we take our responsibilities towards their learning. Indeed, Lucas and Claxton (2010: 163) are right to stress that 'Students often deduce the values of any institution more from the way teachers and other adults behave and from the way the schools actually treat them than from any published statement of belief'.

> *The research is very clear; students who perceive their teachers as caring tend to engage more with the content, take intellectual risks including probing when they do not understand, and persist in the face of failure.*
>
> (Davis et al. 2012: 80)

Principle 5: Support Learner Autonomy

As mentioned earlier, one of the key needs that learners have is for autonomy. Teaching behaviours can be classified as stretching along a continuum from more controlling to more autonomy-supportive (Deci, Schwartz, Sheinman and Ryan 1981). In reality, a teacher is likely to move back and forth along this continuum at different points for various purposes; for example, as Dörnyei and Murphey (2003) explain, in various phases of a learner group's development different degrees of control serve the group well, moving from a more autocrative towards a more democratic teaching style. Research has shown that from the point of view of student engagement with the teacher, more autonomy-supportive teaching behaviours are most effective (Reeve 2006). Autonomy-supportive teachers tend to see themselves as facilitators, acknowledging that learners have much to contribute to the learning process and supporting, but not smothering, learners' own curiosity and inner motivational drives. Such teachers acknowledge learner diversity and seek to organise their instruction in such a way that learners can determine to some extent their own learning. Key behaviours include building in an element of choice where possible, sharing decision-making to include learners as democratic partners and giving students positions of genuine responsibility.

> *An autonomy-supportive style represents the prototype of the sort of interpersonal relationship that facilitates students' autonomous motivation and classroom engagement.*
>
> (Reeve 2006: 234)

Principle 6: Be Passionate About What You Do

This final principle is central for both teacher well-being and learner well-being. Crucially, YOU need to be engaged and enjoy your job in order to be able and willing to invest in engaging your learners with you and the learning opportunities you create. Research has shown how teacher and learner psychologies are in fact two sides of the same coin (e.g. Dresel and Hall 2013; Frenzel and Stephens 2013). Essentially, our physiological states and emotions are 'contagious' for our learners. Quite simply, if teachers are engaged and passionate about their work and their languages, then learners are more likely to be too (Mifsud 2011; Skinner and Belmont 1993). Indeed, in respect to language learning motivation, Dörnyei and Ushioda (2011) contend that the teacher's level of enthusiasm and commitment is one of the most important factors that can affect learners' motivation to learn. Their conclusion coincides with the bidirectional nature of engagement stated above: 'if a teacher is motivated to teach, there is a good chance that his or her students will be motivated to learn' (p. 158).

> *If at the front of the classroom you are not conveying enthusiasm for your material with at least a reasonable level of energy, how can you expect a class full of sleep deprived, distracted students to eagerly tackle whatever you have planned?*
>
> (Cavanagh 2016: 64)

However, teachers are only human and we too quite naturally also suffer occasional lows. The challenge is to maintain our passion for teaching in the long term and recover from any setbacks. As Bentley-Davies (2010: 243) reminds us, 'teaching is a marathon, not a sprint'. For this reason, teachers need to attend to their all-round well-being. If we are overworked or exhausted, we have nothing left to invest in our teaching and no energy with which to cope with the demands of working in a language classroom. We are quite simply better teachers when we are refreshed and motivated. Looking after our well-being as teachers 'is not an indulgence, it is the key to resilience and good practice in action' (Roffey 2011: 133).

REFLECTION TASK 3

The six principles in this chapter highlight the importance of establishing positive rapport to facilitating learner engagement. You may want to take a moment to reflect on how confident you feel that you already teach with these principles in mind. Are there some you find easier than others? Are there any other ideas you would add about why and how to build rapport with learners?

Teacher Actions

The principles outlined above are the building blocks needed to facilitate learner engagement with us as teachers. Although we mentioned some practical ways of realising them, they concerned primarily the social and affective dimensions of relational engagement. Now we want to turn to specific interactional strategies that foreground more the cognitive and behavioural dimensions of engagement with us. Our focus will be on how we interact with learners, because the discourse we use has the potential to influence all relationships and has particular centrality in the language classroom; as Knight (2016: 3) explains, 'one of the most important and powerful ways we can improve our schools is to improve the way we interact with each other'.

Action 1: Take Care With Teacher Talk

> *The power of teacher language cannot be overstated. The language we use with students every day influences how they see themselves, their teacher, their classmates, and their experience with learning.*
>
> (Denton 2007: 31)

How we talk to learners in our classrooms, and particularly how we talk about language learning, has the power to affect not only what they believe about themselves and language learning but also the nature of their relationship to us. There are two levels of interaction we can reflect on: how teacher talk affects learner readiness for interaction, and *what* teachers say and *how* they say it. Firstly, there is the dialogue between teacher and learner, and learner *readiness* for interaction. As we suggested above, we can enhance our communication by ensuring we are approachable. Fundamentally, we have to give learners the chance to communicate. This means giving them the space to talk with us and their peers and showing a willingness to truly listen. In language learning specifically, we need to create opportunities for learners to use the target language actively. At the basic level, this means critically evaluating how much *teacher talk* there is compared to student talking time. Petty (2014: 154) reports that, in general education, teachers talk on average for 60% of lessons and he considers this too much; as he then he adds, 'good teachers know when to shut up!'.

REFLECTION TASK 4

Who tends to do most of the talking in your classes? How many of the learners are actively using the language and for how long? Who is getting more chance to use the language – you or the pupils?

It requires little justification that there need to be sufficient opportunities for genuine communication on personally meaningful topics. Ideally, speaking tasks should offer learners the chance to bring in their own perspectives on topics that are of personal interest and relevance. Of course, as will be discussed in the next chapter, an open speaking climate requires positive group dynamics, so that learners are not afraid to speak up and feel confident that they will not be mocked or rebuked. If we want learners to engage with us, we must make engaging with us as comfortable and easy as possible.

> *As the children leave your classroom, don't pass up the opportunity for some mini-conversations. Remember this is what your discipline is founded on. Particularly with the hard-to-reach brigade, this is an ideal moment as they pass you by to say something positive to them, when they don't have the rest of the gallery in attendance.*
>
> (Toward, Henley and Cope 2015: 132)

The second level of teacher talk is concerned with *what* we say and *how* we say it. We can use our voices to convey our enthusiasm and engage learners in what we are doing by varying pitch and volume, using facial expression and gesture to add emphasis. We can use eye contact and make sure we 'sweep the room' to embrace all our learners in our visual engagement with the class. Our body language can also communicate a lot about our enthusiasm and confidence as a teacher. Somebody slouching, looking at their shoes, hiding behind a desk with their arms crossed, is not conveying the image of an engaging teacher. We can ensure we move around to be near all the learners, respectful of appropriate gender and cultural distances, crouching down when appropriate and generally being an active and visible part of the classroom community. A simple smile can also be infectious and engaging, and, interestingly, can also help reduce your own stress (Kraft and Pressman 2012).

Our choice of words can also have a powerful effect in setting the tone for our relationship. Language can be open, calm, respectful and inviting or can be indifferent and distancing, closing off dialogue. Language can also communicate our faith in all of learners' abilities and potential to improve. While constructive feedback (see below) is useful, it is also important to tell learners what they are doing well and what aspects of their behaviours and approaches we appreciate. Linley (2008) coined the term 'strengthspotting' and argued that most students are in dire need of help in identifying what they are good at so that they can flourish and confidently engage with the teacher and learning. This focus on learner strengths is also an effective way of implicitly fostering a growth mindset in our learners.

> *Just as linguists distinguish between the surface structure of language (the actual words) and the deep structure (concepts), so too does the language of classroom exchanges reveal deep meanings about learning and learners, responsibility and effort, intelligence and enterprise, and so too does this language help to build profound beliefs about engaging learners as capable learners.*
>
> (VanDeWeghe 2009: 62)

Action 2: Be Thoughtful About Feedback

Feedback has been found to be one of the most influential factors on student learning and achievement (Hattie 2009). Essentially, feedback is about providing the learner with useful information about how they have done on a task or how they are approaching it – both outcomes and process. It can be a way of communicating with learners in a constructive, personalised manner, to bridge the gap between current competence and provide direction for progress towards learning goals. As argued above, feedback should ideally point out strengths as well as areas in need of improvement. To be most engaging, feedback is best conceptualised as a form of dialogue; rather than a 'one-way' street (Nicol 2010), feedback functions best as an interactive process in which teachers and learners communicate together about learning and teaching. This communicates to learners that they are actively involved in their learning progress and processes – that is, it makes them agents rather than merely passive recipients. Campbell and Schumm Fauster (2013) report on an approach to feedback with advanced learners in which learners asked questions about their written work and a question and answer dialogue developed across multiple drafts. Another interesting example was presented by Nakamura (2016): she described how the feedback process became an opportunity for learners and teacher to get to know each other through written comments and questions about the content as well as the language.

From the learners' point of view, the most salient form of feedback is the *grades* they receive. The problem with grades is that they can completely undermine our efforts to build rapport with our students, because of the emphasis on the product rather than on the process, and with the preoccupation with comparing, ranking and categorising students. Unfortunately, because of their ultimate importance in every facet of most education systems, grades frequently become equated in the minds of students with a sense of self-worth; that is, they consider themselves only as worthy as their school-related achievements. One way of mitigating this damage is to complement teacher ratings with students' *self-assessment*. This not only shows students that you trust their honesty and judgement but it can also serve as a valuable vehicle to enhance student engagement. For example, Mercer and Schumm (2009) describe a particularly engaging approach whereby learners and teachers work together in developing grading scales: they invited adult learners to discuss collectively the criteria on which a piece of writing of a specific genre should be assessed and which of these aspects they felt were more or less important. The process created transparency, it got learners to reflect deeply on the task at hand and what it involved, and it also engaged them in dialogue with each other and the teacher about the criteria for appraisal of their work.

> *Assessment is the area where achievement-based societies and student-centred teaching principles inevitably clash.*
> (Dörnyei 2001: 131)

Once we help learners to see feedback as part of a joint dialogue aimed at helping them to self-assess and make progress towards their goals, even negative feedback becomes less threatening, particularly if we word criticism as advice (Petty 2014) – feedback will thus be seen as part of the teacher's role as advisor. Emphasising this role is all the more important, because effective feedback has to be informative. Accordingly, Hattie (2009) stresses that for feedback to be useful to students, it must address one of the following three key areas in an informative way: the task itself, the process of working on the task, and/or self-regulation competencies for working further on related tasks. In terms of positive feedback, there tends to be an overwhelming assumption that praise is inherently positive and motivating.

Praise that focuses on the person, however, especially in a generic generalised sense, runs the risk of fostering a fixed mindset, implying that the merit for the praise lies with some innate person-related trait (Mueller and Dweck 1998). In contrast, praise which looks at the process and not the product of learning can highlight the effort, strategies and approach taken, thereby supporting a growth mindset. The most effective forms of praise are specific. If the teacher says, 'Well done, Li Na!', the learner is unlikely to learn much from this as it is vague and unclear. However, if the teacher provides more detailed feedback, such as 'Well done, Li Na. You used some really good linking words that helped the cohesion of your text', the learner can build on this in future work. Essentially, however, any praise given must be genuine and deserved. As Hyland and Hyland (2006: 221) explain, 'students are adept at recognizing formulaic positive comments that serve no function beyond removing the sting from criticisms and do not generally welcome empty remarks'.

> *To be effective, feedback needs to be clear, purposeful, meaningful and compatible with students' prior knowledge, and to provide logical connections. It also needs to prompt active information processing on the part of the learner, have low task complexity, relate to specific and clear goals, and provide little threat to the person at the self level.*
>
> (Hattie 2009: 177–178)

Action 3: Listen to Learners

Knight's (2016) book, *Better Conversations*, discusses how we can improve our abilities to interact and be better conversational partners with our learners and our colleagues in schools. He offers a range of useful, practical guidelines, including displaying empathy, seeing conversation partners as equals, finding common ground, managing our emotions, building trust, being interested in what others have to say, and being humble in reflecting how we can learn from them. However, the core of his guidelines centres around the conversational skill of being a *good listener*. For educators, this means maybe a shift in our perception of how we see our learners as conversation partners. This means not viewing them as an audience to be talked at or as objects to be influenced, but rather as partners to be engaged with in two-way conversations. A healthy interactive 'back and forth' with students is the foundation of respectful engagement with each other.

Importantly, listening requires effortful thinking, concentration and empathy. A first step to enhance our listening abilities is simply not to interrupt, as it may inadvertently send the message that we feel what the learner is saying does not matter or is not as valid as what we are saying (Knight 2016). Another dimension to effective interaction and listening involves use of teacher *wait time*. This refers to the time between a teacher asking a question and either a student responding or the teacher asking another question. According to research, most teachers tend to wait less than one second for responses; in language classrooms this is more likely to be one to two seconds (Shrum 1984, 1985; Smith and King 2017). However, ideally, we should be allowing three to five seconds for learners to respond. Studies show that extending wait time even by just one to three additional seconds can give a greater number of students the space and time to speak up, thereby significantly enhancing the quality of discourse in the classroom and boosting learner engagement (Smith and King in press; Tobin 1987).

> *Listening is an important way to show respect for others. When we really listen, we have a chance to enter into a deeper form of communication. A conversation characterized by people really listening is humanizing for all parties.*
>
> (Knight 2016: 56)

Action 4: Use Questions to Engage

The other side of listening is *questioning*, and how we use this in the language classroom can be defining for learner engagement. In language teaching, the most common structure of discourse in the classroom is known as IRF, which stands for Initiation, Response, Feedback. Typically, it is the teacher who initiates an interaction, often through a question to which a learner responds and which the teacher reacts to with feedback. However, if we get the learners to initiate interactions by getting them to come up with the questions, classroom engagement can be transformed. Wallace and Kirkman (2014: 109) go so far as to argue that, 'learners should be encouraged to ask more questions than the teacher asks'. They warn us that in some classrooms, asking questions is interpreted by learners as a sign of being unintelligent and by teachers as an irritating interruption. Instead, engagement benefits from a culture which views learner questioning as a positive indication of engagement and student-initiated dialogue as a chance for learners to develop higher order critical thinking skills as they reflect more deeply and develop their own curiosity (see Chapter 5 for more practical advice).

The prevailing practice of teachers asking questions reflects an assumption that the primary function of questioning is as a way of checking understanding – in that sense, questions are often no more than mini-oral tests. Walsh and Sattes (2011) are probably right in suggesting that many teachers fail to see the potential in their questions as a rich source of data about learners' overall learning and competencies beyond mere comprehension. In terms of engagement, certain types of questions from the teacher, but especially questions stemming from the learners, can get learners actively thinking about their learning and the tasks at hand.

TYPES OF TEACHER QUESTIONS THAT DON'T WORK WELL

Bonwell and Eison (1991) found that questions were *less* successful if:

- they were too broad or vague and therefore confused students;
- they asked several sub-questions at once;
- they were so convergent that students perceived only one answer was 'right' and therefore hesitated to respond;
- they were factually oriented with one answer.

A particular form of questioning that has been suggested as being beneficial not only for engagement and relationships but also for higher order thinking is what is known as 'academic press' (Fredricks 2014: 142) or what Lemov (2015: 108) refers to as 'stretch it'. This is where teachers make learners stretch their knowledge with additional follow-up questions. The idea is that if the learner provides an appropriate answer to a question, we follow up with further questions, such as more challenging questions or how/why questions, to allow learners to expand on their answers. Not being satisfied with the shortest, quickest or even the first correct answer shows learners you have those high expectations for them all, and models that learning is never done and that there is always more we can do to 'stretch' ourselves. An extension of this process is to encourage learners to listen and respond to each other more. Wallace and Kirkman (2014: 103) propose an activity where students are encouraged to continue the discussion by asking more questions. After a student responds to the teacher's question, this student asks another student a question, and the next student responds and asks another question, and so on. The idea being that the whole class is working together to keep the questioning going. As such, questioning becomes part of classroom life and culture.

Action 5: Deal With Discipline Relationally

A final point we wish to reflect on is the issue of classroom discipline and how this can be addressed from a relational perspective in a way that fosters learner engagement (we shall further discuss this topic in the next chapter from the point of group dynamics). Discipline and, more generally, classroom management, is obviously a topic that can fill a book in its own right (see e.g. Scrivener 2012; Wright 2005) but here we would like to focus only on one aspect of it. Davis et al. (2012: ix) suggest that we need to rethink classroom management, seeing it not as being about managing learners but rather about *managing relationships*. A trusting relationship with the learners is expected to lead to fewer disruptive incidents, and indeed, Marzano, Marzano and Pickering (2003) analysed over 100 studies on classroom management and concluded that teachers who had high-quality relationships with their learners reported approximately 30% fewer behavioural problems in their classrooms.

> *We no longer live in a deferential age where those in authority are automatically revered and respected. Order is not maintained by fear of the consequences of doing wrong. Discipline has to be earned and the key to successful discipline is relationships.*
>
> (Toward et al. 2015: 144)

A frequent challenge for early-career-stage teachers is to find the appropriate professional distance with their learners, fluctuating between being overfriendly or too authoritarian. Perhaps a deep-lying misunderstanding of this difficulty is that there is no contradiction between being a warm, friendly and kind teacher and also having routines, rules and boundaries. These are not a contradiction, quite the opposite in fact. Roffey (2011: 19) makes the distinction between 'being friendly' and 'being a friend'. She explains that pupils do not want to be your friend, although they would doubtless appreciate you being friendly. Moreover, we are in agreement with Quigley (2016: 148) that, 'Rules do not crush the humanity and individuality of our students. Instead, they provide clear expectations for learning to thrive for everybody.' While teachers can seek to develop mutual trust, this does not mean being gullible, and from time to time discipline and correction of misbehaviours will also be necessary (Tschannen-Moran 2014).

> *Too easily, a focus on trust and developing a relationship becomes confused with being liked and not establishing the boundaries for the good behaviour that are needed. The kindest act we could ever commit for our students would be to give them the safety conferred by explicit boundaries of how they should behave.*
>
> (Quigley 2016: 141)

The autonomy-supportive behaviours and the various actions involving pupils in explicit dialogue about decisions - described earlier in this chapter - can contribute significantly to the emergence of a healthy teacher–student relationship. This is sometimes called the 'proactive' aspect of discipline (in contrast to the 'reactive side') because, given good relationships, we can proactively reduce the need for any reactive interventions. However, this 'ideal' perspective seems to be shattered when sometimes, despite our best proactive efforts, conflicts happen and require disciplinary action. At times like this, some teachers may revert back to authoritarian stances so as to prevent such episodes from happening again. The best advice in such situations is, 'Hold your nerve!' Drawing on the principles of group development, Dörnyei and Murphey (2003) emphasise that conflicts are not necessarily bad but can serve a variety of useful purposes: 'they may be the grist for the mill' (p. 141). They argue that conflicts are useful from the group's point of view because they can provide the necessary push for the group to move forward together (see more in Chapter 4).

POTENTIAL BENEFITS OF CONFLICTS

- *Conflicts can increase student involvement:* Heated discussions or even confrontations are the sign that the people who were involved in them care, and if the issue in question can be resolved satisfactorily, the parties will be drawn into a deeper commitment.
- *Conflicts can provide an outlet for hostility:* By bottling things up, conflicting issues do not go away but fester and might develop into deep-seated hostilities. Giving vent to some of the tension can be liberating, provided there is a supportive atmosphere.

> - *Conflicts can promote group cohesiveness:* Contrary to beliefs, confrontations do not necessarily ruin the relationship between people but can actually enhance it; even upsetting interpersonal reactions can be constructive, as they lead to a deeper connection between the parties.
> - *Conflicts can increase group productivity:* Conflict over issues often promotes critical thinking and can help to improve on various task-specific procedures. It would, in fact, be unusual to find a high-achieving group that is not characterised by vibrant disputes that occasionally escalate into rows.
>
> (Wilson 2002)

REFLECTION TASK 5

How have you personally handled conflict effectively in the past? How comfortable are you with remaining patient and keeping calm? What conflict situations are you in, or potentially in, right now and how might they be resolved?

The real question is how we react when discipline is called for. A key rule is to remain respectful. The simple rule of taking a deep breath, issuing a 'look' and counting a few seconds, gives time for your cognition to catch up and helps to stop our emotions hijacking how we respond. It is usually rightly recommended that we should never engage in an argument with a pupil in front of an audience, but deal with incidents quietly in a space out of the room, or after class, in which there is no public humiliation or battle for either of you. In terms of the language we use, it is best to seek to be as unconfrontational as possible. We can simply use a non-verbal signal such as a 'look' or raising your hand to remind and warn learners, or we can describe what the learner is *doing* to remind them of their behaviour, prompting them to reflect on what the desirable behaviour ought to be, rather than telling them what not do. Ideally, we should always use their names to connect relationally, such as 'Samuel, *you're talking* when Pablo is giving an answer to my question'. It is worth bearing in mind when disciplining to name and focus on the *behaviour*, and not some characteristic or trait of the person – it is the behaviour we are responding to and trying to change. Consider the effects instead of saying, 'Samuel, you're selfish and never listen'. This statement suggests a negative personality trait and generalises a single incident to supposed behaviours the learner 'always' or 'never' does. When disciplining, even when you may have an issue with a specific behaviour at a moment in time, it is important for learners to know you believe in them and you still 'care' for them. In particular, following a disciplinary incident, it is important for teachers to demonstrably 'repair and rebuild' (Rogers 2007: 23) their relationship to the learner, to ensure the rapport is not damaged from the experience.

REFLECTION TASK 6

The previous action points all centre around how we interact and communicate with our learners. In this final reflection task, we suggest a series of questions to evaluate your own interactional patterns and relational engagement:

- How at ease are your learners speaking to you in the target language?
- How comfortable are your learners speaking in front of their peers?
- In what ways can you elicit feedback from your learners about tasks and topics?
- Can you think of a strength or positive characteristic for specific learners you work with?
- How many opportunities do you have for really engaging in dialogue with your learners, in written or spoken form?
- What kinds of questions do you typically ask your learners?
- How long, on average, do you wait for students to respond to a question before prompting or moving on?
- To what extent do you use follow-up questions initiated by you or the other learners?
- In what ways could you be more relationally-aware in how you discipline bad behaviour?
- How consciously do you seek to repair your relationship with a learner after a discipline incident?
- What areas of your interaction with learners would you like to work on developing further?

Summary

In this chapter, we have discussed the importance of the relationship between teacher and learner as a basis for all learning engagement, but especially the engagement with us as teachers specifically. We have sought to foreground the importance of putting the relationships we build with learners at the centre of our teaching planning and in-class behaviours. We reflected on six principles to facilitate learner engagement with teachers, especially in affective and social terms. The attitudes and behaviours of the teacher are central. This includes being approachable, empathetic, and responsive to learner individuality, believing in all of your learners' potential to improve, seeking to support learner autonomy, and remaining passionate about what you do.

> *It is not new to argue that relationships matter [in education] but the body of evidence is now quite large and powerful. We can conclude that the connections between people in schools are a driving force in shaping engagement with school.*
>
> (McLaughlin and Clarke 2010: 99)

We proposed five specific action points, which teachers can employ to support these principles and engender learner engagement, particularly in terms of cognitive and behavioural engagement. The key is the importance of balanced, respectful interaction:

- Take care with teacher talk
- Be thoughtful about feedback
- Listen to learners
- Use questions to engage
- Deal with discipline relationally

CHAPTER IN A NUTSHELL

In order to develop learner engagement, we need to work on developing a positive relationship with our students and reflect on how we make ourselves available and interact with them.

IF YOU WANT TO FIND OUT MORE

Davis, H. A., Summers, J. J. and Miller, L. M. (2012). *An Interpersonal Approach to Classroom Management: Strategies for Improving Student Engagement.* Thousand Oaks, CA: Corwin Press. (This book explores how interpersonal relationships lie at the heart of learner engagement.)

Roffey, S. (2011). *Changing Behaviour in Schools: Promoting Positive Relationships and Wellbeing.* London: SAGE. (This book focuses on how to promote quality relationships between teachers and pupils and how such relationships are connected to better behaviour.)

Weinstein, R. (2002). *Reaching Higher: The Power of Expectations in Schooling.* Cambridge, MA: Harvard University Press. (This book reports on the ways in which teachers can hold expectations of pupils and how these affect the learning opportunities the teachers generate.)

4 Positive classroom dynamics and culture

As learning a language is a highly social undertaking, the relationship between peers is arguably as critical for learner engagement as the rapport between teacher and students. Dewaele and MacIntyre (2016), for example, found that anxiety about speaking up in class was more connected to how learners felt in front of their peers, rather than in front of their teacher. Indeed, few would question Fredricks's (2014) conclusion that in order to be able to fully engage in class, learners need to feel that 'the group is important to them, that they are important to the group, and that they will be cared for and supported (i.e. they are in a safe learning environment)' (p. 183). While agreeing with Fredricks in principle, some teachers would maintain that it is not their job to interfere in peer relations as the latter is simply not part of their main teaching objectives. In this chapter we hope to be able to show that peer relations form the foundation of a positive learning culture and that employing strategies to ensure that everyone feels accepted, valued, safe and included in group life is a profitable part of facilitating engaged, quality learning.

> *Some people may feel that the very act of thinking about group dynamics and how we can affect them suggests manipulation. However, as teachers, we are, whether we like it or not, manipulators of people. Whatever we do, or do not do, in the classroom will have its effect, positive or negative, on the dynamics of the group. Since we are in such a responsible position, I think it only fair that we should be aware of our actions and the possible effects they might be having, and should choose to do those things which are more likely to have a positive effect on the individuals we are dealing with.*
>
> (Hadfield 1992: 13)

REFLECTION TASK 1

Every teacher knows that the atmosphere in a group can make or break the teaching and learning experience for all involved. Yet, it is often so hard to pinpoint what exactly it is about the group that works or does not work. Take a moment to think about a class that 'gels' and one that doesn't. Can you identify any aspects that contribute positively or negatively to the classroom atmosphere?

Rationale

One of the core components of self-determination theory that helps us understand engagement needs is *relatedness* (e.g. Ryan and Deci 2017). In Chapter 3, we considered the teacher-learner relationship, which is defining for the whole atmosphere in any learning group and the culture that emerges, and in the current chapter our focus is on the influence the teacher can have on fostering the relationships among learners. We shall argue that teachers can be 'the invisible hand' (Farmer, McAuliffe Lines and Hamm 2011) that engenders group dynamics, peer relationships and the overall socio-emotional climate in class. In other words, besides the more traditional teacher role of providing guidance for typical school-based values, rules and norms, teachers can also play an invaluable part in facilitating positive peer relationships and the construction of peer norms and values that support social interaction and learning.

> *Students' social and academic lives are intertwined. Peers can provide companionship, emotional support, and validation, and they can help with solving academic problems. Students who have positive relationships with their peers have been found to have higher levels of engagement, motivation, and achievement.*
>
> (Fredricks 2014: 161)

REFLECTION TASK 2

Think about a student you currently teach who you would classify as either highly engaged or highly disengaged. Take a moment to reflect on this student's social network in class (their friends and who they hang out with). How accepted are they by their immediate social group and within the class as a whole? How do their behaviours meet or not meet the overall group's norms and values?

A key notion for effective groups and positive classroom culture is '*psychological safety*' (Edmondson 2019). This is the feeling that learners can speak freely in class, make mistakes or suggest ideas without fear that anyone (teacher or peers) will make fun of them, or embarrass, humiliate, reject, resent or punish them for doing so. Everyone needs to feel safe, not only to make mistakes but also to engage fully without risking bullying. Nobody wants to feel foolish, laughed at or excluded - indeed, Kohn (2006: 103) is absolutely right that 'Few things stifle creativity like the fear of being judged or humiliated.' Indeed, humans go to great lengths to avoid feelings of social awkwardness, no matter what age they are! Particularly in the inherently stressful context of using a foreign language, it is vital that teachers develop a culture where psychological safety is the norm, so that learners can be confident of a supportive response from everyone, no matter what linguistic slip-ups they make. Psychological safety does not always mean everyone is in agreement or that nobody faces criticism or correction: it is not false harmony. Rather, it means always treating each other and the shared goal of language learning with respect, accepting differences and being supportive of each other as individuals.

> *In psychologically safe environments, people believe that if they make a mistake, others will not penalize or think less of them for it. They also believe that others will not resent or humiliate them when they ask for help or information. This belief comes when people both trust and respect each other, and it produces a sense of confidence that the group won't embarrass, reject or punish someone for speaking up. Thus, psychological safety is a taken-for-granted belief about how others will respond when you ask a question, seek feedback, admit a mistake or propose a possibly wacky idea.*
>
> (Edmondson 2019: 118–119)

Principles for Positive Group Dynamics and Classroom Culture

What can teachers do to foster a healthy learning environment within their classroom? We believe that the psychological safety of a classroom culture can be best captured by drawing on the principles of *group dynamics*, originally developed in social psychology (e.g. Lewin 1947) and later adopted for understanding educational groups (e.g. Schmuck and Schmuck 2001) as well as group processes in language learning (e.g. Dörnyei and Murphey 2003). Aspects of group dynamics have been successfully linked to motivation to learn (e.g. Dörnyei and Muir 2019) and student engagement (e.g. Juvonen, Espinoza and Knifsend 2012; Lynch, Lerner and Leventhal 2013). Past research has examined a wide range of group characteristics, from group development to group roles; our current focus will be on two aspects in particular: how the quality of the relationship between group members affects their willingness to engage, and how teachers as group leaders can positively influence this process.

> *Although the scientific investigations of group work are but a few years old, I don't hesitate to predict that group work – that is, the handling of human beings not as isolated individuals, but in the social setting of groups – will soon be one of the most important theoretical and practical fields. ... There is no hope for creating a better world without a deeper scientific insight into the ... essentials of group life.*
>
> (Lewin 1943, cited in Johnson and Johnson 2017: 2)

Principle 1: Lead by Example

As noted in Chapter 3, the teacher's actions are defining for the climate and attitudes that develop in class. It is not only what we say but how we act that sends messages to learners about what is acceptable or not. This has been articulated expressively in the Chinese proverb, 'Not the cry, but the flight of a wild duck leads the flock to fly and follow.' The 'lead-by-example' principle, which is one of the main laws of effective leadership in business management, states that leaders set an example and model behaviour through their daily acts. In a similar way, teachers, as group leaders, can also do much to manage the atmosphere and culture that emerges in their classes by how they behave.

> *The most powerful thing a leader can do to mobilize others is to set the example by aligning personal actions with shared values. Leaders are measured by the consistency of their deeds and words – by walking the talk. … Leaders take every opportunity to show others by their own example that they're deeply committed to the values and aspirations they espouse.*
>
> (Kouzes and Posner 2004: 12)

We have discussed earlier the importance of an autonomy-supportive leadership approach which enables learners to become involved and direct their learning experiences to some degree. However, teachers can also be thought of as having one of three styles of leadership: *autocratic*, *democratic* or *laissez-faire* (Lewin, Lippitt and White 1939). As the labels suggest, an autocratic leader has complete control of the group and a laissez-faire leader does little in the way of leadership, leaving the group to their own devices. From a student engagement point of view, neither of these extremes can be seen as especially effective, although we must note that at different stages of group development the optimal leadership style varies somewhat, with a more autocratic style benefiting the group at the beginning and a more laissez-faire at a mature stage (see Hersey, Blanchard and Johnson 2008).

The most effective leadership style in most teaching contexts is usually the democratic one, where the leader leads the group but also shares some power with the group members concerning the decision-making processes. Such leadership tends to be typified by friendly, open communication and better relationships within the group, as well as between the leader and the group (Dörnyei and Murphey 2003). However, it is worth mentioning that being a democratic leader can also be done badly; to know when to take a strong leadership role, when to democratise decisions and when to intervene requires teachers to have a broad range of classroom management and interpersonal skills to draw on (we shall revisit this question in the last Action Point).

> *Democratic leadership is sometimes mistaken for laissez-faire leadership, although, in fact, a 'democratic' leader does exert authority, but in a way that respects the constant need for balance between structure and freedom.*
>
> (Ehrman and Dörnyei 1998: 160)

REFLECTION TASK 3

In his book on *Classroom Management Techniques*, Scrivener (2012: 53) puts three important (and somewhat rhetorical) questions for teachers to consider concerning the quantity of control in the classroom:

1. Is it possible that over-organising by the teacher takes away or reduces the students' own ability or willingness to take decisions, self-evaluate and organise?
2. Would learning be more focussed if students had a larger degree of control over what they did?
3. Would activities actually run smoother and more efficiently without the constant interventions (or possibly interference) from the teacher?

As teachers, we may find that we inadvertently prefer to work with learners who are more compliant and more willing to take part in activities as we intend, as opposed to the more difficult students who can be disruptive or disengaged. The problem is we may directly or indirectly be communicating this to all the learners in class, as well as the specific individuals. One of our roles is to model inclusivity. This means finding the positives in every learner, even those where we may need to look a little harder. Sometimes creativity and originality can be found in those learners who do not conform, and harnessing these positively can be enriching for everyone. A culture of inclusivity means teachers need not only to attend to how they model inclusivity in their treatment of all learners in class, but also to take note of which learners may be excluded by their peers and find ways to consciously ensure they are included. This may involve making explicit decisions about assigning group composition or pair work teams. Ideally, nobody should be left out or made to feel an 'outsider'. However, we acknowledge that this is not always easy, and some learners may prefer themselves for a number of reasons to stay more on the periphery (we shall discuss this issue further below).

REFLECTION TASK 4

What kind of leader do you think you are in your classrooms and, perhaps more importantly, how do you think the students view you? Does this change across time and context? If so, what kind of things affect your leadership style?

Principle 2: Promote Group Cohesiveness

In the work on group dynamics, perhaps the key factor contributing to positive group atmosphere and culture has been recognised as *group cohesiveness*. This refers to the closeness of the group and the feeling of 'us' among the members. If learners feel a strong sense of belonging to a cohesive group, they are more likely to actively participate in classroom life. A cohesive group has a climate of solidarity and unity among the members and is less likely to dissolve or disintegrate into cliques (Forsyth 2019). Moreover, what is particularly important from an educational point of view is that it is also more productive. Johnson and Johnson (2017) explain that under most conditions, the productivity of groups in general is higher than that of individuals working alone, but this productivity further increases with improved interpersonal relationships amongst the students. They report on a meta-analysis of 148 studies involving more than 17,000 early adolescents in 11 countries, which found that as much as 33% of the students' achievement was explained by peer relationships. Knowing the number of other factors that affect success in learning (e.g. aptitude, motivation, family background), this is a massive proportion, and the authors' advice, thus, is unequivocal: 'if teachers want to increase early adolescents' achievement, they should facilitate the development of friendships' (p. 100). Translated into group dynamics terms, teachers should promote group cohesiveness.

FURTHER BENEFITS OF INCREASED GROUP COHESIVENESS

Increased group cohesiveness will typically result in an increase in:

- members' commitment to group goals
- feelings of personal responsibility to the group
- willingness to take on difficult tasks
- persistence in working toward goal achievement
- satisfaction and morale
- commitment to one another's learning growth and success

(Johnson and Johnson 2017: 99–100)

The core components of group cohesiveness include *interpersonal acceptance* (i.e. positive, non-judgemental attitudes towards each other), *group pride* (i.e. appreciation of the group as a whole and being proud to be part of it) and *task commitment* (i.e. collective interest in and commitment to the task – language learning in our case) (Dörnyei and Murphey 2003). Group cohesiveness is obviously a generally positive feature of a class, but too much of it can lead to a lack of individualism and a risk of 'groupthink', that is, a state when loyalty to the group is so strong that all conflict and critical thinking is avoided (Ehrman and Dörnyei 1998). Naturally, it is healthy in any classroom, and especially language classrooms, to retain an openness to diversity of people and opinions, and to also be welcoming to newcomers who may join the group at a later stage. Some of the best discussions in a language class depend on disagreement and a willingness to express this. The key is having a healthy group climate and mutual respect, which allow diverse opinions to be expressed and considered without aggression or rejection of the individual. Harmony within a group does not mean blind, universal agreement.

> *Belonging feels like it happens from the inside out, but in fact it happens from the outside in. Our social brains light up when they receive a steady accumulation of almost-invisible cues: We are close, we are safe, we share a future.*
>
> (Coyle 2018: 25–26)

A particular context in which group cohesiveness is especially strong is in *teams,* and this notion can be useful to guide our understanding of how to build teams, not merely groups in our classrooms. Although 'small group' and 'team' are often used interchangeably in the literature, it may be useful to separate the two terms, with a team being a subset of small groups that is made up of members with a salient, well-defined shared purpose that binds them together into a cohesive unit (Edmondson 2019). This is common, in sports contexts – it is easy to see, for example, that a basketball team will require more in terms of collaboration from the members than, say, a committee. Ideally, we want learners to work together on tasks with a sense of being a team. This 'team feeling' can be engendered through setting team accountability (rather than merely individual accountability) – which is of course typical of sports teams – and by celebrating team success. Of course, people cannot be forced to feel team spirit and group identity; these emerge from the way the members respond to and interact with each other, and this is an area where technology can be very helpful: setting up a group to exchange instant messages or providing a forum or message board can make instant communication effortless and can contribute to setting the tone and enhancing the relational quality in the group.

GOOGLE'S RESEARCH ON HIGH-FUNCTIONING TEAMS

Five factors which contribute to effective teams:

1. **Psychological safety** – team members feel safe, trust each other and are comfortable being vulnerable in front of each other
2. **Dependability** – team members can depend on each other
3. **Structure and clarity** – team members have clear roles and goals
4. **Meaning** – the work and goals are meaningful to the team members
5. **Impact** – the team members feel their work and contribution matters

(Based on Winsborough 2017: 68)

REFLECTION TASK 5

How cohesive do you judge your class to be? To what extent are there positive relationships and a sense of friendship among all members? How closely do the students identify with the group as a whole? How focused are they on working together to help each other improve their language skills? Is there an area (e.g. interpersonal relationships, group pride, task commitment) you feel needs developing?

Principle 3: Promote TEA Among Learners: Trust, Empathy and Acceptance

A prerequisite for a cohesive group is the members' ability to exercise constructive interpersonal skills. These not only lubricate the smooth functioning of teamwork and contribute towards creating a sense of psychological safety, but are also indispensable skills for language learners to communicate with people from diverse backgrounds in various crosscultural settings. From among the relevant aspects of socio-emotional competence, we have chosen to compress core components into the acronym *TEA* – *Trust*, *Empathy* and *Acceptance*.

> *When teachers consciously create caring relationships and teach relationship skills, they build a strong foundation of safety and trust. Studies show that this increased safety and trust result in more cooperation, less conflict, and fewer verbal put downs in the classroom ... In addition, better scores on standardized achievement tests and improved ability to acquire skills have been reported.*
>
> (Hart and Hodson 2004: 16)

Trust is the basis on which social relationships are built. It takes time to generate but, sadly, it can be broken in an instant. Rather than grand gestures, trust tends to emerge from the small daily interactions between people in class. It is dependent on the consistency and reliability with which people act and respond and whether they meet others' expectations and needs. Being able to rely on others and trust how they will respond is a core contributor to psychological safety. In a caring and compassionate classroom, there will be trust not only between teacher and students but also among the students. Key scholars on trust in schools, Bryk and Schneider (2002), propose that trust emerges from four components: *respect*, *competence*, *personal regard for others* and *integrity*. Another definition is offered by Tschannen-Moran (2014), who lists the five facets of trust: *benevolence*, *honesty*, *openness*, *reliability* and *competence*. The different labels, however, do converge into a composite attribute which is arguably the most fundamental characteristic of strong relationships, and what is important to highlight here is that this composite trustworthiness is not only fully under each individual's conscious control, but can also be taught and enhanced by teacher actions.

Empathy lies at the heart of positive relations (see also Chapter 3). It requires a person to try to see the world from somebody else's point of view, imagining not only what they are thinking but also what they are feeling. The aim is not to agree but to seek to understand the other person's thoughts and feelings and communicate this understanding to them. Not only is this a critical skill for us as educators to model in our own behaviours – Carl Rogers (1983) listed empathy amongst the three basic attributes of a good facilitator, alongside acceptance (unconditional positive regard) and congruence (being genuine and authentically connected) – but it is something we can explicitly try to foster in our learners. It is perhaps the cornerstone of positive classroom dynamics and a culture of relational support and kindness. An excellent illustration of an educational intervention focusing on teaching empathy is Gordon's (2009) *Roots of empathy* programme in Canada (see panel below).

ROOTS OF EMPATHY

Roots of Empathy is an international, evidence-based classroom programme that has shown significant effect in raising social/emotional competence and increasing empathy. It is designed for children aged 5 to 13 and involves a detailed curriculum. At the heart of the programme are a local infant and parent who visit the classroom every three weeks over the school year, and a trained instructor who coaches students to observe the baby's development and to label the baby's feelings. Thus, in this experiential learning, the baby is the 'Teacher' and a lever, which the instructor uses to help the participants to identify and reflect on their own feelings and the feelings of others.

(adapted from https://rootsofempathy.org/roots-of-empathy)

Acceptance means creating an inclusive classroom in which every person is accepted by the others for who they are, irrespective of their differences, strengths and weaknesses. It does not mean always having to like a student who, for example, may be disruptive, aggressive or bullying. Such cases will require teacher intervention but in a way that communicates a willingness to listen and seek to understand that person and try to help them.

> *[Acceptance] is prizing the learner, prizing her feelings, her opinions, her person. It is a caring for the learner, but a nonpossessive caring. It is an acceptance of this other individual as a separate person, having worth in her own right. It is a basic trust – a belief that this other person is somehow fundamentally trustworthy.*
>
> (Rogers 1983: 124)

FIVE KEY FACTORS PROMOTING ACCEPTANCE IN GROUPS

1. *Learning about each other:* This is the most crucial and general factor fostering relationships within a group, involving the students sharing genuine personal information with each other.
2. *Proximity, contact* and *interaction:* Proximity refers to the physical distance between people, contact to situations where learners can meet and communicate spontaneously, and interaction to special contact situations in which the behaviour of each person influences the others'. These three factors are effective natural gelling agents, which highlight the importance of classroom management issues such as the seating plan, small group work and independent student projects.
3. *Cooperation toward common goals:* Superordinate goals that require the cooperation of everybody to achieve them have been found to be the most effective means of bringing together – even openly hostile parties.
4. *Extracurricular activities:* These represent powerful experiences, partly because during such outings students lower their 'school filter' and relate to each other as 'civilians' rather than students.
5. *Teacher's role modelling:* Friendly and supportive behaviour by the teacher is infectious, and students are likely to follow suit.

(adapted from Dörnyei and Muir 2019)

Principle 4: Foster a Culture of Collaboration and Support

The 'culture' of an organisation – including a school and a language classroom – refers to a set of emerging norms, values, beliefs and expectations that govern social relations and community life. To put it simply, it is 'the way we do things around here', and Xenikou and Furnham (2013) highlight its durability when they state that culture can be seen as 'what is passed on to new generations of group members' (p. 100). To create a learning environment in which engagement can flourish, we need to generate a culture that values the active investment of students in the learning process. This requires students to be supportive of each other and accepting of those who want to work beyond the norm. In many classrooms, however, this condition clashes with counterproductive peer pressure, that is, the pressure to follow the influence of peers and conform to a 'norm of mediocrity'. Such pressure affects everyone at every age but is especially acute in the teenage years. As a child, one of your parents or grandparents may have warned you 'not to get in with the wrong sort' and there is in fact good logic behind this advice: friendship and peer groups share values and characteristics and there are processes of contagion that ensure that group beliefs are spread among the members. In respect to engagement, this means that we may find friendship groups which are supportive and contribute positively to engagement, whereas others may pressure their peers not to engage. Our aim is to spread 'the engagement bug' across the whole class and create an atmosphere in which being engaged is not something to be mocked or embarrassed about (for more discussion, see Action Point 4).

> *Children imitate friends' school-related behaviours and goals, and these actions and attitudes have the effect of encouraging or discouraging their participation in scholastic activities. The implication is that friends positively influence children's school engagement when they value schoolwork and participate willingly in classroom activities, but have the opposite effect when they disparage school and withdraw or rebel against the academic milieu.*
>
> (Ladd, Herald-Brown and Kochel 2009: 323)

Developing supportive and collaborative relationships also needs learners who know how to work well together. Just putting people together and asking them to successfully cooperate – as we so often do in communicative classrooms – is often insufficient. To help things work effectively, it can be useful to assign individuals specific roles, which not only instruct them about what their specific contribution should be but which also give students a direct inroad into becoming part of the action; to put it broadly, by starting to act out the roles students have something to do – that is, get engaged! – straight away. Action Points 3 and 4 will offer specific advice on what roles to set and when, but here we would like to highlight a possible consequence of a lack of roles: 'social loafing'. This is when an individual does not make much effort in group work, relying instead on others to pick up the slack. Explicit roles can counteract this as they create a sense of accountability and make visible every person's output and contribution.

WORKING WITH PEERS

When working together, peers can influence each other's engagement and cognitive development by:

- Providing feedback
- Debating ideas
- Asking questions
- Asking for justifications
- Providing elaborations
- Sharing strategies
- Offering suggestions and explanations
- Redefining problems

(based on Fredricks 2014: 169)

An often underutilised strategy to foster supportive relationships among peers is *peer mentoring*, in which specifically assigned peers teach and encourage – that is, mentor – each other. If the brief of each peer mentor is to recognise their mentees' strengths and to help them to build on these, peer mentoring can literally do wonders, and not only for the receiver: the mentor will also gain confidence and experience of leadership. Of course, such a process does not emerge spontaneously but requires a structure and format in place, including allocated time, space and some initial training on how best to mentor each other. Peer mentoring is also increasingly used both in secondary and higher education to provide support for new, incoming students so that they can adopt the institute's culture and achieve their full potential. There is no reason why such mentoring provision should not have a prominent focus on encouraging engagement, and as the mentors in such programmes are usually students from higher classes, their 'authorisation' of engagement will be seen by students as a permit to do well.

REFLECTION TASK 6

If you think about your classes, what kind of socialisation culture would you say exists in regard to engagement? Do you witness instances of positive peer pressure to engage with learning opportunities or more pressure to disengage or downplay commitment to learning? What specific behaviours are illustrative of this in your classes?

Principle 5: Resolve Conflict Constructively and Respectfully

The topics of conflict and discipline were already addressed in the previous chapter, but these are such important issues that it warrants some further discussion. No matter how hard we work on teaching interpersonal skills and seek to foster a positive climate in class, there will be occasions when we need to intervene in conflict and exercise some form of disciplining or conflict resolution. How we do this speaks volumes about our values and our relational stance; it is often during these critical incidents that we communicate powerful implicit messages to learners about respect, trust, tolerance, acceptance, compassion and kindness. The challenge is to resolve conflict in ways which meet the expectations of our roles (and responsibilities) as educators and yet which also contribute to building up a positive learner community. The secret of achieving these two things simultaneously is to bear in mind that, as Roffey (2011) points out, in a relational classroom, the teacher can be in charge *without* being controlling. Teachers, by dint of their position, have more power than the students, but this can be used for democratic participation in order to give learners agency and voice in shaping and creating the social context of their classroom and behavioural expectations.

> *Time devoted to initial positive group dynamics is like taking immunity shots before travelling – it can make a lot of potentially serious problems unrealisable. But we still might have a few bumps and surprises.*
>
> (Dörnyei and Murphey 2003: 135)

It is useful to distinguish *disciplining* and *conflict resolution* from each other. Put simply, disciplining follows breaking a rule or violating a group norm. These instances should be addressed consistently and firmly, focusing on the dysfunctional impact of the behaviour, and communicating and enforcing the consequences with respect. The notion of acceptance discussed earlier also dictates that if a student has to be disciplined, it is also important that they should know that the relationship is not damaged by this instance and that they are still appreciated as individuals. Indeed, this is the opportunity for rebuilding trust and showing the relationship is still intact.

> *Children will break rules, even rules they cherish and respect because they helped create them. The way we manage the rule breaking is critical to the development of community. The way we attend to children when the rules are broken is critical to the development of discipline.*
>
> (Charney 2015: 144)

Conflicts are different from disciplinary matters (although they can lead to them) in that they refer to disagreements over issues or between group members. From a group dynamics vantage point, the appraisal of conflict is somewhat ambiguous. Although conflicts were traditionally seen as disruptive (because they impede task performance and spoil student relations), Dörnyei and Murphey (2003), for example, devote a whole chapter to discussing the subject and argue that if they are managed well, conflicts have the potential to be beneficial in at least four ways:

- *Conflicts can increase student involvement* (a heated discussion that is resolved satisfactorily draws the parties into a deeper commitment).
- *Conflicts can provide an outlet for hostility* (instead of festering when bottled-up).
- *Conflicts can promote group cohesiveness* (one of the main principles of group development is that in order to mature, groups need to go through a turbulent stage when issues are aired and resolved).
- *Conflicts can increase group productivity* (by promoting critical thinking and improving task-specific procedures).

> *Disagreement about ideas is a healthy sign as long as intellectual disagreement does not degenerate into sharp interpersonal conflict. Some interpersonal conflict is inevitable and should not be taken as a sign of failure. Nor should it be an opportunity for you to intervene and take over the reins immediately, acting as arbiter, juror, and judge.*
>
> (Cohen and Lotan 2014: 137)

The key notion in constructive conflict management is *negotiation*. Open discussion can defuse disputes and bring people together. Dörnyei and Murphey (2003) stress that the teacher's lead in being able to talk calmly and openly about the issues and to show respect for diverse opinions will provide an important model for the students. Ideally, a conflict is best resolved directly by the opposing parties themselves, but sometimes when the animosity is so great that it prevents constructive interaction, a third party is needed to act as a *mediator*. An important aspect of mediation is to make the two parties see each other's points, to resolve misunderstandings and to encourage a solution where there is no winner and loser. Here the skills of empathy play an important role in helping the parties, not to agree but to try to understand the other person's perspective.

> *Just as conflicts escalate when group members become firmly committed to a position and will not budge, conflicts de-escalate when group members are willing to negotiate with others to reach a solution that benefits all parties. Negotiation is a reciprocal communication process whereby two or more parties to a dispute examine specific issues, explain their positions, and exchange offers and counteroffers.*
> (Forsyth 2019: 431)

DURING MEDIATION, ASK THE PARTIES:

- to describe what happened and how they feel;
- to paraphrase the *other's* position and how the *other* feels;
- to tell each other what they can do to avoid the conflict in the future;
- to search for a solution, going back and forth between the parties;
- to repeat the solution they have found and agreed on.

(adapted from Dörnyei and Murphey 2003: 152)

A specific approach to relational ways of dealing with conflicts and resulting discipline problems can be found in the growing interest in *restorative justice* in schools. This refers to a radical approach to discipline originating in the criminal system but also used increasingly in schools with positive effects such as reduced bullying and antisocial behaviour, improved attendance, better group and community dynamics, enhanced interpersonal skills for the learners, and overall less classroom disruption and more time on task (Evans and Lester 2013; Fronius, Persson, Guckenburg, Hurley and Petrosino 2016; Ortega, Lyubansky, Nettles and Espelage 2016). Essentially, the approach gives each individual in a conflict situation the chance to understand how their behaviour affects others, possibly also through mediation with others in the group. They are encouraged to switch perspectives and listen to each other through open discussions where everyone concerned feels safe and respected. The person who caused the issue has to reflect on ways of making right the wrong. The method may not suit everybody or every school, and there remains controversy about its effectiveness as a challenge to zero-tolerance policy approaches to discipline, but it is certainly an approach which underlines many of the values conducive to engagement - respect, safety, inclusion, relationships, pro-social behaviours, open dialogue and trust.

REFLECTION TASK 7

Think of a conflict you have witnessed in your own or somebody else's class. How do you think the two parties were feeling at that moment? Why might they have acted the way that they did? How did you or the observed teacher feel at that moment? How might this have affected your response in dealing with the conflict? Could anything have been done differently to prevent this happening or to deal with it differently in retrospect?

Teacher Actions

All of the five principles discussed in the first half of the chapter centre on the notion of creating a positive, encouraging and safe classroom environment in which there is a focus on quality relationships among peers, as well as a culture for engaging in language learning. There are many aspects of the behaviour of the teacher as the group leader which can promote such a climate, and in order to offer some practical suggestions we have selected five specific action areas that in our experience are particularly relevant to implementing these principles in language classrooms: connecting learners with each other personally; developing a sense of 'we' and 'us' in the classroom; preparing learners for groupwork and cooperation; structuring the class using the three 'R's - rules, roles and routines; and, finally, fostering democratic learner participation.

Action 1: Connect Learners Personally

A bottom-up strategy for enhancing the whole class dynamics is to work at ensuring that all the learners have some kind of relationship with each other. It is hoped that this personal connection will reduce the risk of cliques, bullying or any learner being excluded. Principle 3 concerned the building of trust, empathy and acceptance (TEA) in the classroom, and key elements of this process include getting learners to have contact and interact with each other, to learn more about each other and to cooperate with each other. An advantage of language education is that there are plenty of opportunities for learners to work together and get to know each other personally during L2 classes. These opportunities can be utilised to consciously work at mixing up the students to ensure they connect with each other personally. Here we would like to highlight three key aspects of the group formation process: using *icebreakers* and *warmers*; the significance of knowing each other's *names*; and the usefulness of *groupwork*.

Icebreakers are designed to be used in the first couple of meetings of a newly formed group or when a large new intake joins the group. According to Frank and Rinvolucri (1991: 9), the purpose of these short tasks is 'to get people to ... become aware of each other as people ... to relax people, get them to unfold their arms, to smile and to laugh. ... In doing these exercises people learn a little about other group members consciously and a vast amount unconsciously'. This latter function - unconsciously collecting information about each other - is vital from the point of view of the development of cohesiveness: seeing the others moving, hearing their voices, talking to them and establishing personal relationships with everybody will result in a strong sense of familiarity surprisingly quickly.

FUNCTIONS AND CHARACTERISTICS OF EFFECTIVE ICEBREAKERS

- Creating opportunities for everybody to talk to everybody else, even if only briefly (e.g. conducting a mini-survey)
- Involving sharing personal information (e.g. self-disclosure games)
- Involving action and movement (e.g. games involving throwing beanbags)
- Moving people around in the classroom (e.g. getting students into various groups)
- Involving humor and laughter (to lighten the atmosphere)
- Utilising various interaction formats (e.g. pairs, small groups, altogether)
- Requiring cooperation (e.g. small-group competition)

Initial ice-breaking, however, might not be enough, because until the climate warms sufficiently, ice has a habit of re-forming. For this reason, most groups need a period of readjustment each time they come together, a time to rejoin the group, to accept each other again, to re-establish relationships, and to remind themselves implicitly of the goals and rules of the group. These are the invaluable functions of *warmers*, designed to be used at the beginning of every lesson.

The significance of knowing each other's names. Not knowing the others' names in the class has a far more serious consequence than most teachers would assume. Students who think that their peers or the teacher do not know their names will often feel that they are invisible in the group - the sense of being anonymous almost amounts to the feeling that one does not exist in that group. Thus, in our haste to get through the curriculum, we run the danger of leaving some students behind, and with a feeling of being insignificant, if we do not ensure not only that we as teachers know learner names but also that the learners know each other's names too.

> *If you don't know their names, students are just anonymous members of class. Knowing and using a name acknowledges each person as an individual, someone you pay attention to and are interested in.*
>
> (Scrivener 2012: 76)

Groupwork is known to be an effective format for practice in communicative language teaching, but from our current perspective its primary importance lies in its creating proximity, contact, interaction and cooperation amongst the members of a small group. There is an impressive body of social research to show that when people work together in groups this affects their feelings for one another in positive ways: they are more likely to form friendly ties and develop trust for one another, and group activities are particularly beneficial in establishing harmonious interracial relations in desegregated classrooms (for a good summary, see Cohen and Lotan 2014).

There are four main options for setting up groups: the teacher deliberately and purposefully allocates groupings; the teacher engenders random groupings (e.g. by drawing lots); the learners choose their own groupings; and a mixture of teacher- and learner-defined groups. Clearly, there are times when it can be beneficial for learners to choose their own partners and especially at the outset if they are nervous, it can give learners security to have familiar friends to work with. However, there is a danger of fixed cliques forming, which are unhealthy for the class of the whole. Teachers may also want to deliberately separate some learners or put specific learners together. Random groupings are popular, especially as they seem 'fair' to all concerned and offer an element of excitement. A mixed version involves the learners picking their own partners but under certain conditions, for example 'not with any person they have already worked with that week or month'. (Action Point 3 will discuss ways of preparing learners for participating in groupwork effectively.)

> *If a teacher wants to produce active learning, then groupwork, properly designed, is a powerful tool for providing simultaneous opportunities for all class members. Small groups are not a panacea for all instructional problems. They are only one tool, useful for specific kinds of teaching goals and especially relevant for classrooms where students have a wide mix of previous academic achievement and proficiency in the language of instruction.*
>
> (Cohen and Lotan 2014: 1)

Action 2: Develop a Sense of 'We' and 'Us'

We saw in Principle 2 that the essence of positive group dynamics is that the learners share a sense of cohesiveness that emerges from positive group relationships, task orientation and group pride. Ideally, we want all the learners to identify and feel a sense of belonging with the group as a whole. However, we are also aware how difficult this can be in some cases. Forsyth (2019), for example, discusses a continuum of inclusion/exclusion in a group stretching from maximum group inclusion to maximum exclusion or ostracism. Understanding group membership on a continuum helps us to understand two facets: (1) the group may accept members to differing degrees, and (2) different learners may need and want to be involved to varying degrees. As an educator, we want the group to be accepting and open to all members, with a flexibility for individuals to commit in a way and at a pace they feel comfortable with.

One of the most remarkable aspects of groups is that given appropriate conditions for group development, a 'we' feeling can emerge *regardless of*, or even *in spite of*, the initial intermember likes and dislikes - in a well-functioning group, initial attraction bonds are gradually replaced by a deeper and steadier type of interpersonal relationship: *acceptance* (Dörnyei and Murphey 2003). How can this happen? The previous Action Point already presented some ways to promote the 'gelling process' within a group, and the following six factors have also been found highly instrumental to this effect.

- *Shared goals*. It is useful to initiate explicit discussions about what we want to accomplish in the class and how students can see themselves using the learnt language in the future. At the beginning of the school year, the group can be encouraged to set specific goals that they want everyone to achieve and to reflect on ways to ensure that collectively the whole group can reach these targets.

> *Creating engagement around a clear, simple set of priorities can function as a lighthouse, orienting behaviour and providing a path toward a goal.*
>
> (Coyle 2018: 210)

- *Extracurricular activities* can be a powerful way to form bonds. They can offer a chance to create shared memories and experiences which can gel the class together more tightly, and savouring the positive memories together can foster the positive group identity. Not only do students lower their 'school filter' during these times and act more like their real selves, but these activities can usually offer students a variety of positive roles to experiment with and, if successful, to adopt. Companies sometimes organise cohesion-building outdoor experiences for their employees which include a series of challenges that they must deal with as a team (e.g. rock climbing or whitewater rafting). While undergoing such joint hardship together, people tend to do things for one another to lessen the difficulty and to overcome the obstacles, which in turn enhances solidarity and affiliation. Coping with a difficult situation together creates a sense of group achievement and becomes an indelible element of the group's history.
- *Competition* is an interesting dimension to consider in respect to group cohesiveness. There is a recognised rationale for organising competition

with other classes, in order to strengthen the within-class bonds through functioning as a team, and small-group competitions within class can serve the same purpose. However, competition should be used with caution: it can indeed boost motivation, be great fun and strengthen group cohesiveness, but used poorly, it risks isolating some learners, creating in and out-groups, having winners and by default also losers, as well as focusing on the output / end result as opposed to the process of learning. Shindler (2010) offers some guidelines for 'healthy competitions', including having only rewards of symbolic value, keeping competitions short and sweet, ensuring everyone feels they could win, and making sure the process and not the winning are foregrounded.

- *Group legend.* A further important factor fostering cohesiveness is *group legends.* Hadfield (1992) underlines that successful groups (and, we may add, also youth gangs) often create a kind of 'group mythology', which includes giving the group a name and inventing special group characteristics (e.g. a dress code) in order to enhance the feeling of 'groupness'. Group members may also be encouraged to establish group rituals, create a semi-official group chronicle, prepare 'group objects' and symbols (such as flags or coats of arms) and find or create appropriate group mottoes and logos.
- *Public commitment and investing in the group.* Public commitment to the group strengthens a sense of belonging, and can be made more salient by formalised group agreements and contracts. Wearing school colours or t-shirts are another way of doing this. In addition, when members spend a considerable amount of time and effort contributing to the group's goals (e.g. completing a major project), this will increase their commitment towards these goals and towards the group in general. In other words, psychological membership develops faster after some personal involvement in acts of actual membership, especially if publicly acknowledged.
- Finally, in a section focusing on 'we' and 'us' it is necessary to also talk about the discrimination between 'us' and 'them' – that is, *defining the group against another* – as a possible group-building tool. The reason why we need to address this question is because this strategy is extremely powerful but equally dangerous. Dörnyei and Murphey (2003) warn us that although the rivalry between classes (as in a sport competition), for example, is highly effective in uniting people within each class, it can easily shift into stirring up emotions against the outgroup in order to strengthen ingroup ties (i.e. 'us' versus 'them') – indeed, politicians sometimes deliberately create external enemy images in order to strengthen their popularity and their country's internal unity. Within and between classes, we need to take care how and when an 'us-and-them' discourse emerges.

WHO WE ARE – AN ALL-STAR CLASS! (CLASS DISPLAY)

Everyone has strengths and it is important for individuals and the groups to recognise these strengths in each other. Early on in a group's time together, it can be useful for the group to survey themselves, each reporting on something they are good at - related to language learning or otherwise. This can be displayed as a group collage (digitally or on a poster). During the term, as the class gets to know each other, other activities can include getting peers to compliment each other and add positive comments to the group collage when somebody does something kind for somebody else. Supporting learners in looking for the good in each other and ensuring everybody's strengths are recognised is invaluable for the group liking and appreciating each other.

Action 3: Prepare Learners for Groupwork and Cooperation

Groupwork has the potential to produce more active, engaged and task-oriented learner behaviour than any other teaching formats, and in their authoritative overview, Cohen and Lotan (2014: 3) report that even students 'who usually do anything but what they are asked to do' become actively engaged with their work and are 'held there by the action of the group'. However, we should not assume that students instinctively know how to work with each other in a constructive and cooperative manner; they will need to perform some communicative functions in which they may not have any experience - especially in the L2 - and they may need to adjust their mindset to working in tandem with others rather than purely pursuing individual rewards (as is traditionally the case in education). The three basic strategies to prepare learners for groupwork and cooperation involve relevant *skill-building*, *norm-setting*, and *role assignment*.

FIVE WAYS OF MOTIVATING COOPERATIVE LEARNING IN SMALL GROUPS

1. *Structuring the goal.* Groups work towards a single team product (e.g. joint performance).
2. *Structuring the rewards.* In addition to individual scores/grades, some sort of team score is also calculated and joint rewards/grades are given for the group's overall production.
3. *Structuring student roles.* Assigning roles to every group member so that everybody has a specific responsibility (e.g. 'explainer', 'summariser', or 'note-taker').
4. *Structuring materials.* Either limiting resources so that they must be shared (e.g. one answer sheet for the whole group) or giving out resources (e.g. worksheets, information sheets) which need to be fitted together (i.e. the jigsaw procedure).
5. *Structuring rules.* Setting rules which emphasise the shared nature of responsibility for the group product (e.g. 'no one can proceed to some new project/material before every other group member has completed the previous assignment').

(adapted from Olsen and Kagan 1992)

Building required skills. In order to function efficiently in a groupwork setting, students need to know how to carry out language functions in the following five areas:

- asking for other people's opinion, help and clarification;
- helping and encouraging each other, and showing others how to do things;
- negotiating ideas and giving reasons and explanations;
- giving constructive feedback and managing differences of opinion;
- working out compromises and coming to a consensus or joint decision.

Performing the necessary language skills will require some L2 input (e.g. conventionalised expressions and phrases associated with each linguistic function) as well as some controlled practice, for example as part of role-play activities. The good news is that a communicative language teaching syllabus can accommodate such practice seamlessly.

Setting special norms for group behaviour. Group tasks involve a major change in traditional classroom norms, which are usually centred around paying attention to the teacher and following his/her instructions. Cohen and Lotan (2014) explain that the norm of 'equal participation' is the fundamental cooperative rule to internalise, which can be broken down to a set of behavioural requirements such as (adapted from Ehrman and Dörnyei 1998: 264):

- Be responsive to the needs of your group.
- Encourage others, praise helpful actions and good ideas.
- Take turns, pay attention to and respect other people's opinions.
- Consult your teammates before making a decision.
- Do not dominate but make sure everybody participates.

In Action Point 4 we shall discuss further how group norms in general can be established.

Assigning group roles. Groupwork tasks usually benefit from student role allocation as a way of avoiding problems of disengagement, domination and interpersonal conflicts, through ensuring that everybody has something specific to do. Some generic, task-independent roles that have been successfully used in groupwork activities include:

- *facilitator*: keeps the group on task;
- *encourager*: encourages contributions from each member;

- *resource person / information-getter*: communicates with the teacher and other groups to receive information, advice, materials and feedback;
- *summariser*: summarises key ideas on paper and highlights disagreements to be resolved;
- *recorder*: writes up the group decision and acts as the group's spokesperson;
- *time-keeper*: makes sure that the group makes appropriate progress in the allotted time period.

These generic roles can then be complemented by roles specific to the tasks (e.g. overzealous police officer, cheeky reporter, complaining passer-by). Similar to the cooperative skills discussed above, in many cases it may not be sufficient simply to assign the roles, as students may also need language input and practice to be able to perform their roles effectively.

Action 4: Structure Using the Three 'R's: Rules, Roles and Routines

Sometimes classroom communities function smoothly without any intervention but more often than not, the quality of group dynamics is enhanced when the teacher intentionally creates some internal 'structure' in the group. Following Cowley (2013), let us consider three key 'R's as the main ingredients of a facilitative learning culture: *rules*, *roles* and *routines*. As we shall see, these structural components mirror some of the elements of effective groupwork discussed above, but this time they are applied at the whole-class level.

Rules. Class rules – also called 'group norms' – exist so that everyone can feel safe in working together and joint learning can be accomplished. Some group norms are explicitly imposed by the school or the teacher, but the majority emerge spontaneously as the group develops in time. It is important to realise that real group norms are inherently *social products* and, therefore, in order for a norm to have an impact, it needs to be explicitly discussed and then accepted by the majority of the members as a necessary condition for the smooth running of the class. To ensure this 'buy-in', we may initiate an explicit brain-storming exercise early on in the group's life to produce a pool of potential class rules, followed by a process of prioritising, negotiating and selecting. Such a discussion of why the group wants a particular rule and how it will make everyone feel is also an important part of developing interpersonal skills, empathy and an ability to reflect on the effect of a person's actions on others.

GROUP MEMBERS WILL ACCEPT AND FOLLOW A NORM WHEN THEY:

1. Recognise that the norm exists.
2. See that other members accept and follow the norm.
3. See the norm as helping to accomplish the goals to which members are committed.
4. Feel a sense of ownership for the norm (which usually happens when someone was involved in establishing it).
5. See the norm is being enforced immediately after a violation.

(adapted from Johnson and Johnson 2017: 250–251)

Once prepared, the 'officially' recognised group norms may be displayed on a wall chart to serve as a visible reminder of the rules the group has accepted. One final thing about group norms: it is important to emphasise here that the saying popular in educational circles 'Practise what you teach' is very relevant to them. The personal example the teacher sets in adhering to established norms is a prerequisite to maintaining them in the long run.

SAMPLE SET OF CLASS RULES

For the students:

- Be on time for class.
- Do your homework.
- In small group work, help each other stay in the L2.
- If you miss a class, make up for it and ask a classmate what the homework was.

For the teacher:

- Finish on time.
- Homework and tests should be marked within a week.
- Always give advance notice of a test.

For everybody:

- Listen to each other.
- Help each other.
- Accept each other and encourage each other.
- Do not hurt each other or make fun of each other's weaknesses.
- It's good to take appropriate risks in language use.
- It's OK to make mistakes.

(adapted from Dörnyei and Murphey 2003: 37–38)

Roles. The second R is about the learners having certain *roles* in the class. This can help each learner feel involved and will also give them a sense of accountability for their contribution, thereby reducing the risk of 'social loafing' – everybody hates it when some people simply do not pull their weight. We considered in the previous Action Point a list of useful student roles to enhance engagement in groupwork, and the same principle holds for the whole-class level: when students are given a named responsibility (i.e. a role), they can feel very satisfied with the part they play in the group process. If we think about it, the group norms discussed above identify a set of behavioural standards that are instrumental for the group to function well, and roles carry the same function further by assigning a set of expected behaviours to the role-holders so that they can fit into the smooth and productive functioning of the group.

What roles shall we set? This will partly depend on our specific aims, but we may recruit the students themselves to draw up a long-list of useful roles and then to choose a role for themselves. At other times we may want students to challenge themselves in new roles that may be out of their comfort zones. Many educators will be familiar with the notion of Vygotsky's (1978) Zone of Proximal Development (ZPD), which refers to the distance between the things a learner can currently do and those skills they are close to being able to do but for which they may need the guidance and input of someone more capable, be that a teacher or peers. The most effective learning comes when learners work within their ZPD, being stretched but not overstretched, to develop their skills and competences. Learners may need their role explained to them and role cards can be useful in this respect – there is no reason why these should not be made by the students themselves. Some roles may be more social or group management-based, while others may be more academic or task-based; accordingly, Cohen and Lotan (2014) distinguish between 'how' roles and 'what' roles, the former referring to *how* the process of learning should be done (e.g. facilitator, discussion moderator) and the latter to *what* is being learnt (e.g. resource finder, secretary/recorder). The following panel presents a fuller list of example roles that have been recommended in the literature.

EXAMPLES OF POSSIBLE LEARNER ROLES

- *Clarifier*
- *Contributor*
- *Coordinator*
- *Energiser*
- *Evaluator*
- *Fact-checker*
- *Harmoniser*
- *Information/Opinion seeker/provider*
- *Initiator*
- *Resource manager*
- *Secretary/Recorder*
- *Summariser*
- *Time-keeper*

(adapted from Dörnyei and Murphey, 2003)

Routines. The final R refers to the value of routines for groups. Later, when focusing on task design, we will stress the value of variation for engagement (see Chapter 6), and so it may sound counter-intuitive to now highlight the value of recurring routines, yet in terms of group dynamics, they can be invaluable. Just like norms, rules and roles, routines also concern desirable behaviours, but this time these are not described in terms of general expectations in line with the ethos of the class (i.e. a group norm) or with a certain class job (i.e. a role), but rather as concrete acts to perform at a specific stage of the lesson. In a recently observed class of young teenagers in a secondary school in Austria, the teacher walked in and all the students were already behind their desks with pieces of paper in their hands. It transpired that every Friday they start the last lesson of the week with a fun, quick-fire game, and they were enthralled, excited and ready to go even before the teacher entered the room. It was a form of shared knowledge and pattern of action that was part of their classroom culture.

Interestingly, having a routine also means that you can sometimes break it for extra-special effect by *not* doing what students expect and thereby creating surprise and novelty. In addition, routines are also useful classroom management techniques to help everyday things run more smoothly. They can offer a default scenario for dealing with the person who comes to class late or for a learner to ask to be excused for the bathroom. Establishing routines often requires an investment of time and patience, but their benefits for creating engaging learning conditions are manifold.

REFLECTION TASK 8

What rules and routines govern your classes? Have any of these behaviours simply emerged from your preferences over time? Would any of these benefit from being explained more explicitly or the rationale clarified? How consistent are you in enforcing classroom norms? How much input have learners had in them?

Action 5: Foster Democratic Participation

Johnson and Johnson (2017) explain that the field of group dynamics originated from concerns about democracy after World War II, and was seen as a scientific method to strengthen democracy, solve social problems, protect against the reappearance of fascism and reduce racism. It was hoped that training people in cooperative group skills would promote the effective functioning of democratic social systems. Cohen and Lotan (2014) report empirical studies that suggest that this hope is not completely unfounded. In one investigation, for example, when a mixture of young people were given a collaborative task, those who came from classes using cooperative groupwork displayed far more helpful and collaborative behaviour than those coming from classrooms where only whole-class instruction was in use.

Another study by Gillies (2002) showed that training in small-group and interpersonal behaviours can have lasting effects: in her study, even two years after their initial cooperative training, children proved to be better at collaborating and helping each other than their untrained counterparts.

These and other similar investigations evidence that a democratic teaching style that allows learners to make decisions and to discuss, plan and carry out tasks on their own can have beneficial socialising effects and can teach students skills that are critical for adult life in a democracy. Bearing these high stakes in mind, let us examine briefly how such democratic participation can be fostered in language classrooms.

> *Lewin and others saw group dynamics theory as one way to bridge the gaps among science (i.e. theory and research), public policies, the solution of social problems, and democratic practices. Inherent in the theory and research on group dynamics is a mandate to improve the effectiveness of democracies ...*
>
> (Johnson and Johnson 2017: 479)

In their summary of group dynamics in education, Schmuck and Schmuck (2001) conclude that leadership behaviours that involve stimulating and encouraging student interaction, organising groupwork regularly, initiating discussions about how the class is going and facilitating greater student choice will result in more mature groups. It is important to note, however, that the increase of democratic participation in the classroom can only be gradual – one may rightly argue that at the beginning of a group's life a teacher cannot be as 'democratic' and 'facilitative' as with a fully matured, cohesive group. In agreement with such concerns, Heron (1999) set up a fairly straightforward system concerning optimal facilitation. According to this system, at the outset of group development, the facilitator exercises all the power and makes all the major decisions *on behalf of* the group, in order to offer a clear framework within which early development of cooperation and autonomy can safely occur. Once participants start acquiring the necessary knowledge and skills to manage themselves, more power and responsibilities can be shared with the group in governing the learning process; the facilitator can negotiate the curriculum with the students and cooperatively guide their learning activities. Finally, when the group has reached maturity, students are ready for even more power to be delegated to them so as to achieve full self-direction in their learning, that is, to find their *own* way and exercise their *own* judgement. The task of the facilitator at this stage is to create the conditions within which students' self-determination can safely flourish.

Thus, the essence of fostering democratic participation in the classroom is to correctly gauge the optimal speed and manner of relinquishing direct leadership over the group. All this boils down to *delegating authority*, that is, passing on to the students part of the responsibility for getting the work done efficiently and effectively. This is not abdicating responsibility – after all, you will still hold the students accountable – but rather taking a more background role and enhancing self-leadership within the group. We would like to reiterate that delegating authority is not an abstract, theoretical exercise but a very hands-on, step-by-step process: it involves specific teacher action to create opportunities - preferably during every single lesson - for learners to go beyond merely following task instructions, by giving them a say first about how to perform certain aspects of the task and then also about what tasks to perform. That is, delegating authority involves, in effect, engaging learners in a qualitatively new mode.

> *When the teacher gives students a group task and allows them to struggle on their own and make mistakes, she has delegated authority.*
>
> (Cohen and Lotan 2014: 2)

REFLECTION TASK 9

How active are your learners in decision-making or influencing their own rights, responsibilities and conditions of learning? What structures, committees or voting bodies exist in your setting as part of school or classroom policy, and how are learners involved? What could you do within your class to foster more democratic participation on the part of the learners?

Summary

In this chapter, we have explored the role of group dynamics in engaging learners, with a special focus on peer relationships and classroom culture. We have argued that these represent the foundations from which learner engagement can flourish. The teacher's primary leadership role in this respect involves creating a safe environment for the learner group to develop and gradually become a mature, productive unit, characterised by cohesiveness and collaboration. The specific actions we can take to facilitate the positive group groundwork for engagement include:

- mixing up learners so that everyone in class knows everyone else personally, thereby strengthening bonds across the group and ensuring that everyone is integrated;
- developing a sense of 'we' and 'us' in the class, to help students forge a group identity and a sense of cohesion as a community;
- preparing learners for groupwork through building relevant interpersonal, collaborative and linguistic skills, through setting cooperative norms and through assigning appropriate group roles;
- structuring classroom life around the 3 'R's - Rules, Roles and Routines - to help things run smoothly and get everyone involved and accountable;
- fostering democratic participation by creating channels for consulting learners and ways of integrating their voices in various aspects of decision-making.

> *As a focus on relationships has been the fastest growing area of engagement research in the past 15 years, we have gone quickly from the realization that 'relationships matter' to understanding that few things may matter more.*
>
> (Shernoff 2013: 152)

CHAPTER IN A NUTSHELL

For learners to be willing to engage in class, they need to feel safe and accepted as valued members of a cohesive classroom community, who also have specific responsibilities for their own and the others' learning.

IF YOU WANT TO FIND OUT MORE

Dörnyei, Z. and Murphey, T. (2003). *Group Dynamics in the Language Classroom.* Cambridge: Cambridge University Press. (The core book on group dynamics in language teaching, balancing insights from research with practical advice.)

Kohn, A. (2006). *Beyond Discipline: From Compliance to Community.* Alexandria, VA: ASCD. (A controversial but thought-provoking book that invites us to reflect on our main assumptions as teachers. It includes theory and philosophising as well as some practical ideas.)

Merrell, K. W., and Gueldner, B. A. (2010). *Social and Emotional Learning in the Classroom: Promoting Mental Health and Academic Success.* New York, NY: The Guildford Press. (One of many possible books which explain what SEL – Social and Emotional Learning – is and how it can be integrated into teaching programmes. A good blend of rationale and practical guidance.)

Roffey, S. (2011). *Changing Behaviour in Schools: Promoting Positive Relationships and Wellbeing.* London: SAGE. (An insightful book on promoting prosocial behaviours and positive relationships to maximise engagement and reduce discipline issues. It also briefly addresses the important related issue of teacher well-being.)

5 Initiating engagement with learning tasks

REFLECTION TASK 1

When you start a new book or watch a film, the first few pages and minutes are critical. This is where the author or director grabs your attention, gets you hooked and draws you in. Think of a book or film that properly captured your attention from the first page or opening scenes. How did it do this? What made you want to read and watch on? What ideas does this give you regarding design principles for teaching tasks?

Teachers are constantly competing with a whole host of distractions in class, and the challenge for language educators is to cut through all of that, to grab the learners' attention and to get them to delve in and stay submerged in the tasks which will help them learn and grow. In the next two chapters, we have split the relevant strategies and techniques to achieve this into two categories: the first is concerned with how to generate the initial engagement and get learners hooked (current chapter), the second with how to keep them involved and engaged (Chapter 6). Of course, the two areas are closely interrelated as they overlap and feed into each other, so in some ways this split is a little arbitrary; yet, the division helps to clarify two different types of triggers and ongoing drives for engaged behaviour. However, before we start exploring task design, let us briefly address two preliminary issues, *distractions* and *terminology*.

Distractions. Because one of the key issues in designing engaging tasks is to combat distractions, we can make our job easier by tackling some of the obvious disruptions. Classic examples of these include student tiredness and peer discord. If the learners are tired or have been sitting for too long, a short power break with some physical movement or exercise and an oxygen boost will be helpful to get them back on track. Regarding peers, it is worth giving some careful thought about seating and grouping arrangements to ensure the most effective learning partnerships and groups (as discussed in Chapter 4).

The biggest contemporary distraction, however, is the issue of the ubiquitous mobile phone. If the students' phones are not needed for the task at hand, then they should be put on silent (not vibrate - even that noise is known to mentally distract people) and put away in bags, desks or cupboards where they cannot be reached easily. Alternatively, some teachers collect phones in a box at the front of class where they are visible but utterly unreachable! If the phones are being used for learning purposes, then that will need to be managed accordingly. For example, teachers can employ tighter task time frames so as to leave learners little freedom to wander off into other phone distractions. If the task has deliverables and a fairly tight (but realistic) schedule, students will not be able to do much else if they are to complete the task. Naturally, phones should then be put away again once the task is complete rather than left on the table, tempting students to engage with them instead of the lesson.

Terminology. As outlined briefly in the introduction, these two chapters will focus on how teachers can trigger and maintain learner engagement. In fact, we think of teachers as *designers of learning experiences*. This is not meant to be merely some jargonistic new terminology, but is intended to reflect a fundamental shift in thinking about what teachers do. Inspired by innovations in technology about 'user experience design' (e.g. Garrett 2011), it equates the learners with the users and underlines their experience in the learning tasks as the key aspect of what we focus on. We have found that there are several design principles in psychology that we can draw on to create engaging and learning-rich experiences. This perspective asks us to look at what we are doing through our learners' eyes, possibly more so than in traditional learner-centred techniques. Finally, before we proceed, we need to note how we employ the term *task*. We use the term to refer generically to any language learning activity in class which has a clear set of objectives and is purposefully designed to foster language learning and use. We do not use it in the specific meaning assigned to it in task-based learning approaches, although it can include such an understanding of task.

> *Instead of thinking of teachers as performers, I prefer to think of them as designers of experiences for students. I assume the essential skills that teachers need are those associated with designing work for students that students find engaging.*
>
> (Schlechty 2011: 3)

Rationale

Let us assume that we have developed the foundations of engagement as proposed in the previous chapters. We are ready to grab our students' attention and not let go. *Attention* has been described in educational psychology as 'the ultimate currency of our classrooms' (Mccrea 2017: 39), because without attention, no learning can take place. Yet, similar to other currencies, attention is a limited resource and there are many demands on it at any one time. The challenge, therefore, is to design attention-grabbing learning tasks, but, luckily, this may not be as daunting as it sounds! Sometimes the simplest tasks can be highly engaging when they follow the principles of what guides and captures our attention – just think of some classic party games such as pass the parcel or a treasure/scavenger hunt. Obviously, it is easier to engage learners when they are fundamentally interested in a subject, but learners can also be lured into a task by generating curiosity, challenging them to think, posing a puzzle or problem, or developing a storyline that draws them in. Essentially, the brain focuses on what it perceives as being important and therefore the ultimate goal of task design is to make the learners' brains sit up, notice and attend to the task at hand.

> *We all have an excess of things that try to command our time and attention. And attention is pretty critical, right? If your learners aren't paying attention, then it doesn't matter what kind of learning experience you've created – they aren't getting much from it.*
>
> (Dirksen 2016: 123)

Principles for Initiating Engagement on Task

In a study by Antonetti and Garver (2015), the authors suggested eight principles for student engagement (some of which overlap with our suggestions in this book) and found that employing at least three of the principles led to a dramatic increase in engagement, where 86% of learners displayed genuine, deep engagement. This suggests that sometimes less is more, and in a similar vein, in his book on motivational strategies, Zoltán suggested that we should aim to become 'good enough motivators', rather than striving unreasonably to achieve 'supermotivator' status (Dörnyei 2001: 136). What we need is *quality* rather than quantity: a few well-chosen strategies that suit both the teacher and your learners might be sufficient to create an engaging climate in the classroom – in fact, some of the most engaging teachers often rely on a few basic techniques! There is a good chance that many educators reading this book already use some aspects of the following principles, so they may only need to add in one or two further ideas to boost their learners' engagement. The palette of options should not leave teachers feeling overwhelmed, but is rather offered as a selection from which to choose as suits their needs and preferences.

We will look at several principles for getting and keeping learners engaged throughout this chapter and the next. In this chapter, the focus is on creating learners' initial engagement with a task. As Ainley (2012: 293) says, 'students' initial reaction to the task sets a direction for their level of engagement'. So, how do we get learners 'hooked' into our task, active and curious to continue?

> *The beginning is the most important part of the work.*
>
> (Plato)

Principle 1: Design for the Learners in Front of You

REFLECTION TASK 2

How much do you know about your learners' interests? Can you name one thing each learner in your class is passionate about? As language teachers, we are privileged to often get a greater insight into our learners' lives beyond the classroom than is typical in other subjects. Ideally, we can build on that knowledge as a connection for engagement. Consider how you could enable learners to bring in their passions to class daily, as well as explicitly on larger tasks.

Every teacher recycles materials and tasks, which is quite normal and necessary to stop us from burning out. The good news is that even small tweaks can enhance a task and make it more engaging. When preparing classes, it can enhance the effectiveness of our materials if we consider the specific group of students we work with rather than thinking of generic learners, and maybe pick one or two individuals to focus on, reflecting on their needs and interests. When planning our next lesson, we can make sure we think of another set of specific learners, so we keep concrete examples of learners in mind but vary who they are for our planning. Designing tasks with a specific set of learners in mind will strengthen the connection between the materials and the learners (Antonetti and Garver 2015). This principle comes first as it is the basis for initiating engagement as well as maintaining it. It underlies all good task design.

> *In one instance, a student told a member of the Schlechty Centre staff that he never knew his teacher cared about whether he found the work engaging. Now that his teacher is asking him about how he feels about the work he is assigned, he feels more like a partner with his teachers than a student, and he tries to "help the teacher think up ways to make the work more engaging". This is not a bad place to begin.*
>
> (Schlechty 2011: 25)

Any design process begins with the need to understand the audience (Dirksen 2016). For our language learners, we identify five core areas: the participants' needs, preferences, wants, current performance and contextual conditions. These can be addressed by five questions that will guide this section. The answers to these questions constitute the kind of needs analysis that helps teachers to know what design factors to build into tasks.

1. *What do learners need to learn?* The purpose of this question is to keep a focus on curriculum commitments and learning objectives. Engaging tasks alone are not enough – tasks must also be effective for learning. The question also sensitises us to the fact that rarely do all learners

in one class need the same support, input and instructional design. Effective differentiation is about keeping shared goals but offering alternative pathways to get there, in order to meet diverse learner needs and different starting points.

> *The starting point for differentiation will always be about getting to know your learners better, as far as is humanely possible, so that you can plan the right kind of learning for them. Invest time in thinking lessons through ahead of time, to help you figure out the right activities to support and challenge all the learners in your class.*
>
> (Cowley 2018: 33)

2. *What are the learners' current abilities?* All learning takes place from where learners currently are. Only when we understand each learner's current competencies and proficiency levels can we appreciate how far they can realistically be expected to stretch. As mentioned in Chapter 4, the most effective learning comes when learners work within their Zone of Proximal Development (Vygotsky 1978), attempting things that they can do with help and support but not being stretched too far. It is also important to ensure that we do not only focus on the weaknesses and areas for improvement, but also help them become aware of their strengths and areas they can build on.
3. *What do learners like to do?* Every teacher and learner we know insists that they have certain preferred ways of organising how they learn, such as choosing what time of day to study, degree of background noise they can tolerate and the kinds of techniques they like to use, such as highlighting, writing memos or audio-recording notes. Yet, there is little reliable practical advice for educators on how to work with or acknowledge these kinds of individual preferences. Learning styles are controversial notions in psychology, and empirical research offers little support for the kinds of taxonomies that typically exist (see e.g. Dörnyei and Ryan 2015). For the purposes of this chapter, perhaps the most important lesson is simply to remind ourselves that people like to learn in different ways and, from an engagement perspective, providing variety is highly energising. The other dimension of the *like* question concerns what learners are interested in, what they like to work on, talk about, think about and do. Finding out what interests a learner and connecting to that is the key to opening up engagement.

> *When individuals have an interest in a task to be accomplished or subject matter to be learned, they have focused attention, goals and learning strategies; they are more likely to feel self-efficacious and be able to self-regulate. Depending on how developed their interests are, they persevere to understand more. They can be expected to expend effort without it feeling effortful, seek feedback, make an effort to find additional resources, and create opportunities for themselves that allow them to more fully engage their interests.*
>
> (Renninger and Hidi 2016: 33)

4. *What do learners want?* This is different from what they need or what they like – learners have their own agendas in terms of their goals and what they perceive of as being of value or relevance. The question of learner beliefs has long been recognised as a decisive factor in guiding learner performance, and expectancy-value theory (see e.g. Wigfield and Eccles, 2000) has drawn attention to how the perceived value of an activity affects engagement. Thus, it is important that we make the value of a task explicit, and effective task design aims at reducing the gap between the learners' desired value and the task's delivered value. Especially at the outset of a task, it is very helpful for learners to see the link between their personal preferences for learning and what the task has got to offer.

> *If we intentionally have students generate work, products, and responses that reveal their cognition, opinions, and attitudes, then it becomes much easier to get to know each of them. This knowledge, in turn, can help us design more effective and meaningful instruction.*
>
> (Antonetti and Garver 2015: 69)

5. *What are learners' lives like?* As we saw in Chapters 1 and 2, learners do not come to our class as abstracted beings living in a social vacuum. Research is fairly unequivocal that learning is affected by a complex tapestry of social and contextual influences such as race, social class, ethnicity as well as the demographics of age and gender (see e.g. Kessels, Heyder, Latsch and Hannover 2014; Lee 2002; White 1982). Planning our teaching to display sensitive awareness of this diversity and to accommodate differences in a positive way may be a vital inroad for our learners to find a connection to the tasks in class. We can, for example, reflect on the specific wording that we and our learners use when talking about different social and ethnic groups; additionally, in all subjects but especially in the language classroom, it is vital to

understand and accommodate learners' linguistic heritages and the various languages they may bring into class with them. These can be made valuable resources for learning an additional language and can be seen as a form of linguistic capital which learners can share, connect to and explicitly build upon.

CHALLENGING QUESTIONS FOR LANGUAGE EDUCATORS ABOUT THE SOCIAL AND CULTURAL CONTEXTS OF OUR WORK

- Does the way in which teachers talk about and use languages minimise or empower other speakers?
- Do a teacher's approaches to, and theories of, language learning limit or respect diverse capacities for learning?
- Do observations about learners by teachers and peers disparage or dignify diverse language learning processes and outcomes?
- Do learners have a chance to express their authentic selves in ways which are valued and respected by teachers and peers?
- Does the approach to language teaching content and design transform or maintain the social status quo?

(adapted from Birch 2009: 3)

Principle 2: Get Learners Emotionally Invested

REFLECTION TASK 3

Emotions are no longer thought of as only being positive or negative but rather as how they may function for a specific person at a specific moment in time. For example, pride can sometimes be seen as negative (e.g. the assumption of arrogance and self-interest in the expression 'pride comes before a fall'), but actually having a sense of pride in what we do can motivate us and drive us to persevere (DeSteno 2018). Consider the emotions below and reflect on how or in what contexts these could function in a positive way for learning and engagement:

- *Awe*
- *Compassion*
- *Anger*
- *Disappointment*
- *Excitement*
- *Anxiety*
- *Surprise*

All learning is imbued with emotions, which can be both facilitative or inhibitive. They focus our attention, amplify our perceptions and influence what our memory attends to and stores (Smith 2018). As the reflective task above illustrates, the function of emotions is not always straightforward: under certain conditions, both positive and negative emotions can activate learners, although some lead to more positive, sustainable, long-term engagement, others less so. The challenge is for teachers to generate the kinds of emotions that activate engagement and draw learners into the tasks so that they are willing to invest energy and effort. Arguably, one of the most effective emotions for task-level engagement is *situational interest,* which is triggered by a specific task situation. This contrasts with *personal interest,* which is more permanent and reflects things of personal value where the interest endures across contexts (we shall further discuss this distinction in Chapter 6).

> *When faced with a classroom of students who are potentially drowsy, stressed, and exposed to multiple sources of competing stimuli both external (the smartphone in their laps) and internal (nagging worries about whether they're going to pass the calculus exam they have next), your best route for grabbing everyone's attention and directing it to the material at hand may well be to tap into your students' emotions using your activities and assignments.*
>
> (Cavanagh 2016: 36)

Task design can captivate learners emotionally on three levels, in its *physical appeal, activity appeal* and *content appeal.* At the most basic level, the visual channel of perception can be an impactful route to emotional engagement. Aesthetically pleasing materials can arouse learners' attention at the initial stage, a principle known by all advertising agencies. In this respect, technology can be highly effective in creating attractive ways of presenting tasks, but it needs to be used with care, as it can easily turn into a distracting factor by misleading students as to what is truly relevant for the learning task at hand (see e.g. Fisher, Godwin and Seltman 2014). In other words, irrelevant physical appeal can work against the second level of appeal - *activity appeal* - which is concerned with the emotions learners experience when working on the task (see also Chapter 6).

Ideally, learners should feel sufficiently competent and capable of doing what is expected of them and should experience the process of working on the task as interesting and enjoyable. A sense of mastery and autonomy are key. Relevant factors to consider in this respect are the *mode* of working, the *medium* of working, the *social structure* of working and the *form of task output* they create. Some particularly pertinent questions include:

- How much time, freedom, choice and resources do learners have on the task?
- What different language skill areas are being employed?
- Where, with whom and in what ways do they work with others?
- How pleasurable and attractive is it for learners to create the task output?

The third level for building emotional appeal to learners – *content appeal* – is through the choice of topic of the task. Sometimes the themes prescribed by curricula and coursebooks are inherently engaging for the age group and specific group of learners we are working with, but at other times the many compromises that coursebook writers need to make to satisfy (and more often, to avoid offending) all the diverse audiences result in topics that can range from bland to outright boring. This, however, perhaps also offers an opportunity: teachers can create an emotional hook to draw students into the topic by inviting them to add aspects that examine the subjects from a fresh and exciting perspective or which link to highly personal or relevant interests in respect to the topic, especially in terms of localising content. For example, exploring human connections (by adding real-life emotions), personal attitudes, local relevance, additional narrative elements (i.e. stories behind the main plot) are all effective ways to engage learners emotionally. If the topic is something like 'animals', pupils can look for stories of animals in the media, such as rescue stories, animal welfare stories or unusual animal behaviour stories. Learners may want to report on their own pets or animal encounters, or they may want to talk about local animal volunteer opportunities or protection groups. Essentially, making the learners care about the topic and the characters or want to know more about what happens next can be powerful emotional attractors.

REFLECTION TASK 4

Boredom has been associated with four conditions: the degree of arousal (low or high); the degree or monotony or repetitiveness; how pleasant or unpleasant the task is; and how much freedom or constraint the individual has. Reflect on the hypothetical scenario posited in light of this by Keller (2010: 90):

Imagine sitting in a class in which you are finding it almost impossible to stay awake. Assume it is a class that you do not want to take (unpleasantness), you can't leave until the bell rings (constraint), the teacher speaks in a monotone voice (low arousal), and is very redundant (repetitive). It is the perfect scenario to induce boredom! And sleepiness. Is this scenario realistic or an exaggeration of reality?

Principle 3: Curiosity Captivates

> *The cure for boredom is curiosity. There is no cure for curiosity.*
>
> (Attributed to both Ellen Parr and Dorothy Parker)

We start off life curious. Anyone who has spent time with young children knows the endless series of 'Why?' questions which riddle any conversation. Throughout our lives, curiosity drives much of our behaviour and certainly a great deal of our learning. Some people remain more curious than others and there is some debate about whether curiosity may be a personality trait and whether there is a personality variable called 'Need for cognition' (Cacioppo and Petty 1982). However, the fact is that a huge proportion of a nation will tune in for the next episode of a soap opera when the previous one ended on a cliffhanger; indeed, the seventeenth-century English philosopher, Thomas Hobbes, described the 'desire to know why' – that is, curiosity – as a 'a lust of the mind' (1985: 124). Teachers thus have a powerful tool at their fingertips!

> *... curiosity resembles scratching a mental or intellectual itch.*
> (Livio 2017: 64)

Scholars often distinguish between two types of curiosity: (a) *epistemic curiosity,* which refers to the general drive for learning simply for the reward of the pleasure of knowing more, and (b) *perceptual curiosity,* which is aroused by novel, surprising or ambiguous stimuli – it is the uncomfortable although not totally unpleasant itch that needs to be satisfied (Leslie 2014). As educators, we want to ignite our learners' curiosity by arousing their 'mental itch' to know more and we also want to tap into their general curiosity about the world around them for lifelong learning. Education specialists such as Kohn (2013) and Robinson (2013) bemoan the state of many contemporary education systems, which they feel have essentially crippled learners' general epistemic curiosity through the endless batteries of standardised tests. We remain more optimistic, believing that despite the challenges that many stifling education systems pose for teachers in harnessing epistemic curiosity, there are strategies to tap into this powerful fundamental human drive.

> *Rather than just getting more people to school and university, therefore, the new challenge is to find ways of making more people hungry to learn, question and create.*
> (Leslie 2014: 9)

So, how can we tap into the curiosity to learn new things? One way is to begin with the curiosity learners bring with them to class. From adolescence onwards, there are certain key topics that typically capture the thinking and imagination of all humans, such as the meaning of life, love, fairness, equality, life in the universe, how the planet works, well-being, altruism, the role of education, the implications of democracy, globalisation, etc. Many of these topics can be connected to key twenty-first-century learning objectives and themes such as health literacy, democratic principles, social justice, harmony and intercultural communication. Epistemic curiosity can also be built further on by encouraging the quest for *depth* of knowledge, for example by allowing learners to explore the nuances of controversial or surprising phenomena within some project work. Thus, the key is letting learners find out things for themselves and not presenting them with information – offering them opportunities to discover things on their own. This discovery approach is crucial for fostering epistemic curiosity. For language learners, this principle applies not only to topics that may be addressed through language, but also to allowing learners to work out the rules of language and how it functions for themselves.

GUIDED DISCOVERY APPROACH TO GRAMMAR

One increasingly popular approach for teaching grammar is what is known as the *guided discovery approach* or the *inductive approach*. To illustrate the approach and how it facilitates curiosity, we will outline possible steps in learning a clear, uncomplicated grammar rule. It is often helpful for learners to work with peers when taking this approach. Some coursebooks also include this in a simplified form, in terms of example sentences which ned to be examined for learners to complete a rule. Typical stages in the discovery approach include:

- *Step 1:* Learners are exposed to authentic language in context such as articles, blog entries, extracts from books, etc.
- *Step 2:* Through guided questions prepared by teachers and/or peers, learners analyse the language in use, trying to deduce a rule.
- *Step 3:* Learners can be encouraged to find more examples of the language and rule in use, seeking to prove themselves wrong before they commit to stating the rule.
- *Step 4:* Learners present their understanding of how the language works and their rule to the rest of the class. This can be done creatively.
- *Step 5:* The class discusses the rules to check they all agree and whether they find any exceptions.
- *Step 6:* Learners try out applying the rule (more structured or more freely, depending on what you feel is more appropriate for the learners) in order to test the applicability of the rule. They can be encouraged to look for evidence to prove or disprove the suggestions.

REFLECTION TASK 5

Take a look at the coursebook you are currently teaching with or at a popular coursebook for your teaching context. Look at the topics addressed. There are two questions related to different curiosity triggers worth reflecting on:

1. Is the topic authentically relevant to learners' own lives?
2. Is it a topic that could be leveraged to stimulate epistemic curiosity (desire to learn more)?

All topics can be made interesting but in reality some topics will pique learners' interest from the outset more than others. It can be useful to reflect on the types of topics we are working on from the learners' perspective, but we may also simply ask them what is of interest to them.

Perceptual curiosity is triggered by the itch that must be relieved. This feeling can come from two main sources: (a) the novelty and surprise type of itch, or (b) the puzzling, ambiguous or gap-in-information type of itch.

Both attention-grabbing strategies are used widely in advertising and as good cliffhangers in films or books, as well as by many websites that want users to click links. We should note that there is a peculiar characteristic of the second type of perceptual curiosity triggered by a gap in our knowledge: one needs to have a certain degree of knowledge about the topic to be aware of what one doesn't yet know, otherwise there is nothing to be curious about, or one simply doesn't know what to be curious about (which is sometimes referred to as 'Meno's paradox'). Loewenstein (1994) explains that people need to be aware of their 'ignorance' and perceive a gap before it can trigger curiosity, and Leslie (2014) calls this the 'zone of curiosity', in line with the parallels to Vygotsky's Zone of Proximal Development (1978). The lesson for teachers is that providing some knowledge might be a first step for creating curiosity to know more.

Principle 4: Concentrate on Task Set-Up

As designers of learning experiences, teachers often put a lot of thinking and creativity into the task experience from the learners' perspective, but a key part that can easily be overlooked is the *set-up* of the task - that is, the part where we lay out what will be done, give instructions and direction as we get them engaged and look ahead to the task. The difficulty with task instructions is that we can go wrong with them both when they are too short and when they are too long. On the one hand, *KISS* (Keep It Short and Simple) remains one of the best pieces of advice for instructions - after all, who wouldn't agree that rambling and potentially confusing sets of initial directions can destroy any learner interest and undermine the task? In the language classroom, things are further complicated by the need to use the right level of the target language and to ensure it is readily comprehensible for your learners.

> *Most of the outcomes that you desire in your classes depend to a great extent on your ability to promote clarity within your environment. Clarity within the classroom has been found to correlate positively with student achievement, level of engagement, and student satisfaction ... And most classroom management dysfunction is related to a lack of clarity in some form.*
>
> (Shindler 2010: 17)

We like the slogan of 'Never explain, demonstrate!', because actions speak louder than words and a concrete example can bring a task to life more than any amount of explanation. Yet, this is also a double-edged sword, because the absence of any explanation would omit one of the key aspects of task instruction, that is, the communication of good reasons as to why the particular activity is meaningful and important - if we want our students to give their best when engaging with a task, they need to see the relevance and value of what they do. Moreover, a key dimension of task set-up that must be clear is the expected outcome or goal of the task.

Learners need to know what is expected of them and how this will be assessed. Having a clear sense of direction will help them to keep focus, remain on task and evaluate their own progress towards task goals. These goals, in turn, must be well articulated, specific (in other words concrete and clear) and measurable (somehow quantifiable so you can see how much of the goal has been completed). A classic study in education by Bandura and Schunk (1981) showed that students who were given specific, short-term goals achieved greater than 20% more work completed than those with vague goals or distant goals. This shows that having a clear focus and an understanding of exactly what needs to be done makes a difference to student progress.

A final important dimension of task set-up is 'whetting the students' appetites', that is, raising the students' expectations of something interesting and important to come. You can do this by projecting intensity and enthusiasm when you introduce the activity, and by pointing out something interesting or important either about the content of the activity or the procedure of task completion – if there is nothing to point out, this might be a good indication that something is altogether wrong with the task. Naturally, if you start every task in the same way always, this is going to lose impact over time as well, so the point is to remember that this initial setting-up stage is also worth reflecting on, given how impactful it can be.

TASK INSTRUCTIONS

Five things to bear in mind when presenting a task – although not all may be relevant every time, depending on the kind of task you do:

1. Get everyone's attention before you begin and then Keep it Short and Simple.
2. Describe what students will be doing step-by-step, and model the activities if it is easier than to explain.
3. Be clear about what the product or output will be when finished and how it will be evaluated or utilised.
4. Help learners find value, utility, purpose and meaning in the task by emphasising the learning opportunity in the task.
5. Whet the learner's appetite by pointing out something interesting about the task.

Principle 5: Learners Need to be Active to Engage

This final principle may seem so obvious that it doesn't need saying, but we think it is good to be reminded. While people can thoroughly enjoy sitting back and taking in a good film or theatre performance, very few teachers have the charisma and persona to pull off an engaging performance when they are the 'sage on the stage'. Yet, so much of classroom time is spent with the teacher being active in the front and the students being passive – when it should be the other way round! Rather than taking the stage, teachers should 'set the stage to engage' (King and

King 2017: xv). This means that teachers should design for engaging learning experiences where the main actors are the learners, not the teachers. Quite simply, no theorising can change the fact that mastering active communication skills requires engaging in active language practice.

REFLECTION TASK 6

Language teachers are familiar with discussions about the ratio of Teacher Talking Time (TTT) to Student Talking Time (STT) (see also Chapter 3), with the ideal being more STT than TTT. However, we should also look at how much Teacher Activity (TA) is in relation to Student Activity (SA) in each class. When designing lessons, do you think of the TA/SA ratio? What active roles are teacher and learner engaged in at any one time?

In the psychology of gaming, one key reason why video games are engaging in a manner that, for example, watching a film is typically not, boils down to *action*. In games, the participants are the actors who define what happens to them, actively making choices that direct the action. They are not the audience, quietly watching what happens to others. The reason for the shift in popularity from films to games that is typically observed in youth culture is exactly the fact that the gamers are the agents of change – they are the actors exerting control and taking action (Rigby and Ryan 2011). This notion of active involvement is central to engagement and provides a valuable lesson that educators can learn from the way games have captured people's attention. Furthermore, it reflects the more general trend that today's learners are quite simply used to more interactive forms of learning and information-seeking.

> *One must learn by doing the thing, for though you think you know it, you have no certainty until you try.*
>
> (Sophocles)

One way to increase the general level of active involvement in the classroom is to immediately get learners to do something hands-on at the start of class. This may involve moving things around or holding things or physically engaging with something. This can then be combined with a focus on employing all the five senses in teaching, which can lead to more memorable multisensory learning (Cowley 2009). It is also acknowledged that when learners experience something for themselves, it tends to be more emotionally memorable and they have a deeper connection to it.

This also links to the idea of making the most of class trips, excursions and exchanges, which take language learning beyond the confines of the classroom, put learners at the heart of communication contexts and make the learning and use of the language as hands-on and active as it can possibly be. In class, we can make tasks more interactive by working with online resources, such as voting apps like Plickers or Kahoot, but also by using more traditional cards and realia or props that learners can physically move around. Movement and getting learners physically active is also part of an 'active learning' approach (Bonwell and Eison 1991). This can be as simple as having learners do a role play or, as mentioned earlier, it can be introducing a power break in the middle of a session to re-energise learners.

Teacher Actions

The principles outlined above set the stage for designing engaging tasks. The focus in the following actions is very much on creating that initial spark that gets learners involved. We are mindful, however, that unless initial engagement is sustained, it risks being only a fleeting gimmick which may grab the students' attention and interest but which is easily dropped and does not lead to any deep or meaningful learning. The actions in this section alone will not drive the deep engagement over time that leads to learning but they will help to set learners off on a pathway of engaged learning. The key message of this chapter is that how we set up and begin a task is critical to capturing their engagement - first impressions matter a lot in education. We are in full agreement with Plato that 'the beginning is the most important part of the work', and therefore it is important to invest time, thinking and planning into our starters of the lesson in general and how we begin specific tasks in particular. So, here are some suggestions on how to hook the learners and get them on board.

> *You never get a second chance to make a first impression.*
> (Source unknown)

Action 1: Start With Deliberately Small Steps

> *A journey of a thousand miles begins with a single step.*
> (Lao Tzu)

As the saying goes, 'How do you climb Everest? By putting one foot in front of the other.' It is indeed often the taking of that first step that is so difficult. If we can get our learners to take the very first step at the initial stage of a task, this will create momentum and we have a stronger chance of keeping them working on the task. The key is that the first step in the process should be attractive and manageable. Indeed, this is how gaming gets players hooked, by drawing them in with an attractive interface and easy first success (Rigby and Ryan 2011). This will get learners active straight away and will lead to an instant reward mechanism through a sense of success, mastery and progress. This is also true of the whole class: we often use initial *warmers*, that is, short introductory games at the beginning of a lesson. Like the first level in a game, a warmer should be fun and allow students to have some success in using the target language. This gets students in the right frame of mind, both in terms of becoming an active group member and switching from their mother tongue into the L2 mode.

> *The evidence of observing hours of lessons shows that the first few minutes are key: Students are restless by nature, so any teacher who demonstrates they have a clear purpose and expects active student participation in the first five minutes is more likely to grab their students' attention and get the lesson off to a flying start.*
>
> (Bentley-Davies 2010: 80)

Thus, the key to beginning a class or a task is to get on with it straight away without too much fuss. It is useful to have routines in place to manage the administration you may have to do at the outset of class, in order to speed up that process and so that you can get the majority of learners straight on task doing a quick activity, while you deal with the initial paperwork and individual student issues (Cowley 2013). It is worth noting that active starter activities can actually be used throughout a lesson as energisers to boost learner vitality as well as to get them thinking and active, and possibly also switching the pace or focus if need be.

REFLECTION TASK 7

Compare these two lesson starters:

1. *With a partner, you have two minutes to brainstorm everything you know about 'homelessness in this country'.*
2. *With a partner, write three statements you believe to be true about homelessness in this country. You have two minutes.*

Both are likely to get students active but the first is rather vague and very open so although they may initially engage, learner enthusiasm and focus can wane, although it does have a time limit which helps them to focus on the task. The second one also sets up a form of prediction, so that students will have a chance during the lesson to check whether their assumptions were true or not. This may also be a good chance to challenge stereotypes and reflect on social justice issues. It also ensures contextualised language use in full sentences.

Starting with a *personal element* is also a good first step in a more complex task sequence. It is a first way into a topic and can be facilitated through questions, discussion statements, ranking tasks, picture prompts, guessing games, drawing up lists and interviews, among others. Students usually find it motivating to discuss themselves and everyone can experience success doing this. If this step can also create positive emotional resonance for the learner, the effects can be even stronger in terms of engagement.

> *Personal experiences are factually concrete and emotionally valuable. As a result, acknowledging student experiences and using them in the learning process stimulates intrinsic motivation.*
> (Raffini 1996: 232)

Here is a dilemma to finish with: Should a warmer review the last lesson or focus on setting up this lesson? Or is it possible to do both things at once? Many education approaches recommend (for obvious reasons of recycling, revising and priming previous learning) using the first five minutes of a lesson to revisit what happened in the last session. We wonder, however, if this is a sufficiently engaging way of spending the crucial first five minutes. Admittedly, a revision can be done in an interesting way, for example, by asking learners to become the teacher and teach one key insight from the last class to others, by getting learners to create quick quizzes for each other on the last lesson, or by using activities such as sort the jumbled statements, spot the odd one out, annotate a picture or text, or complete the opinion polls with clickers. Still, perhaps, it might be best to keep starters fresh, original, manageable and fast-paced – after all, the beginning is the start of everything that follows. In addition, if warmer activities are connected to the lesson topic and do things like arouse curiosity about the topic or set up an information gap (e.g. a knowledge gap) then they can serve a dual function. What do you think?

Action 2: Build in Surprise and the 'Wow' Factor

REFLECTION TASK 8

Think about your online reading behaviour. What is it that makes you click on a link and then continue reading beyond the headline? These actions can give us some clues about the attractors that can draw us into doing something, as well as the drives that keep us engaged with it.

A key principle for the initial stage of engagement is to create curiosity, and many of the following teacher actions revolve around this principle to some extent. The first such action is to go for the 'wow' factor. Building in surprise or novelty sets the brain on edge and heightens our attention with a greater focus and concentration – ideal for initiating engagement. It also ensures that what we do learn is then stored better in our memories (Fenker and Schütze 2008). Surprise is connected to the brain's pleasure centre, which means we actually get a reward and a dopamine boost in the brain from the experience of surprise, which supports engagement and memory.

Surprise can be achieved in various ways. It involves breaking expectations or challenging assumed knowledge, and it creates an emotional response which can range from excitement and amazement to shock and disbelief. Interestingly, research has shown that unexpected rewards are valued more than expected rewards (Berns, McClure, Pagnoni and Montague 2001). Our attention is greater for those things which surprise us and break expected patterns and norms. In classrooms, we can build in surprise at various stages and levels. For example, if you are introducing a new topic, we can confront learners with a surprising prompt. To create surprise at the start of a lesson, you could begin with a surprising statistic, an unexpected fact, a common misconception, or a hidden talent/secret about a famous person. Did you know, for example, that there are over 84 million active teachers? Want to know in which sectors and in which countries they worked, as well as what salaries they earned? If so, check out 'Our World in Data' (https://ourworldindata.org/teachers-and-professors) – we bet many of you are about to do that, which shows the strategy at work!

> *Our attention is so splintered that having a single focus is almost impossible. Unless we're surprised. Surprise unifies our attention and gives us a deep experience right here in the present.*
> (Luna and Renninger 2015: 14)

In our teaching, we tend to have certain routines and there are expectations that the learners have about what happens in class and school. If we can disrupt their patterns of expectation, then we can capture their attention. If we can deal in an unusual way with the ordinary, then learners may be surprised and become engaged by the novelty of the task. It can be a simple twist on the usual; for example:

- If we normally provide students with a reading task copied on to white paper, try copying on to coloured paper and cut into paragraphs that they have to reconstruct, or try posting the different coloured paragraphs on the walls of the room and asking them to move around the room to read the text.
- If you typically set up a role play by allocating roles on cards, try handing out cards with nothing on them, or just a picture, and ask learners to devise roles. Then collect the role cards created by the learners and redistribute them for a different type of role play designed and enacted by learners. You could even ask learners to video themselves performing a role play.
- Try teaching from a different point in the room, so that learners experience the classroom space differently.
- Do something dramatic, such as teaching about a festival or holiday with everyone in costume or moving the class outdoors in summer to explore language and spaces beyond the class.
- If you always use the same online platform, try a different resource or let the students choose or create activities instead of you.
- If you start the lesson by collecting homework, don't – start with a fast-paced game and then collect the homework.

It is about varying the norms, avoiding the rut and sparking an interest in the task at hand and the class as a whole. Surprise them! Do the unexpected and get students also to do the same – as we all know, variety is the spice of life.

SURPRISE ME!

What things can you work on in your classroom setting to bring in an element of surprise? What would be a novelty or surprise? What would challenge the expectations, routines and norms of practice?

- Surprising *content* – facts, figures and images
- Surprising *format and mode* – online tools, interactive platforms, hands-on activities, coloured cards and pens
- Surprising *set-up* – location, groupings, seating, teacher
- Surprising *output* – posters, vlog, performance, song

Novelty is also about *variation*. On the one hand, as we have discussed earlier, there can be some comfort in having certain routines and habits built into classroom life. Indeed, learners often appreciate the security of doing tasks they are familiar with and feel safe and positive about. On the other hand, learners can explore something new which is exciting and creates curiosity but which also inherently incorporates a degree of risk for the unfamiliar. For the most part, too much of the same thing gets dull and boring – no matter how dazzling that activity may have been at first. The more they do it, the more it loses its sparkle and ability to wow.

> *Surprise stems from appraising an event as unexpected, and interest follows when people further appraise the unexpected thing as within their capacity to understand.*
>
> (Silvia 2017: 101)

An initial 'wow' factor can also be achieved through the aesthetics of how we present tasks. As mentioned earlier, in the digital and highly visual world of our learners, aesthetics can define engagement. Indeed, designers of websites, games and coursebooks spend a lot of time and budget thinking about the layout and attractiveness of materials. First impressions count! People are more willing to engage when something looks visually appealing, with an attractive interface. However, we should also reiterate that the physical appeal may not always contribute meaningfully to the task; indeed, there is some research that found that learners can be distracted by visuals in unhelpful ways (Harp and Mayer 1998; Thalheimer 2004). On the other hand, other research indicates that learner motivation *can* be boosted with emotionally engaging images, provided they are at least peripherally linked to the main topic or task (Park and Lim 2007). This is reminiscent of the use of humour (see Chapter 3), which can also be an effective tool when it is relevant to the task at hand.

> *Although Novelty and Variety can lead to engagement fairly quickly, there is always a danger that students become engaged in the novelty of the activity and not in the learning.*
> (Antonetti and Garver 2015: 93)

Action 3: Build in Mystery and Puzzles

Everyone loves a mystery or a puzzle. Humans are neurologically wired to satisfy curiosity as our brains seek to make sense of the world around us. Every time we hear the ping of an e-mail or message, we need to solve the mystery of who it is or what the message is about. The ping alone sets off our curiosity antennae. In teaching, we can generate that curiosity by creating some healthy confusion, uncertainty, mystery or puzzlement. Let us now consider a number of practical ways of doing so.

A classic method of generating interest is through creating a sense of *puzzlement*. Puzzling elements can be brought into teaching in a myriad of ways. For example, you can employ traditional puzzle formats such as jigsaws, crosswords, quiz shows, treasure/scavenger hunts, logic puzzles, riddles, word games, visual illusions and pattern-guessing games. These are popular leisure activities for many people, as they stimulate thinking and unleash the drive to want to 'resolve' the puzzle (Davies 2014). Naturally, they need to be used meaningfully in ways relevant to the topic or language issues being worked on, but one productive way of producing these adaptations is to involve the students themselves – after all, creating a crossword puzzle can be as interesting as solving it.

REFLECTION TASK 9

How do you create initial curiosity currently in your teaching? What kinds of starter activities do you use? How effective do you find the following?

- Outline a mystery
- Pose a question to solve
- Hold a quiz
- Use provocative visuals
- Partially reveal a picture or play part of an audio or video recording
- Present a dramatic picture and ask 'What happens next?'
- Present ambiguous statements and ask learners to predict if they are true or false
- Ask learners to predict the questions they think the text will answer
- Ask learners to guess the answers to comprehension questions before they read or listen

Many communicative language tasks are designed around some form of *information gap*, where the need to communicate with each other stems from one person knowing something that the other person does not.

However, where such activities sometimes fall short is on the relevance or interest of the task per se and on the authenticity of the need-to-know. Is the gap just one to be filled for the purposes of completing a task that is overall lacking in real meaning and purpose or relevance? One way of making the need-to-know element more genuine is to adjust the artificial content; for example, one of the standard information gap tasks is giving directions where one person has a map and the other person asks directions to places on the map, and this could be made more meaningful by using a map of the school and turning it into a treasure hunt through the school, following directions. Alternatively, if the students are going on an exchange, get a map (or use an online map) and use real locations such as the hotel or the various places you will visit. Even better if, again, the students themselves are involved in creating these treasure hunts / direction puzzles for each other.

Task-based learning (TBL) approaches usually involve problem-solving, puzzles and simulations of some kind. These engage learners by using language as a functional means to an end. Typically, students work in pairs or small groups, using the language to interact and communicate on how to meet the demands of the tasks, which are often challenging and have a clear purpose and outcome beyond language learning goals. For example, in an ESL setting, learners could identify a problem in the local community, such as reported in a local newspaper or brainstormed from their own experiences. In groups or as a class, they could work on proposing a way of addressing the issue and how they could help or seek help in practical terms. One example could be thinking of ways to teach people digital literacy skills. In an EFL setting, learners could be given the task of finding a partner school in an English-speaking country to liaise with. Each group would have to find a school online, do some research about the suitability of the school and how they could approach them. The groups would then present their suggestions for the class to vote on which school to approach with a concrete suggestion for an e-partnership. There are also smaller-scale TBL tasks such as role play, discussions, voting, interviews, etc. (for further examples, see Nunan 2004; Willis and Willis 2007).

Another way of prompting curiosity and deeper thinking is to provoke learners in a way which leaves them wanting to respond or to know more. Using provocations is the foundation of many approaches to critical and creative thinking. There are several strategies of provocation, which can include: making a seemingly untenable statement or crazy idea that is explored for grains of truth or usefulness; asking moral and ethical questions to provoke thinking and discussion; using wishful thinking ideas to fantasise; posing 'what if' questions; presenting contrasting or opposing viewpoints; using concrete examples and stories; or exaggerating a scenario to show ideas taken to extremes. Of course, the provocation should be an invitation for learners to join the task on their own terms (rather than alienate or anger them). For example, learners could be asked to think about the world without money and how it could function, or they could be asked to think of one thing they could change to improve life on Earth, or they could discuss a dilemma such as the Robin Hood dilemma: you witness somebody robbing a bank but then giving the money to homeless people - do you report this or not?

> *We confuse the practice of curiosity with the ease of access to information, and forget that real curiosity requires the exercise of effort.*
>
> (Leslie 2014: 19)

Action 4: Create Cliffhangers

We all love a good cliffhanger, and skilful novelists and TV series writers know how to exploit this to good effect to keep us hooked and desperate to find out what happens next. Imagine if we could harness the same feeling for teaching. A cliffhanger depends in psychological terms on an effect known as the 'Zeigarnik effect'. This refers to the Russian psychologist Bluma Zeigarnik, who noticed that the waiters and waitresses in a restaurant in Vienna could remember orders in the process of serving them but completely forgot and erased them from memory once the order was complete (cited in Alter 2017). This effect is due to the tendency for humans to want closure and resolution. An incomplete task will intrude on your thoughts and you are drawn back to it with a desire to finish it. It stays in our memory more strongly as long as it is unfinished. In the same way, ambiguity and unresolved plot lines leave us frustrated and yearning for a neat, 'proper' ending... To be continued!

> *This suspense is terrible. I hope it will last.*
>
> (from *The Importance of Being Earnest* by Oscar Wilde)

REFLECTION TASK 10

'Clickbait' is a term used to describe online content such as a visual or a headline that is designed to make readers want to click on the link to find out more. It is designed to be attention-grabbing. It often draws on all the kinds of strategies in these first three action points - surprise, mystery, puzzlement, information gaps and cliffhanger prompts. In the coming days, make notes of the kinds of clickbait you encounter online - but beware those used to get you to purchase or spend money or to take you to dubious sites! Focus on those regular websites which may take you to other news stories or articles. What strategies are they using and how do they relate to the actions and ideas suggested in this chapter? Can you think how to 'clickbait' your students' attention at the start of a task or class? (This could even become a project involving the students themselves to do the research!)

We can also use people's desire to know more to get learners' attention at the start of the task (and indeed repeatedly throughout a class) by using a cliffhanger. As with a good thriller or TV series, the trick is not to reveal all the information at once but to hold some back and plant the seed of an idea. It is all the more powerful if we can make the cliffhanger emotionally loaded. So, how can we create an initial cliffhanger? Asking questions that people feel a need to have an answer for is one strategy. For example, for someone interested in films: Which famous film is reported to be getting a sequel? What part-time job did actor X do before he became famous? What was the most outrageous demand made by an actor on a film set?

To use these kinds of strategies well means knowing your audience and knowing what your learners would want to know more about, what is relevant for their lives and interests more broadly, and how we can tap into that. We can use strategies such as making content personal, connecting to famous people and our interest in gossip, using hyperbole and exaggeration, asking questions, using emotionally strong language (amazing, terrible, shocking, outrageous, etc.), eliciting a sense of exclusivity or insider secrets, working with lists, or creating some sense of controversy, ideally using actual facts or true statements that shock or create polemics. Such prompts work most effectively when they are short and to the point. See examples in the reflection task below.

REFLECTION TASK 11

If you work with teenage learners or have teenage children, think whether these headlines might pull them in or not and what 'clickbait' strategies they are drawing on:

- *Not cool – these trends are finished*
- *This has to be THE greatest travel adventure of all time*
- *What the internet knows about you*
- *Bet you didn't know this about BTS / Baby Ariel, etc. (insert any popular band, actor or YouTube star!)*
- *Why do we yawn?*
- *5 things you must do this summer break*
- *Under-16s to be allowed only one hour online per day*
- *Secret hacks for learning vocab – Never fail a vocab test again!*
- *Click here to find out what you and Cruz Beckham have in common!*

A numerical trick is often an easy way to harness the sense of dissatisfaction that emerges from the Zeigarnik effect and it is therefore also a typical clickbait strategy. Firstly, how driven are you on your social media sites to see 100% completed on progress bars or fully completed pie charts? Do you feel that if it is already 90% complete, you may as well finish off the task? And since you have read five of the six chapters in this book, do you feel you may as well read on? Starting a task with a progression bar or number of subtasks to complete can be a lure, especially if we ensure the first one is completed quickly and relatively easy to generate an immediate sense of progress (see also Action Point 5). For example, completing the first step may take users straight to 1 out of 5 completed or 20% completed. If this is visible on a progress bar or chart, it can be a powerful motivator to continue to complete the chart / progress bar and would be thus instrumental for getting learners hooked and engaged.

Secondly, we can create a numerical-based cliffhanger by saying we will talk about three top tips for doing something and leave getting to number three until a little later. The brain will wait around for the third point needed for completion, at least for a certain amount of time. We also have a love of lists, which is why many online writers and presenters organise things around a numbered list - these articles are called 'listicles'. For example: 3 things you need to know about engagement; my top 10 favourite teaching novels; 5 simple steps to a perfect essay; 10 commandments for motivation! It is also why learners like to create lists too and are unhappy if they cannot complete the whole list. These are particularly effective when the list goes backwards from ten to one with lots of build-up, as people are really curious to know what is number one. Typically, the number one spot is taken by a controversial item to get people to comment and share the list.

> *The Zeigarnik effect reveals a tendency to experience tension and even intrusive thoughts about goals one has engaged in that are left incomplete. It appears to bother us whenever we don't finish what we start. Some psychologists refer to this as a lack of closure. By contrast, completion of a task brings a feeling of relief and pleasure. In short, unfinished business heightens internal tensions, and completion of tasks releases it, which feels good.*
>
> (Rigby and Ryan 2011: 109)

Action 5: Use Questions to Trigger Curiosity

Socrates, the Greek philosopher, probed his students and colleagues through a process of continual questioning. The 'Socratic method' is still popular among lawyers but is also increasingly used in education as one way of promoting critical thinking skills. Whether asking questions or being asked questions, questioning is a highly effective way of engaging learners and is a valuable strategy for teachers to have in their toolkit. Getting learners to formulate and respond to questions makes learners actively think about and engage with content. Not only is this more engaging, but it is also a more effective way for learners to learn in lasting, memorable and transferable ways.

SAMPLE QUESTIONS FOR THE 'SOCRATIC METHOD'

- What do you think?
- Why do you think so?
- Is this always true?
- Can you give an example?
- Can you think of an exception?
- What is the consequence of what you are saying?
- How does this affect you or someone/something else?
- Do you think this was a good question?
- What would *you* ask?
- What would you answer?

Sadly, the vast majority of questions that teachers typically ask are merely knowledge recall questions, whereas questions which promote critical thinking, analysis, comprehension, evaluation, synthesis and transfer are more effective for deep learning (Walsh and Sattes 2011). The effective use of questioning is not about 'testing' rote-memorised answers but about using questions to get learners to think for themselves, connecting to prior knowledge and personal experiences and reaching their own understandings. For example, instead of asking what happened, we can ask learners to think why somebody might have acted in a certain way, or what they were feeling at the time, or what the implications of their actions might be. Such questioning can serve as a key trigger for curiosity as well as creativity (Berger 2014).

> *quality questioning activates and sustains interactions and relationships between students and teachers, between students and the content, and between teachers and the content in ways that increase both student engagement and achievement.*
>
> (Walsh and Sattes 2011: 11)

Finally, does it always have to be the teacher who poses the question? We have indicated more than once before that many tasks can be prepared and run by the learners themselves – which is an engaging task in itself! – and here, too, learners can be the ones to think about a topic and generate the questions to be answered. Even when working with a reading or listening exercise, learners can be encouraged to think of questions the text could answer and then find out if it does or not. Then they can prepare questions that the text does answer as a sign of comprehension rather than writing answers to *your* questions. This can even be turned into a small-group task, with each group writing questions for the other group. Following a listening or reading task, students can also be asked what questions they still have about the text and characters or content. As appropriate, this could be the start of them researching online to find answers or doing creative writing to create answers to any further questions they generated.

REFLECTION TASK 12

Often we are unaware of how we use questioning in our teaching, but research suggests that many of us are less-than-effective questioners. It can be helpful to conduct an audit of our use of questions. You can either record yourself teaching or ask a colleague to observe your class and make notes about your use of questions. Noting all the instances of questions you use, try to categorise what function each question has and whether it is really prompting learners to think and get engaged or whether it is more a 'performance' or simple knowledge recall question. Those types of questions will be necessary, but student engagement can be better served with a range of questioning types and formats.

Summary

Teachers are designers of engaging, meaningful learning experiences. This chapter offered some ideas on how to design with engagement, especially initial engagement, in mind. There are five principles that may guide our task design. The first is to think specifically and in very concrete terms about the actual learners we intend to use a task with. This ensures we maximise the appropriateness and relevance for those learners. We also need to get all learners emotionally invested in the learning tasks, ensuring that learners find their own connection to what is being done. The third principle is perhaps key for the initial stage of a task or class - we have to create that curiosity itch that learners are driven to scratch. In addition, we need to think carefully about how we begin a class or a task - the start-up is critical in capturing and sustaining, or at least not losing, learner engagement. This affects both the types of tasks we choose to start off and how we give instructions. The final principle is perhaps the most obvious - learners have to be active to learn and be engaged. We want them working and doing something straight away, whether that be hands-on, physically active or simply working on a task and thinking. To achieve these principles, we propose five key teacher actions:

- The initial step in a task or class is the most critical one - it shakes learners up, gets them hooked and puts them in the right frame of mind.
- One way to get learners' attention is to build in surprise and 'wow' factor, that is, grab the learners' attention and trigger their curiosity through activities that surprise or are novel in some way.
- The second way to provoke curiosity is by employing strategies which trigger puzzlement, mystery, confusion, ambiguity or some gap in knowledge or information.
- We can also trigger engagement through the use of cliffhangers designed for learners to want to know what will happen next or how an unfinished business will be completed.

- Finally, questions are another powerful strategy that can set learners thinking and make them more active, and putting them in the questioning seat can be even more engaging and powerful for learning.

However, getting students initial engagement is only part of the story. If you want to know how to keep their engagement, turn to the next chapter!

CHAPTER IN A NUTSHELL

Teachers can design specific tasks to get learners active, curious and emotionally invested in wanting to learn and do more.

IF YOU WANT TO FIND OUT MORE

Cowley, S. (2018). *The Ultimate Guide to Differentiation: Achieving Excellence for All*. London: Bloomsbury. (This is a highly practical, no-nonsense book which offers realistic and sustainable ways for teachers of all subjects to adapt their teaching to meet individual learner needs.)

Dirksen. J. (2016). *Design for How People Learn* (2nd ed). San Francisco, CA: New Riders. (A book that also positions teachers as designers of learning experiences. It offers useful principles with vivid illustrations in a highly accessible format.)

Leslie, I. (2014). *Curious: The Desire to Know and Why your Future Depends on it*. New York, NY: Basic Books. (An excellent book that explains various theories of curiosity in a highly accessible manner and with a clear plea for the value of promoting curiosity in all of us.)

Rigby, S. and Ryan, R. M. (2011). *Glued to Games: How Video Games Draw us in and Hold us Spellbound*. Santa Barbara, CA: Praeger. (This book does not take a position on whether games are a positive phenomenon or not but it does explain the psychology of why they are so addictive and why they capture our attention. It contains vital lessons for designing engaging learning tasks – not necessarily games- or tech-based.)

6 Sustaining engagement on learning tasks

REFLECTION TASK 1

What is your understanding of persistence? When is it healthy and when not? Can you think of a time when you had to persist when faced with a challenge which required effort and time? What helped you to keep going?

In this book, we have made a (somewhat artificial) division between initiating and maintaining engagement. This is because to awaken the initial curiosity and to engage learners at the beginning of a task requires a somewhat different set of strategies from building on that initial spark of engagement and converting that energy into positive persistence so learners stay on task. In reality, of course, the two sets overlap and interact with each other, together producing sustained engagement. It is also worth reiterating here at the outset that our goal is not merely to keep learners busy. We want meaningful engagement which leads to actual learning. Therefore, our focus in this chapter will be on activities that go beyond keeping students merely active.

> *It is important to consider the differences between authentic engagement and mere 'on-task' behaviour. Getting students to be on-task is not the goal; the goal is for them to be engaged in something meaningful that leads to learning.*
>
> (Harris and Bradshaw 2018: xiv)

Rationale

Let us assume that we have created the right kind of groundwork conditions in the classroom for learners to feel willing and able to engage. Then we have also caught their attention and successfully got them involved in a language learning task. Now we have to keep them there – maintaining their attention in the face of competing distractions. In reflecting on how this can best be done, a very helpful source of ideas has been the psychology of video gaming. If video games can be engaging to the point of addiction, we can surely draw lessons from them about designing healthily 'addictive' language learning tasks!

REFLECTION TASK 2

Have you ever played a video game or app and found the time just zooming past with you unable to put the game down? If so, that experience resonates with millions of people worldwide. There are various reasons for why people get so absorbed in gaming. Think of your own experience and what explanation you would give.

Gaming is an escape from reality into a story or world where typically you are the hero and the agent of your destiny. You are not just being told a story. You are the story. You have control over what happens to you and you are actively creating the direction of your pathway through the game. You have agency and can experience feelings of success and progress with a risk of failure, but failure which has no consequences, given you have the chance to replay, practise and improve - that is, to *learn* - until you master one level and progress to the next. The emotions you feel in a game are real and powerful, and the context of the game is often attractive, stimulating and appealing. Increasingly, gaming is also highly social and interactive, leading to collaboration and sharing of resources, ideas and strategies for success. It is not difficult to see how such an experience can be engaging, empowering, positive and often addictive.

Of course, gaming heavily relies on advanced digital technology. In this book, we have been conscious of wanting to support a range of teachers in diverse settings, some who will have access to technology and some who may not. For those reasons, we have championed principles which can be employed in more traditional or resource-poor environments as well as in settings rich in technology opportunities. In the twenty-first century, for many, technology is commonplace and offers rich potential for education, but we feel that technology is not the ultimate answer to all our educational needs but constitutes merely another set of learning tools. Like all tools, digital technology can also easily become mere gimmickry if it is employed without clear learning intent. That said, the psychology of gaming *can* provide valuable insights, which form the core of this chapter. We seek to go beyond a simplistic gamification approach and to reflect on principles and actions inspired by gamification that get to the heart of the psychological experience.

> *Game designers incorporate a number of strategies and tactics for engaging players in 'gameplay'. These strategies and tactics may provide instructional designers with new methods for engaging learners.*
>
> (Dickey 2005: 67)

Principles for Maintaining Engagement

When we talk about task engagement, learner action is key, and all tasks need to maximise the action space for learning. This is not to say that teacher-led input has no place in an engaging classroom - quite the contrary, some teachers can engage with captivating stories, cleverly posed questions and skilfully scaffolded frameworks for learners to follow. The point, however, is that when we design a task, it is important to think of what is asked of our learners at every stage of our lesson. How much opportunity are we generating for them to be active, both mentally and in terms of behaviours? After all, 'task' is but a name for a specific language learning opportunity, and a good task follows a design that maximises learning potential, with learner action being the defining criterion.

Principle 1: Provide Cognitive Challenge

Experiencing challenge in learning has got a bad reputation; in efforts to make learning feel manageable, challenge has mistakenly been viewed as something to be avoided. Yet, *appropriate* challenge - also known as 'desirable difficulty' (Bjork & Bjork 2011; Leslie 2014) - can contribute positively to learner engagement and also to the depth of learning. Teachers know from experience that tasks which are too easy or too difficult, leave learners bored, frustrated and often tempted into poor behaviour. Instead, when learners feel competent but have to invest effort in working on a desirably difficult task, they are likely to remain engaged. A further benefit for learning is that people are more likely to remember what they have had to expend effort on learning, according to memory studies (Bjork and Bjork 2011; Tyler, Hertel, McCallum and Ellis 1979).

> *Making things easier can come at a cost - there can be hidden value in difficulty. It's a principle that seems to apply with special force to the way we learn. The harder things are to grasp or memorise, the more our brains rise to the challenge.*
>
> (Leslie 2015: 90)

The notion of an appropriate level of difficulty in learning is not new. Vygotsky's (1978) classic notion of the Zone of Proximal Development (ZPD) is concerned with exactly that. It breaks up learning zones into the zone of what a learner can do - the 'inner zone' - and what a learner cannot yet do, the 'outer zone'. In between is the ZPD, which is the zone of things which a learner *could* be able to do with support and guidance. The key here is the appropriate level of challenge for each individual's level of competence, accompanied by the kind of support they can positively respond to. Approaching the issue from a different perspective (as part of his 'flow' theory), Csikszentmihalyi (2002: 52) also states that there is a 'golden ratio between challenges and skills' where 'enjoyment appears at the boundary between boredom and anxiety, when the challenges are just balanced with the person's capacity to act'.

> *We need to get our challenges "just right". The point is we need to adjust the level of difficulty just above the learner's current achievement level. If the teacher succeeds in doing this, the learners will be presented with a challenge and the stage will be set for the optimal learning success.*
>
> (Hattie and Zierer 2018: 70)

It is noteworthy in this respect that Hattie (2003) shows that an important difference between expert and inexperienced teachers is that the former set more challenging tasks for learners, to push them and engage them more actively in thinking for themselves. As he summarises, expert teachers set 'challenging and not merely time-consuming activities, they invite students to engage rather than copy, and they aim to encourage students to share commitment to these challenging goals' (p. 9). This approach is reminiscent of the importance of holding high expectations for all learners and employing challenging questions (see Chapter 2).

Yet, Puchta and Williams (2011) highlight a specific problem in language education, namely, that as we often need to keep language simple, there is a danger of also simplifying cognition at the same time. This is best illustrated by the infamous activity so common in the 1960s, whereby a teacher holds up an object, say a pen, and asks the class, 'What colour is this pen?' And all learners, who are cognitively mature, are meant to answer, 'The pen is blue.' Such dumbing-down in stating the obvious can lead to frustration and boredom for learners who may be restricted in their linguistic expression but not in their ability to exercise their thinking. We are convinced that given the openness of the topics and methodological approaches language teachers can draw on, cognitively stimulating tasks and methods can be integrated into any language class. Think about classic categorising activities such as having to decide which animals fly, swim, move on land or two of these or all three, using a three-circle Venn diagram. The main language used is vocabulary for animals but the learners have to think of which category to place each animal they know in and this encourages critical and more complex cognitive thinking (see e.g. Puchta and Williams 2011).

> *There is a danger when activities are designed for second language learners of removing any intellectual challenge in the attempt to make the activity linguistically comprehensible. Children are frequently disenchanted by over-simple activities which are designed to suit their language level but are often way below their cognitive potential and therefore fail to provide a challenge. In presenting a cognitive challenge, we aim to keep learners engaged in the activity.*
>
> (Puchta and Williams 2011: 7)

So, what constitutes a cognitively challenging task? Figure 1 presents Bloom's classic taxonomy of various facets of thinking (Bloom 1956), proposing six categories of increasing complexity. The bottom three levels of the model are said to represent lower-order thinking skills (LOTS) and the top three levels represent higher-order thinking skills (HOTS). Ideally, we want more of the HOTS and less of the LOTS, moving away from mere rote learning and memorisation. Moreover, teachers need *not* begin at the bottom of the list and work up, but could begin a session with the top category of 'creation' and then end the lesson with an exit ticket checking on what the learners 'remember'. We find this taxonomy useful in reminding us of the kinds of activities and tasks that promote higher-order thinking (e.g. creating something original, forming and defending an opinion, or comparing and contrasting perspectives) and which in turn are likely to be more engaging.

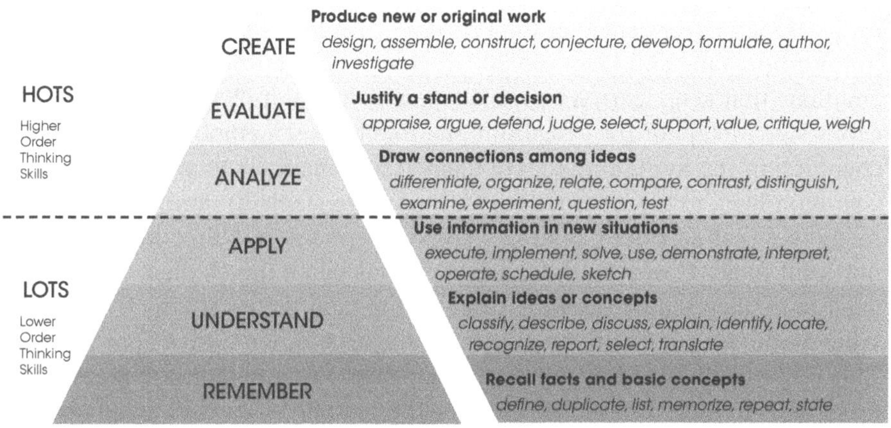

Figure 1. Bloom's taxonomy of facets of thinking (Bloom 1956) © Vanderbilt University Center for Teaching

Another valuable way of promoting cognitive challenge is to consider the distinction between *convergent* and *divergent thinking* (Guilford 1967). Convergent thinking refers to searching for a single best, correct answer to a question or problem. Divergent thinking is open, creative thinking, exploring multiple possible options. In theory, both convergent and divergent tasks can be engaging but more divergent tasks tend to foster richer, higher-order thinking and lead to more creativity. By means of illustration, a relatively simple divergent task could be giving students an everyday household item (e.g. paperclip, rubber band, fork or coin) and asking them to come up with as many uses as possible for it. A more challenging task would involve students picking words from a hat and trying to find a meaningful connection between them (e.g. sun and car; water and television; plastic and dentist). Especially in a language classroom, more discussion and interaction is likely to be fostered through tasks and questions that demand more divergent responses and thinking, but the two types can also be combined, with an initial divergent brainstorming phase to be followed by narrowing the discussion to more limited, convergent options.

> *Creativity is intelligence having fun.*
>
> (often attributed to Albert Einstein)

Principle 2: Maximise Enjoyment, Minimise Boredom

> *Students' brains are not simply waiting to be filled with information. Instead, students' emotions must be activated, attention captured, and memory supported, so that learning becomes something that is intrinsically motivated and can be transferred to real-world experiences.*
>
> (Posey 2019: 4)

Throughout this book, we have stressed the importance of emotions for learning at every stage of the process – 'We feel, therefore we learn' (Immordino-Yang and Damasio 2007). Now, we turn to the kind of emotions that keep learners engaged on a task. Haidt (2006) used an expressive metaphor for explaining the role between emotions and rational cognition in the human mind. He likened our emotions to an elephant and cognition/logic to the rider sitting on top of the elephant, and the point he made was that no rider can drag a six-ton elephant in a direction it does not want to go. However, there are occasions when the elephant allows itself to be directed by the little rider on top, and the most effective way is when both work in harmony and reinforce each other's drives positively. This is the essence of the current principle for sustaining task engagement: tasks need to have 'emotional pull' for the learner to get their elephant interested and moving along that path.

Traditionally, emotions have been seen as being either positive or negative but that dichotomy has increasingly been challenged. We all know that a degree of healthy anxiety can bring out the best in our performance, although we certainly would not want to be deliberately creating learner anxiety. Rather, most teachers and students would agree that, ideally, all learning should be enjoyable; as most teachers would expect, enjoyment is positively correlated with learner achievement (Pekrun, Goetz, Titz and Perry 2002). Enjoyment refers to positive feelings of being satisfied or happy to be taking part in an activity. It is about ongoing feelings of pleasure while working on a task (Ainley and Hidi 2014). This, however, does not necessarily imply that every single aspect of the learning process needs to be equally fun. Learning *can* be fun, but fun must be used in education to focus attention and learning, and not as a distraction (Schlechty 2011). Sometimes teachers use fun activities to diffuse tension or to offer a break, which are clear pedagogical purposes. However, teachers are not there to entertain learners and keep things fun all the time, but to engage them in meaningful learning tasks. When well designed, such learning processes should be enjoyable, but the key is that they should contribute to task-specific cognitive engagement.

Indeed, similar to mastering any skill, the acquisition of language skills also requires controlled practice that is likely to be less 'fun' than other creative aspects of using the skill. Yet, many musicians, for example, do not mind doing the scales on the piano or practising difficult movements again and again. How do they keep up their positive attitude during such 'drilling'? Often, they see such practice as a necessary part of a broader process of learning, working towards larger, long-term goals and visions of themselves as becoming better piano players. They endorse 'pre-living' the positive affective experiences of future related tasks where their skills can be meaningfully employed (see Chapter 6 in Dörnyei et al. 2016). In this way, the same is true for language learners: even the less glamorous skill-building activities will not seem pointless but are connected to the bigger picture of language learning.

REFLECTION TASK 3

Can you think of an activity related to your work as a language teacher that you enjoy? What makes it enjoyable? What aspects of it give you pleasure? What role does interest play? How important is your sense of competence and autonomy in enjoying the task? What lessons can you draw from your own experiences for learner enjoyment?

Let us now turn to *boredom*, the ultimate deactivating emotion we are seeking to avoid. Pekrun et al. (2010: 532) define boredom as 'an affective state composed of unpleasant feelings, lack of stimulation, and low physiological arousal'. Mann (2016: 16) explains that boredom is about how we spend our attention and describes it as 'the opposite of engagement'. Her book is quick to point out that there can be benefits to boredom in terms of unconscious thinking, relaxation, creativity and protection against overstimulation, but, in the context of the classroom, we generally want to reduce learner boredom in the quest to boost learner engagement. Yet, alarmingly, Pekrun et al. (2010) report that boredom is one of the most frequently experienced emotions by pupils in schools. In the 2016 High School Survey of Student Engagement, a staggering 83% of students reported feeling sometimes or often bored in school, with the main reason given that the material was not interesting (NAIS 2017).

> *All of us can relate to the feeling of being trapped in a situation that is irrelevant, meaningless, and uninteresting. Unfortunately, for many students that describes their school experience. They are trapped in situations that they perceive as meaningless. Personal perception is a key idea when attempting to understand boredom and engagement.*
>
> (Harris and Bradshaw 2018: xii–xiii)

On the whole, teachers seem to be aware of possible causes of boredom in their classes, although, according to Daschmann, Goetz and Stupnisky

(2014), they rarely think of themselves as a possible cause. The most common reason given by 91% of learners in Daschmann et al.'s study was the characteristics of *instruction*, that is, how the subject was being taught and, in particular, how monotonous this felt. This is actually good news for teachers, as it means that one of the key perceived causes of boredom is within their control as designers of learning opportunities. Using diversified instructional strategies and ensuring learners are active seem to be two obvious approaches to bear in mind when tackling learner boredom, but this is only part of the bigger picture, because another useful perspective on boredom is that it can be understood as an inability to sustain attention and stop the mind from wandering (Carriere, Cheyne and Smilek 2008). Let us consider this for a moment.

We have pointed out at various points in this book how central the concept of attention is to understanding engagement. Some theorists suggest that problems in attention can be the cause of boredom. In other words, learners who find it hard to focus their attention on the task may become more easily bored. This, however, is a dynamic relationship, because it is also true that if learners find a task boring, it will understandably be more difficult for them to keep their attention focused on it (Macklem 2015). In any case, it is safe to conclude that another key strategy to employ for countering boredom is designing learning activities to capture and keep learners' attention, which is why Macklem (2015) suggests ensuring that tasks are cognitively activating, connected to learner interests, involve discussions, projects, art, games and role play, and provide opportunity for interaction and cooperation. Larson and Richards's (1991) study of boredom and under-stimulation offers further valuable insights in this respect, as they show that the students rated 'hands-on' subjects and socially interactive contexts where they could get actively involved as the least boring. This bodes well for language classrooms, which are often interactive and communicative in design.

> *How we feel during the learning event can enhance or impair the way in which we attend to such events, how we store information received during the event and the ability to retrieve stored information after the event. Specific emotions such as curiosity can enhance while others such as boredom can impair.*
>
> (Smith 2018: 7)

One possible source of boredom from the learner perspective can be coursebooks which may seem inappropriate culturally, constraining, anxiety-inducing or downright useless (McGrath 2006). Yet, coursebooks can also serve as a useful form of structure and guidance, also enabling learners to see a sense of progress as they move through it. And the good news is that not all coursebooks are inherently boring! When coursebooks are humanistic in design or adapted accordingly, they can do much to affect deep learning (Tomlinson 2012). The challenge for teachers is to work with and adapt their coursebooks in ways that are engaging and suited to the specific group of learners. Indeed, learners themselves can be challenged to personalise and localise the coursebook to suit themselves as individuals and as a group (McDonough, Shaw and Masuhara 2013) by creating quizzes, projects, forms of creative expression or alternative content and tasks.

SOME WAYS OF ADAPTING COURSEBOOKS

- Leave things out
- Add materials, images and other resources
- Shorten an activity
- Extend an activity or add further examples
- Modify or rewrite text or activities
- Replace texts
- Reorder the activities
- Alter the instructions
- Build in options and choices for learners

(adapted from Maley 2011)

Principle 3: Captivate Attention, Engage Interest

REFLECTION TASK 4

When did you last get so absorbed in something that you did not notice the passing of time? What were you doing? How did the activity keep your attention? Our ability to focus our attention depends on the task and our relationship to it.

The previous discussion on tackling boredom in the classroom highlighted the significance of learner attention, and we can submit, more generally, that if learners are not paying attention, they are not engaged. This warrants further discussion on how to captivate attention and engage interest. In the previous chapter, we discussed several strategies that can help to get our learners' attention, but there are some further points to bear in mind when thinking about *retaining* this attention. To start with, attention can be 'bought' through extrinsic rewards but this is not a guarantee of real, deep learning. Ongoing attention has to go together with learners' own commitment and investment in wanting to work on the task.

> *Attention can be focused through fear and the threat of punishment, but those who are attentive because of fear and threat are not engaged. Neither are those who pay attention and persist because they place a high value on some reward that is extrinsic to the work. Commitment, attention, and persistence must be present to justify the claim that the student is engaged.*
> (Smith 2018: 7)

No matter how committed to the task, everyone can be distracted by something more appealing in that moment, whether that be an internal train of thought or an external distraction. That means the first thing to do to sustain attention is to reduce external distractions so that it is easier for the learner to concentrate on the task; indeed, Davenport and Beck (2001: 58) claim that, 'the most important function of attention isn't taking information in, but screening it out'. Many of you will be familiar with the 'Gorilla Experiment' (Simons and Chabris 1999); this now famous study asked participants to watch people in white or black t-shirts throwing a ball to each other and concentrate on counting the number of passes of the ball. In the midst of the game, a person dressed in a gorilla suit came into the middle of the players, faces the camera, bangs on its chest and leaves.[1] Amazingly, over 50% of the participants never even noticed the gorilla. The test was an excellent example of selective attention in action and refers to a phenomenon known as *Inattentional Blindness*. It showed how humans, when focusing on one thing, struggle to also focus on an additional thing at the same time. As we have established in Chapter 5, we only have a limited amount of conscious attention, which is why we struggle to multitask and pay attention to several things at the same time. For us as teachers, the clear implication is that if we want students to focus on the learning task at hand, we need to reduce their attention to other peripheral, irrelevant distractions in the environment or to at least reduce the number of external distractions. We want to avoid our learning task being the gorilla that the learners go blind to!

REFLECTION TASK 5

Inattentional Blindness (IB) has now been noted in various people such as pilots (rather worryingly), drivers, bankers and witnesses of events (Hattie and Yates 2014). Can you think of examples of it in school? Could there be instances where learners have IB to what is being said or written when they are cognitively overloaded, distracted or under stress?

The key to staying focused on task is the characteristic of *persistence*. This refers to a learner continuing to work and expend effort on a task, even in the face of difficulties or distractions. To strengthen a learner's resolve and will to persist, we can boost many of the competencies discussed in Chapter 2, including grit – a learner with a sense of competence and a growth mindset will be much more likely to persist on a task. Other skills which foster persistence are metacognitive skills. Metacognition refers to being aware of and able to think about one's own thinking; it involves, according to Williams et al. (2015: 133), 'thinking about and understanding how we learn, as well as regulating and controlling our learning'. If learners have a mature 'metacognitive grip' over the learning process – that is, they can understand their learning objectives, can evaluate their

1 The video is freely available on the internet: www.theinvisiblegorilla.com/gorilla_experiment.html

learning, manage their time, set goals, understand what they are doing – then this will activate self-regulatory skills to continue and persist in a task. Ideas for supporting metacognition include, for example, keeping a learning journal, having a goal-setting buddy to compare goals and progress together with, or maintaining a personal progress log.

The easiest way to keep learner attention is to appeal to their *interest*. As was already mentioned in Chapter 5, interest can be individual (personal interests) and situational (triggered by the situation). If a learner is fundamentally interested as an individual in a topic or subject, it is relatively easy to generate and maintain situational interest. The challenge is to create sufficient situational interest for those who may have low individual interest. Situational interest emerges from the interaction of individual interest, including prior experiences, with situational variables which influence the learner's experience and behaviour during the task (Knogler 2017). Such variables have been found to include hands-on tasks, opportunities for collaboration, well-structured learning tasks with the chance for exploration and discovery, stimulating and appealing input, links to learners' lives and pursuits, appropriate challenge, and opportunities for meaningful choice (e.g. Abbott 2017; Chen, Ennis, Martin and Sun 2005; Schraw, Flowerday and Lehman 2001). Most of these factors will sound familiar by now, as they have emerged in various places in this book before – these are, indeed, the staples of any recipe for task engagement.

In language learning specifically, there has been increasing attention on 'interest' and how to foster this in language classes although research remains sparse (see Tin 2016, for a book-length consideration of this topic). Some of the factors believed to influence this complex construct in language learning include: teacher talk (Tin 2016); choice of topic (Cabot 2012, cited in Renninger and Hidi 2016); choice of activity types such as kinaesthetic drama approaches (Rothwell 2011); working with technologies (Stepp-Greany 2002; Wang and Vasquez 2012); and text-based factors such as layout, language and content (Eidswick 2010; Hidi 2001).

STRATEGIES TO PROMOTE INTEREST

Keller (1983) devised a model of motivational design that included the category of interest in lessons and he proposed five strategies to promote interest:

1. Use novel or paradoxical events to trigger interest
2. Use anecdotes and stories
3. Mix the familiar and unfamiliar for optimal challenge
4. Use analogies to make the strange familiar and the familiar strange
5. Support student inquiry and questioning

Principle 4: Utilise the Power of Unpredictability

One generally observed human trait is that we are drawn to the familiar and we feel safe with certain routines, rituals and a degree of consistency. Yet, curiously, we are also attracted to what is novel and new. Engagement can be found in the ideal combination of the two. Within language classrooms, consistency and predictability can be good at reducing cognitive load and creating security, but too much and learners take things for granted and go blind to and/or ignore certain aspects of the task. In essence, we lose their attention. In contrast, *unpredictability* has been found to keep us alert, and even to contribute to addictive behaviours in respect to technology and gambling (Rigby & Ryan, 2011). To illustrate this, all we need to think about is why we constantly check our email/smartphone for new messages. If your inbox is anything like ours, most messages are quite unrewarding and uninteresting, but just sometimes, unpredictably, there is an exciting email in the mix. Not knowing when or if such an email may come keeps us checking.

REFLECTION TASK 6

Predictability can kill interest, which is why even the best activities or the most dazzling technological tools can lose their lustre if over-used. Think of tasks you frequently use. Do they have a typical format and procedure? Is there a way you could challenge or mix up the expectations and do it differently to what the learners are anticipating? Do you have an element of surprise you can insert into a familiar task?

Especially in gaming, the strategy of utilising unpredictable rewards is a core method of keeping gamers hooked (Rigby and Ryan 2011). This has sound neurobiological basis. In an interesting and frequently cited study by Berns et al. (2001), the researchers showed that the effects of a reward on the brain system were greatest when they were administered in unpredictable ways. Dopamine, which is linked to feelings of pleasure and enjoyment, is released more in the case of unexpected rewards than when people expect or anticipate when the reward will come. The implication is that some degree of surprise and unpredictability is beneficial for holding our attention and keeping us engaged – the level of change is like retriggering initial engagement (discussed in Chapter 5).

REFLECTION TASK 7

Think of your own teaching context and one of the most recent classes you taught. Would it have made sense to vary any of the following elements during the class?

- *Seating arrangements*
- *Grouping*
- *Movement*
- *Timing/Pace*
- *Modality*
- *Materials*

A particularly engaging approach which also generates higher-order thinking (see Principle 1 above) is the problem-based approach to learning (PBL) (see also Action 5 below). Problem-based learning centres round the idea of getting students to work on a complex, real-life problem, typically of their choice, although sometimes the problem is presented by teachers (Amador, Miles and Peters 2006). The main aim is to have learners work together, generally in small groups, to seek possible solutions to the problem. They have to generate ideas, discover relevant knowledge and concepts, propose decisions, defend and justify choices and present findings to others. PBL not only helps to explore the subject matter thoroughly, but it also enables the development of transferable twenty-first-century skills such as collaboration, critical thinking, reasoning and problem-solving, as well as authentic language use for genuine communicative purposes. The teacher's role is to provide resources and guidance, and to facilitate the process, which should be largely learner-driven in PBL designs.

> *Because PBL [problem-based learning] uses an assortment of methods associated with student engagement - active, collaborative, student-centred, and self-directed learning focused on realistic problems and authentic assessments - we might expect that it would lead to increased student engagement.*
>
> (Allen, Donham and Bernhardt 2011: 26)

Principle 5: Stagger Accomplishments

REFLECTION TASK 8

Alter (2017: 97) reports on the finishing times of marathon runners. He notes that there tend to be a surge of finishers at times such as 2:59, 3:29, 3:59 and 4:29. Why do you think that is the case and how does it relate to maintaining engagement?

Goal setting explains why in the marathons, people push themselves to reach milestones and are compelled by the goal to give that extra effort to complete under the specific time markers of three hours or three-and-a-half hours, etc. Goals can be powerful motivators to help people achieve and push themselves to their best. *Incremental goals* are small, frequently-spaced goals that are used to break down a larger, more distant goal into more manageable chunks. They use 'proximal' (close, near) goals to signpost the journey towards more 'distal' (distant) goals. Setting such incremental goals makes it easier for learners to evaluate their own progress and keep track of their journey. As they accomplish an incremental goal, they get a boost to their sense of success, which reinforces their sense of competence to keep on track to the ultimate final goal. Dörnyei et al. (2016) liken such a motivational boost to hybrid cars, which differ from traditional cars in that they not only use up fuel while moving but also generate some at times, resulting in significantly larger driving range; similarly, incremental goals can offer the extra boost that will help to sustain task engagement much longer than would be if students worked towards one final goal.

Although not all lessons or tasks lend themselves equally to such an elaborate goal structure, the idea of incremental goals or milestones is broadly useful. For teachers, it can prompt reflection on what exactly learners are being asked to do, what check points there could be and what milestones might be passed. For learners, reaching such task check points can offer a motivating sense of progress – after all, as the saying goes, 'success breeds success'. Having clear goals, which set suitable levels of challenge, is known to be linked to learners' performance, as well as to their sense of confidence (Hattie 2009).

> The progress principle: *of all the positive events that influence inner work life, the single most powerful is progress in meaningful work.*
>
> (Amabile and Kramer 2011: 76–77)

There are many ways to set incremental goals and make the progress visible. In gaming, progress bars show how far along someone is, for example, in completing a quest, or when we fill in a profile online, it often tells us what percentage is complete. This breaking down a process or progress towards an end goal into chunks can keep us on track to reach 100%. A creative way to mark progress is to provide learners with a piece of a puzzle with each stage completed, but the whole picture or word or clue only becomes apparent once all the parts and stages have been completed. Learners can also have a 'progress card' booklet and collect stamps to complete the booklet. So, in accordance with the point we already made in Chapter 2 (Action 2), the key is to help make the progress learners are making – along with the successes and accomplishments – *visible* for the learners to draw energy from, as well as for the teacher to keep track of where learners are up to on task.

A GOAL-SETTING TOOL

A popular and useful mnemonic for setting effective goals is **SMART**:

- **S**pecific (clearly defined and unambiguous)
- **M**easurable (can be measured to what extent you have achieved it)
- **A**chievable (realistic)
- **R**elevant (relevant to what you ultimately want to achieve)
- **T**ime-bound (with a clear time frame – start and end points)

A core dimension for ensuring a sense of progress is that learners know how to *self-assess* their own advance. This principle is reflected in sports and recreation by the popularity of pedometers tracking one's steps, or in weight-loss systems by plotting calories consumed on one's smartphone, etc. The availability of various metrics and clear progress criteria for students can help to make their development more tangible, and the feedback from teachers also plays a vital role in keeping learners moving forwards with clear direction, sense of progress and accomplishment. Feedback can have some of the most powerful effects on learning, so it needs to be used in a thoughtful and informed way (for a useful guide in language teaching, see Nassaji and Kartchava 2017). It is important for educators to provide encouraging, but at the same time realistic and honest, feedback. Feedback is most constructive when it provides specific information that helps learners to know how to bridge any discrepancy in performance or competence between their current state and their desired targets, while also offering advice on what steps are needed to get there.

EFFECTIVE FEEDBACK

Hattie and Timperley (2007: 86) suggest that effective feedback must answer three major questions:

1. *Where I am going?* (What are the goals?)
2. *How am I going?* (What progress is being made toward the goal?)
3. *Where to next?* (What activities need to be undertaken to make better progress?)

Teacher Actions

The focus in the second half of the chapter is on actions which help to maintain learners' engagement, by keeping them on track as well as by sustaining their effort and will to continue on task. We would like to stress that not all the actions will be pertinent to all kinds of tasks, and, similarly, not all actions will be suited for every purpose or type of learning activity. However, we hope that every teacher may find some relevant ideas to select from and to implement in combination with actions from other chapters.

Action 1: Utilise the Power of Stories

REFLECTION TASK 9

What has your day been like so far today? Where did you spend it? What happened first and what happened later? Who were the heroes and villains of the day? What emotions have you experienced? What were the causes of events and your emotional responses? This is your story. Did you hear or read any other stories today? How much story did you note around you?

Stories are an essential part of being human. It is how we make sense of the world, no matter what age we are (McAdams 1993). Narratives engage us in an active process of meaning-making. So much of our lives centres around the stories we tell, and are told, about ourselves and the world around us. Stories have an incredible emotional pull and can awaken curiosity in the form of empathy and human interest. They help us create coherence in what we experience and our natural tendency is to look for a narrative format in what we hear and read. We are drawn in by stories out of interest for what happens to the characters and the suspense of waiting for the plot to unfold. Stories about people are especially compelling (Davies 2014), as our fascination with gossip shows. We might even say that as teachers we have similar aims to the writer of a novel: in class we want to create enjoyment, trigger interest, captivate attention and awaken curiosity with a degree of uncertainty of how the story will end. Like writers, teachers can make learning engaging by using stories.

> *Story is one of the most powerful cognitive tools students have available for imaginatively engaging with knowledge. Stories shape our emotional understanding of their content. Stories can shape real-world content as well as fictional materials. It is this real-world story-shaping that promises most value for teaching.*
> (Egan 2005: 2)

An important benefit of using stories in education is that research has shown that our brain remembers information more effectively when it is presented in story form, because the story structure is typically familiar to us and easy to relate to (see e.g. Graesser, Singer and Trabasso 1994), and because the content information is connected together. Think about a novel you have read and how you can still remember a lot of relatively complex relationships and events from it, simply because they are held together with a storyline. It is also easier for us to process storied information because it allows us to more clearly see the underlying interactions and causes between different aspects of the story. Working with stories and narrative formats has traditionally been a popular approach when working with young learners (see e.g. Wright 2008), but it is important to note that stories can be used to enhance learning at any level and age, including all way the up to tertiary level and beyond (McDrury and Alterio 2003). In sum, stories make sense to us, they appeal to us and they stick with us – whatever our age.

The use of stories can be employed in any discipline, and Egan (2005) argues that any content can be taught through stories from the teacher or better still, the learners or a collaborative combination of both. Students can be encouraged to think, use their imagination and develop their creative skills and cognitive flexibility by generating their own stories about a range of topics. In language education, we not only employ written or oral stories (also, increasingly, visual or enacted stories) as input, but we also often ask learners to create their own stories in spoken or written form, in short or long formats – thus making them the storytellers. With the advent of digital storytelling tools, the attractiveness of creating stories has been enhanced even further by incorporating interactive formats and attractive visuals (see, e.g. tools and apps such as Storybird, Storyboardthat, Mystoryapp). Egan even suggests that we can get learners to invent stories about language itself on a meta-level to explain and reinforce learning. By way of illustration, he suggests telling learners to imagine that a new family with three children have moved in next door. Their kids are called: Their, There and They're. The students are split into groups and each group gets one of the kid's names and builds a story about the character of that child from their name. So, Their is very selfish as he has his ego – 'I' – tucked inside his name. Learners then together build up a story around these characters which reflects the spelling as well as the meaning of their names. Learners can also create stories to explicitly highlight tense use or linking words.

SOURCES OF STORIES AND NARRATIVE FORMATS

These examples of where we can see the story format may provide inspiration for teaching in terms of using them as input or forms of output for learners' own work.

- Novels, short stories, (auto)biographies
- News stories
- Poems
- Songs
- Oral storytelling
- Pictures and comics
- Drama, including role play
- TV, film, YouTube
- Games
- Dance
- Mime

Dörnyei et al. (2016) argue that centring a task or a project around an unfolding storyline, whereby parts of the story are shared/created gradually and incrementally to build tension and maintain interest, is a natural way of producing an engaging temporal frame that can help to sustain student involvement. A task design following this approach requires a central, engaging narrative to foster student interest to discover or invent what happens in each new sequence of events, and this core axis can even be a visual narrative such as a film, a TV miniseries or a student performance. Teachers can use a storyline pulled out of a topic or content in flexible ways, either as an introductory hook or as the main form of input, or even as the framework for the entire task pitched as a story. The final form will depend on the language levels of our learners, their interests, our teaching objectives and our resources.

EXAMPLE OF A SUCCESSFUL STORYTELLING PROJECT

Tsou, Wang and Tzeng (2006) report on a project with an EFL teacher and her pupils in an elementary school in Taiwan. They had two groups work with storytelling – one in a more traditional manner and one using a multimedia storytelling website. This website managed the storytelling process administratively for teachers, and allowed learners to construct their stories online and also replay and share the stories again later. Tsou at al. note the concerns teachers may have about an already overloaded curriculum and a perceived lack of experience for integrating storytelling. Yet, they show that the learners in the experimental group not only improved in their language skills and confidence, but the teacher herself was also positively impressed by the progress, stating, 'The Website is really magical to me and my class'. Despite possible reservations, this teacher found the combination of storytelling, language learning and the use of multimedia to be worthwhile.

Action 2: Make the Learner the Hero of Their Task

> *Simply put, video games seem to have the ability to not just* tell *us a story, but to let us actively* live *it, making opportunities for bravery, heroism, and gratitude not the exception, but the norm. That's pretty powerful stuff.*
>
> (Rigby and Ryan 2011: 2)

As we discussed in Chapter 5, one reason why gaming has become so popular is that the gamer is the *hero* of the action. It means the story is directed by them, reflects their actions and decisions, and creates feelings of success, ownership and autonomy as real as in any non-virtual experience. If we use stories, they are more engaging if the learner is the hero. There are two main ways that learners become the heroes of their learning to keep them engaged for longer: through (a) *participatory planning and design*, and (b) the use of *personalised pathways* during tasks.

Participatory planning and design is driven by principles of self-determination theory (Deci and Ryan 2002). When designing a learning task, teachers usually have clear educational outcomes in mind but learners can be involved in the planning and design processes of learning tasks and, indeed, whole lessons or series of lessons. They can discuss possible ways of practising the language and strategies to achieve the planned learning outcomes. Not all ideas will be feasible, but thoughtful discussion will help learners become more metacognitively aware of their language learning processes and the purpose of various tasks. Their abilities to contribute meaningfully to the design of their own learning tasks will develop gradually. Not only will such contributions improve their sense of autonomy, but they will also ultimately enhance their decision-making skills, higher-order thinking skills and their ability to self-regulate their learning. As with most democracies, this is not a free-for-all situation; there will be agreed rules and frameworks, but these can be challenged and debated, with decisions being voted upon. Learners can get involved to different degrees, depending on age and experiences, at all stages of the task design process.

> *A democracy is more than a form of government; it is primarily a mode of associated living, of conjoint communicated experience.*
>
> (Dewey 1922: 101)

Personalised learning stems from approaches to differentiation, which refers to when teachers adapt their teaching to respond to individual learner needs and profiles. It has been typically discussed in respect to accommodating gifted/talented learners or vulnerable learners (such as those with special educational needs), as well as its use in virtual learning environments where personalising learning is easier in practical terms (e.g. McLoughlin and Lee 2010; Russell and Riley 2011). In this section, we propose a form of personalisation that involves personalised pathways through tasks. What do personalised pathways look like? One increasingly popular method is the use of 'choice boards' (or 'learning menus') (see Cox n.d.). These are platforms for the teacher to offer different options, either for a whole unit, a larger project or even a single class or set of tasks. These options can then be presented to learners as a graphic organiser in the form of a noughts and crosses (tic-tac-toe)-style board – nine options in total, three in each row (although it can theoretically be more). Learners normally select one task from each row of the board, although they can extend and do more options if they wish. Sometimes, the mid-point of the board is labelled 'student choice' and the learners themselves can offer a suggestion of what they would like to do in the context of this work unit or task. More simply, a teacher can simply present a 'menu' of choices – with starter, mains and dessert – that students have to select from, and a number of side dishes as optional additional tasks – possibly including different levels of difficulty. Sometimes teachers may simply use the same activities already planned but presented in this different format which allows learners choice over sequence and content.

> *Sometimes students may not make the best choice during a lesson, but the empowerment associated with making a choice will promote engagement and can deepen their understanding about their own learning strengths, challenges, and needs for improvement.*
>
> (Posey 2019: 88)

Finally, let us highlight three additional points regarding participatory learning and personalised pathways. First, they lend themselves to be combined with technology-based approaches, as they enable learners to create their own 'playlist' of tasks based on options presented, inspired by previous activities, assessments and learning objectives when managed digitally. Second, the learner-involvement process often works best when learners reflect on specific lessons they have learnt and strategies adopted, and share these with the whole class. In this way, students can learn from each other and teachers can keep track of which tasks are proving challenging and may need more scaffolding. Third, through facilitating learner contributions, future passions and interests can be generated too (Renninger and Hidi 2016). For example, imagine you are teaching a class of B1 learners, aiming to cover the writing of instructions using imperatives. Learners can be asked to prepare instructions for their classmates to introduce something important to them, for example, how to build a model plane, how to identify a green woodpecker in woodland or how to do a popular dance move. If the language focus of another lesson is a lexical field such as cooking, learners can select their favourite foods and dishes to describe.

SARAH'S STORY OF WORKING IN A LEARNER-CENTRED MANNER

Twenty years ago, when I started teaching, I was enamoured with learner-centred approaches and wanted learners to be actively involved in decision-making, exercising their autonomy as much as they could. I failed miserably in my first attempts. I had made the fundamental mistake of forgetting that while learner-centred teaching seemed normal to me, it wasn't for my students. I was starting where I was as a teacher with my experience and not where the learners were with their experiences. My learners suffered a 'teaching-style culture shock'! After a number of teaching mishaps, I had a rethink and began the process afresh with slow, small steps towards a more democratic, autonomy-oriented and learner-centred classroom. I learnt to really think of the learners first, starting off from what they were ready for and making more gradual changes to my teaching style. I built up the courage to keep trying, taking things a step at a time and really listening to the learners along the way. I am still on the journey today.

Action 3: Allow 'Levelling Up', 'Replay' and 'Differentiated Rewards'

There are three key features of computer games that keep players hooked and which have important lessons for education: (a) the notion of *levelling up* and always being at the optimal level of challenge; (b) the permission to fail by *replaying* until the level is mastered; and (c) *differentiated rewards* that suit the task and player. We will reflect on how we can use each of these in all kinds of tasks to maintain learner engagement.

Levelling up. One key feature of engaging tasks is that they challenge learners at the right level of competence (see Principles 1 and 5, this chapter) by gradually increasing the level of difficulty and rewarding accomplishments.

In gaming, this is referred to as 'levelling up'. The notion is that you work on one level and when you have completed it or gained sufficient points, only then do you have access to move on up to the next level or gain new tools or abilities for your character. Reaching the next level and unlocking the next set of tasks is not a punishment or extra work, it is something the person strives for with curiosity and interest. The point is that the levelling up is marked in some way for the learner, so they can feel the sense of progress and accomplishment as they move up to the next level. The approach is beneficial for learners to make progress, be aware of it, to be motivated to move on to the next level and to remain at an ever increasing optimal level of challenge.

In teaching, the task design associated with levelling up involves – obviously – dividing up learning objectives into levels and sequences so that when one level is successfully completed, the learner is allowed to move on and unlock the next level of tasks. The simplest way is to create a basic set of three levels (beginner, intermediate and advanced) for a specific task goal (Kapp 2012). This may in fact reflect the normal process of scaffolding the difficulty of tasks in a lesson, but the point here is to explicitly gamify that process, making the progress up through the levels explicit. Another way that a player's progress through levels is marked in games is through the use of 'experience points'. As players gain experience at a particular level by completing tasks, they gain experience points, and once they reach a certain number of points, which typically coincide with increased experience and competence, they can move on to the next level (for an example in a college course, see, Sheldon 2012).

> *As players advance in experience and accomplishments, they periodically reach milestones that offer greater power, privileges, or options. The system works in games because it provides clear goals (i.e. thresholds for advancement) and subsequently rewards players in ways that further enable activity, growth, and satisfaction.*
>
> (Rigby and Ryan 2011: 148)

Replay. If we structure levels into our learning design, we can also allow for 'replay' options for those who are not yet able to move up to the next level. As Kapp (2012: 48) explains, 'The replay button or do-over gives the player permission to fail'. Being allowed to fail encourages learners to explore with curiosity and without fear; they can try things out without worrying about possible negative consequences. In language learning, the option to fail can be liberating for linguistic experimentation and risk-taking. It can push learners to use new language and move out of their linguistic comfort zones. Feedback on experiments with language will help students learn and improve their language skills, pushing them to the edge of their ability and growing in competence. For example, in language learning, we can encourage learners to experiment by having them deliberately use new language and show us in writing by using a different colour for a new expression – we can even set a minimum of one new thing per text. Maybe they normally write in blue but anything they write in green is treated as an experiment and never treated as an error. If they use it incorrectly, they get feedback on how to use it more appropriately next time and encouraged to try again in green, until they feel they are ready to move this language use from green to their regular colour! As language teachers, we very often stress to learners that mistakes are just part of the learning process, but sometimes our feedback and assessment structures tell a different story: typical school tests and exams often leave little scope for a positive, exploratory attitude to mistakes. A key consideration is that if a student needs a 'replay', then they are likely to need more teacher support or maybe even different tasks. An ideal design is when learners can acknowledge their need for a replay without fear or embarrassment, thereby triggering scaffolded support from the teacher. Replay is not repeated failure; it is the option for more play.

> *In games, unlike many other activities, exploring failure and what it means is a valued approach. Players enjoy failures in a game, or at least use them to progress. The idea of failure is part of the game ethos. No one expects to successfully navigate and win a game the first time he or she plays it. In fact, people expect to fail – and look forward to the lessons learned during the failure process.*
>
> (Kapp 2012: 48)

Differentiated rewards. Rewards (often in the form of grades) have a troubled and confused past in education. Kohn's (1999) popular book, *Punished by Rewards,* drew wider attention to the possible problems with rewards and how they are used or rather misused. In a meta-analysis, Deci, Koestner and Ryan (2001) showed that extrinsic rewards can indeed undermine intrinsic motivation under certain conditions. If the reward is expected, tangible (i.e. gold stars, money, prizes, best player-type awards) and contingent, it risks destroying the intrinsic pleasure of the learning experience, as the learner will focus on doing the task just to get the reward and not to improve their skills or gain pleasure from the task itself. In other words, a reward attached to the task often does not direct attention to the task itself but rather serves as a distraction as students adopt a 'reward-grabbing' or 'grade-grabbing' attitude. There is also the danger when using rewards for reinforcing behaviours that learners are being controlled and manipulated, and not actually learning the desired behaviours themselves but merely complying through the use of what amount to bribes.

So, what does a healthy reward system look like for learners – and is there such a thing? Well, key is that we should think of a 'reward' in a new way, leaving the traditional sense of a tangible bribe behind. There is no harm in rewarding students in the form of encouragement: everyone benefits from praise, and sometimes during a task, learners need some positive encouragement to keep their engagement up and help them stay on task. Also, we can always reward progress and improvement - something which moving through levels or acquiring experience points would do automatically - and in this way, in effect, the progress becomes the reward. Care needs to be taken not to reward test scores or outcomes; it is the process and not the product of learning which needs to be at the centre, ensuring that every learner has the chance of a reward and not only the more able ones. Another approach is to word the outcomes of tasks in terms of what the learners will be able to do afterwards, so that this can serve as a form of incentive: 'You will be able to write a blog post on your hobby in a popular blogging style'. Cowley (2018) also suggests the option of asking the learners themselves what kind of meaningful reward they would want; a colleague of hers reported that learners chose a YouTube video connected to the subject to watch at the end of a session when they completed their class group work early. Indeed, learners are in the best position to suggest what would appeal to them as a perceived but meaningful privilege.

REFLECTION TASK 10

Think of a lesson you taught recently. Can you think of ways in which you could bring in the structure of levels, replay and rewards the next time you teach this lesson?

- Can you set three levels for the task?
- How can you evaluate when it is time to move up to the next level?
- Can you build in an option for a learner to replay by adding another set of practice to achieve the same goal?
- Could you use an experience points system to help learners progress through a task?
- What kinds of positive encouragement can you give learners during a task?
- How could you formulate learning objectives as more desirable incentive goals for learners?

Action 4: Chunk the Lesson and the Task

Chunking a lesson is a strategy that many good language teachers already use. When faced with education goals for a semester, teachers usually break these down into chunks, and within a lesson those goals are broken down into further lesson segments and sequences. Thus, chunking can be a way of making a bigger task more manageable; it is often used to break large goals into incremental ones (see Principle 5) and to scaffold tasks in terms of increasing levels of difficulty. Presenting one chunk at a time and thereby allowing time for practice before moving on to the next, is a simple but effective way to help make learning more digestible.

However, there are other ways a lesson can be broken into chunks to help think about learner engagement in lesson design. Chunking can be done on the whole lesson level and/or on the task level. On both levels, thinking in terms of chunks means creating intervals when you could create a break, change the pace, switch the action, or introduce a new hook for the next stage. It is a bit like inserting several new triggers to keep up pace and attention, but, at the same time, it is worth remembering that some longer tasks may be so engaging that if learners are actively in flow, we do not really want to disturb or break that focus. The notion of chunking is not necessarily new, but this is a way to consciously reflect on designing lesson chunks with engagement in mind.

KEY POINTS ABOUT CONCENTRATION

Petty (2014: 416–417) notes that 'A variety of student activity is vital to maintain concentration'. He lists the following key points about a one-hour lesson:

- Sometimes student concentration drops off completely, often during teacher talk.
- Changes of activity produce an increase in concentration.
- Concentration is maintained for longer when students are active.

For chunking on the whole lesson level, one popular approach designed around the idea of chunks is structuring the class into *learning stations* or *islands*. Stations are usually created 'physically', in that tables are made into islands or groups within the classroom – typically 4–5 for a class of 20–25. Each station has a different activity or set of tasks (and this can include the use of technology). Tasks can be collaborative, individual and one at least can be teacher-led. The process can be designed in two main ways. The first way is to ensure each task lasts a similar amount of time, put learners into groups, and rotate the groups around the stations allowing a set number of minutes for each activity. Alternatively, learners can move around the stations at their own pace in any order they want. The point is that the class is chunked into a series of interconnected but not necessarily chronologically sequenced activities. Sometimes teachers use an overarching worksheet with information drawn from each station for students to complete. It is a hands-on, active classroom design that allows for personalisation as well as chunked pace and diversity. It may take some time to establish this format the first time it is used, but learners soon become accustomed to it.

SEVEN TIPS FOR EFFECTIVE STATION WORK

1. Have one topic that you can find at least 4–5 sets of activities for – keep overall coherence
2. Vary task types – cover different language skills and styles of tasks
3. Allow time to reorganise furniture into stations

4. Plan and monitor timing carefully – for example, use a countdown clock on a projector to display the time for all to see
5. Avoid sequences of tasks, so that there is no particular start/end station
6. Provide clear instructions on each station so learners can get started without you
7. Think about a type of output to keep learners focused and ensure they visit and work at all the stations (e.g. one worksheet to complete, covering all stations)

For task-level chunking, teachers could think about using *energisers.* These are short activities designed to do exactly what they say – break up longer tasks and insert some energy into the learners and the class. They are sometimes also called 'brain breaks', for obvious reasons! They work best when they are kept relevant to the task – although with younger learners, taking a fun power break such as 'Simon says...' or a singalong can also have its place. A good energiser should be fun, relatively short, and involve some movement to get oxygen flowing to the brains. Here are three examples of possible energisers that could work in secondary school:

- *Mime break*. Ask learners to stop working, turn to their partner and mime one of the words or sentences they have been working with from their books. Their partner has to guess the sentence. Alternatively, have the first student ask a question and the second student answer with a mime. Suggest some possible questions to help them get started (e.g. What are you having for lunch? What are you doing tonight?).
- *Physical feedback*. The class can be asked to give feedback of where they are up to on a task, or how much more time they need for a task, or even what they think an answer to a question or opinion is, by asking learners to go to the corner of the room that represents where they are at, what they need or what they think. (You will need to either label the corners of the room or make a key on the board.)
- *Positive peer power*. Students get up and find a partner from another part of the room who has something in common with them. This can be something physically visible (e.g. both wearing glasses), or something they know (e.g. both have a pet dog), or it could even be the fact that they are all in the same class. When they move over to their partner, they should try and guess what the other thought they had in common, or simply just use the opportunity to tell each other one encouraging comment.

> *Exercise improves learning on three levels: first, it optimizes your mind-set to improve alertness, attention, and motivation; second, it prepares and encourages nerve cells to bind to one another, which is the cellular basis for logging in new information; and third, it spurs the development of new nerve cells from stem cells in the hippocampus.*
>
> (Ratey and Hagerman 2009: 53)

Action 5: Work with CLARA Principles

The final action point is one that really applies to the whole book and has been touched on in several chapters (see Chapters 4 and 5), but we feel this is so critical to engagement that we chose to make this the last suggested action to reinforce its value. There is a broad family of instructional approaches - project work, problem-based learning, inquiry-based learning, genius hours (working for set times on personal projects) and passion projects - which are known to be highly engaging due to certain common features in their design. Although they have different origins and have several unique elements, they also share the core characteristics that they are intended to foster exploration, discovery and inquiry, and are directed by learners who take a strong, active role. We have identified five features that are central to them under the acronym of 'CLARA' (see panel below).

CLARA APPROACHES ARE:

- **C**hallenging
- **L**earner-centred
- **A**ctive
- **R**eal-world relevant
- **A**utonomy-rich

All these instructional designs involve learners working for an extended period of time - from over several classes to a whole term - on a particular topic, question or puzzle, presented by the teacher or developed by the learners themselves (see e.g. Muir in press). Students have to work on creating some kind of output that will be made visible to an audience - online or in person. Learners can work alone, but, more frequently, they work together and collaborate with others. The tasks are typically challenging but also interesting, allowing learners to direct the focus and follow their own interests and passions to varying degrees. Learners are active and not only do they practise their language skills in authentic, meaningful, communicative ways, but they also develop critical and creative thinking skills. The teacher creates the structure and framework for the project but then takes more of a guiding role as facilitator and resource. Typically, these project-based approaches rely strongly on digital literacy skills, and learners often use technology to source information, communicate with others, manage their learning and create their output. Many of the characteristics of these kinds of teaching approaches have been linked to increased engagement (see e.g. Ainley 2012; Assor, Kaplan and Roth 2002; Blumenfeld et al. 1991; Buchanan, Harlan, Bruce and Edwards 2016; Christenson et al. 2012; Reeve 2012).

> *Although there obviously will be individual differences in student reactions, projects can be designed to include elements that are likely to enhance most students' interest and value, including variety, challenge, choice, cooperation, and closure in the service of answering real questions. In addition, by considering students' prior knowledge and thinking skills, projects can be designed to support students so that they feel able to succeed.*
> (Blumenfeld et al. 1991: 393)

Not all teachers and learners feel comfortable embracing project-based approaches and Blumenfeld at al. (1991) note the importance of suitable structural support for those wishing to work with such an approach. They suggest technology can play a valuable role in project work as a resource and tool for learners, as well as a way of organising and managing the process for teachers. They draw attention to the fact that learners may need to be taught *how* to research for and work effectively on projects. Similarly, teachers themselves may need guidance in how to form suitably divergent puzzles or questions for projects and how to guide the learners so that the learning during the project, and not the project product, remains foregrounded. In this regard, there are many useful online resources to draw inspiration and courage from where other teachers share ideas and experiences with project work.

DEVELOPING A PROJECT-BASED MINDSET

In discussing the conditions for effective project-based learning (PBL), Dörnyei et al. (2016: 168–172) offer the following points about developing a PBL mindset:

- *Being prepared to alter one's professional role.* When setting up a project, teachers need to take on less commonly assumed pedagogical roles, such as that of coach, coordinator, mentor and – most importantly – facilitator.
- *Rethinking the teacher-student relationship and embracing the ethos of co-construction.* When PBL is successful, students *co-create* the project-learning environment, and learners are more likely to be engaged when they sense that the final goal is something they have *ownership* of.
- *Being prepared to embrace excitement.* PBL can create a tangible goal to work towards and about which learners can become excited. For teachers, it can also reveal an enthusiasm in our learners which is contagious!

> - *Being prepared for failures.* It is inevitable that not all group projects will be successful, especially when the students – and perhaps even the teacher – are unfamiliar with PBL. But, the mindset is to learn from the failures and try it differently next time. We can model the mindset of growth we wish to see in our learners.

For language teachers, who may not feel that it is possible to go for a full project approach within the constraints of the learning environment they operate in, the CLARA principles (i.e. Challenging, Learner-centred, Active, Real-world relevant, Autonomy-rich) can be helpful as they can equally be applied to smaller, regular tasks. To illustrate how this might work, let us take the example of a typical discussion task on a specific topic and the possible steps it could go through:

- The class choose a topic to discuss – it can be entirely learner-generated or selected from a pre-prepared teacher list. (Learner-centred)
- Students choose who to collaborate with and the size of the group they want to work in. (Autonomy-rich)
- Groups are asked to come up with a highly contentious statement reflecting an extreme view on this topic. (Challenging)
- The topic and statements should concern the world around them. The activity of justifying and defending one's opinion is also a real-world skill. (Real-world relevant)
- All the statements are collected together on the board or screen and then individuals rank each statement in terms of how much they agree with it. If there are too many statements for the time available, the whole class should select those they wish to focus on. (Learner-centred)
- In small groups, they try to reach consensus on their statements, with each individual explaining their rationale to the others. Then, as a group, they select one statement and opinion and try to convince their classmates to agree by making an 'elevator pitch', a short presentation that should last as long as a ride in an elevator. The others in class can vote with clickers on how persuasive they found each elevator pitch. (Active)

THE SIX CRITERIA OF THE FRAMEWORK FOR HIGH QUALITY PROJECT-BASED LEARNING (HQPBL)

1. Students learn deeply, think critically, and strive for excellence.
2. Students work on projects that are meaningful and relevant to their culture, their lives, and their future.
3. Students' work is publicly displayed, discussed, and critiqued.

4. Students collaborate with other students in person or online and/or receive guidance from adult mentors and experts.
5. Students use a project management process that enables them to proceed effectively from project initiation to completion.
6. Students reflect on their work and learning throughout the project.

(Source: https://hqpbl.org/)

Summary

To be engaged, learners need to be active, but it also helps if they are interested, enjoying their work and feeling challenged but competent. This chapter has closely built on the material in the previous chapter which centred on triggering engagement, focusing here on ways of maintaining engagement on tasks. We proposed five core principles, concerning providing learners with the appropriate level of challenge, ensuring positive emotions on task, keeping their attention and interest, reducing levels of predictability, and ensuring an ongoing sense of accomplishment and progress. These can be best achieved by having the foundations in place from Chapters 2–4 and by having created the right starting condition of a task. We offered five specific action points that support the principle of sustained engagement:

- working with stories and narratives to keep learners emotionally hooked and interested as well as supporting their ability to process and remember;
- making the learner the hero of their own learning by involving them in task design and helping them to personalise their learning;
- utilising game design elements such as 'levelling up' tasks by providing a structure of levels which serve as milestones for achievement, allowing for replay moments and using judicious reward systems;
- chunking the lessons and tasks into smaller segments, such as through the use of stations or by integrating brief intervals such as energisers or brain breaks;
- working with CLARA principles drawn from approaches such as project-based learning to foster challenge, learner-centredness, active learning, real-world relevance and autonomy-richness.

CHAPTER IN A NUTSHELL

Maintaining task engagement depends on learners being active on a task that is set at their optimal level of challenge, and is characterised by a positive emotional tone and a supportive design structure.

IF YOU WANT TO FIND OUT MORE

Dörnyei, Z., Henry, A. and Muir, C. (2016). *Motivational Currents in Language Learning: Frameworks for Focused Interventions.* New York, NY: Routledge. (This book offers an innovative theory of intensive, long-term motivation that promotes sustained learning, and presents its classroom application in various project designs.)

Nunan, D. (2004). *Task-Based Language Teaching.* Cambridge: Cambridge University Press. (A useful overview of issues involved in task-based language teaching with practical advice grounded in research and theory.)

Posey, A. (2019). *Engage the Brain: How to Design for Learning that Taps into the Power of Emotion.* Alexandria, VA: ASCD. (This book focuses on the emotional side of the brain but offers practical classroom strategies designed to enhance student engagement and learning.)

Renninger, K. A. and Hidi, S. E. (2016). *The Power of Interest for Motivation and Engagement.* New York, NY: Routledge. (An academic book that teases apart these three interrelated constructs. Not immediately practical but extremely useful for understanding the nature of interest and its role in learning.)

Conclusion

> *Engagement behaviors are responsive to teachers' and schools' practices, allowing for the possibility of improving achievement and attainment for students.*
>
> (Finn and Zimmer 2012: 99)

The principal assumption underlying the material in this book has been that engagement is key to successful learning in general, and to language learning in particular. If learners are not paying attention and do not become engaged in their work, then learning simply cannot take place. Therefore, we genuinely hope that it is empowering for teachers to learn that engagement can be consciously crafted and generated - there are specific actions that teachers can take to positively impact on learner engagement.

This book has drawn on a host of disciplines and has led us through varied fields of education, business management, leadership studies, psychology and gaming among others. This means we have drawn on a substantial body of relevant literature in our attempt to provide an informed understanding of the topic, as the reference list indicates. Our choice of principles and suggested actions has inevitably been based on a subjective selection from a broader potential menu, in accordance with our understanding of the field (and especially motivation theory and other dimensions of psychology) and our own practical experiences as educators. We do hope that despite any omissions, readers will find the material comprehensive yet not prescriptive or overwhelming.

It has definitely not been our intention to imply that a teacher should use all the actions every lesson and all the time. Instead, we hope that teachers will see this as a palette to select from, as suits them, their learners and their context. Each teacher will need to start where their learners are and what they feel comfortable with. For some, this may mean just small adjustments to their current practices, at least at the outset, but it is the sense of exploration and reflection on how to engage learners actively in their language learning that we hope to foster. For those who wish to read further into a particular facet of engagement or learning design, each chapter provides a brief list of annotated references.

The book started by outlining what engagement is and why we think this is important to understand in language teaching. Chapter 1 moved on to outline the backdrop against which language teachers work. We reflected on the range of contextual factors that tend to be out of the direct control of teachers and yet which can impede or enhance learner engagement in the classroom. Chapters 2, 3 and 4 were all concerned with creating the psychological foundations on which engagement rests. Without a facilitative mindset in learners, positive teacher-learner rapport and a good group climate, task engagement will be much more difficult to achieve, no matter how great the resources and tasks. In Chapters 5 and 6, we focused on task design and what teachers can build into their lessons/tasks to trigger engagement and sustain it over time. We noted the strong role played by emotions and curiosity, as well as the need for a tangible sense of progress and appropriate levels of challenge.

Having considered how best to conclude a book with such wide-ranging materials, we thought it may be useful to offer a summary of the main points in a table format. If the previous chapters have resonated with you, we would like to invite you to take your time to have a look at the table and read through the principles and action points, reflecting on them from three specific points of view:

1. Which of them are already part of your current practice, either fully or partially? (We are confident that every reader of this book will be encouraged by identifying a good number!)
2. Are there any aspects of any of the *familiar* principles/actions that you would want to further strengthen in your practice in the future?
3. Are there any principles or action points that are *new* to you, in the sense that you have not consciously considered them in the context of your teaching? If there are, then it is only you who can decide whether they are worth experimenting with or whether they are not relevant to your specific context (or whether they are simply not useful).

There is one point we would like to reiterate. In Chapter 5 we already referred to Zoltán's argument that teachers should aim to become 'good enough motivators' rather than striving unreasonably to achieve 'supermotivator' status, which would most likely lead to burnout (Dörnyei 2001: 136). We believe that the same applies to strategies to engage learners: we do not think for a moment that anyone should (or could) apply all of the methods listed in the table. Quality is more important than quantity; a few well-chosen strategies that suit both you and your learners might take you beyond the threshold of the 'good-enough engager', creating a safe and involving climate in the classroom. And we are convinced that the conclusion about motivating teachers is also true of engaging teachers: some of the most effective practitioners often rely only on a few basic but well-selected techniques!

THE CONTEXTS OF LEARNER ENGAGEMENT

Learner engagement in class is connected to attitudes and beliefs stemming from a host of contextual factors that affect both the learner and the school.

- **Principle 1:** Recognise that individual languages have sociocultural status and social capital
- **Principle 2:** Connect language learning in class to life beyond the classroom
- **Principle 3:** Families are a valuable resource for learner engagement
- **Principle 4:** School priorities, curricular relevance and testing policies have a bearing on engagement
- **Principle 5:** Whole-school culture can cultivate or kill learner engagement

THE FACILITATIVE LEARNER MINDSET

Learners are more likely to engage with language learning if they feel competent to do so and have some ownership and control over their development and experiences.

- **Principle 1:** Promote a sense of competence
- **Principle 2:** Foster a growth mindset
- **Principle 3:** Promote learners' sense of ownership and control
- **Principle 4:** Develop proactive learners
- **Principle 5:** Develop gritty learners

- **Action 1:** Think and act like a coach
- **Action 2:** Make learning progress visible
- **Action 3:** Discuss beliefs explicitly
- **Action 4:** Build in choice and voice
- **Action 5:** Teach how to learn

TEACHER–STUDENT RAPPORT

In order to develop learner engagement, we need to work on developing a positive relationship with our students and reflect on how we make ourselves available and interact with them.

- **Principle 1:** Be approachable
- **Principle 2:** Be empathetic
- **Principle 3:** Be responsive to learner individuality
- **Principle 4:** Believe in all your learners
- **Principle 5:** Support learner autonomy
- **Principle 6:** Be passionate about what you do

- **Action 1:** Take care with teacher talk
- **Action 2:** Be thoughtful about feedback
- **Action 3:** Listen to learners
- **Action 4:** Use questions to engage
- **Action 5:** Deal with discipline relationally

POSITIVE CLASSROOM DYNAMICS AND CULTURE

For learners to be willing to engage in class, they need to feel safe and accepted as valued members of a cohesive classroom community, who also have specific responsibilities for their own and the others' learning.

- **Principle 1:** Lead by example
- **Principle 2:** Promote group cohesiveness
- **Principle 3:** Promote TEA among learners: Trust, Empathy and Acceptance
- **Principle 4:** Foster a culture of collaboration and support
- **Principle 5:** Resolve conflict constructively and respectfully

- **Action 1:** Connect learners personally
- **Action 2**: Develop a sense of 'we' and 'us'
- **Action 3:** Prepare learners for groupwork and cooperation
- **Action 4:** Structure using the three 'R's: rules, roles and routines
- **Action 5:** Foster democratic participation

INITIATING ENGAGEMENT WITH LEARNING TASKS

Teachers can design specific tasks to get learners active, curious and emotionally invested in wanting to learn and do more.

- **Principle 1:** Design for the learners in front of you
- **Principle 2:** Get learners emotionally invested
- **Principle 3:** Curiosity captivates
- **Principle 4:** Concentrate on task set-up
- **Principle 5:** Learners need to be active to engage

- **Action 1:** Start with deliberately small steps
- **Action 2:** Build in surprise and the 'wow' factor
- **Action 3:** Build in mystery and puzzles
- **Action 4:** Create cliffhangers
- **Action 5:** Use questions to trigger curiosity

SUSTAINING ENGAGEMENT ON LEARNING TASKS

Maintaining task engagement depends on learners being active on a task that is set at their optimal level of challenge and is characterised by a positive emotional tone and a supportive design structure.

- **Principle 1:** Provide cognitive challenge
- **Principle 2:** Maximise enjoyment, minimise boredom
- **Principle 3:** Captivate attention, engage interest
- **Principle 4:** Utilise the power of unpredictability
- **Principle 5:** Stagger accomplishments

- **Action 1:** Utilise the power of stories
- **Action 2:** Make the learner the hero of their task
- **Action 3:** Allow 'levelling up', 'replay' and 'differentiated rewards'
- **Action 4:** Chunk the lesson and the task
- **Action 5:** Work with CLARA principles

Three Central Themes

As we have reflected on the range of principles and actions ourselves, we noticed three strong recurrent themes: *the power of positive emotions, empowering learners as partners in their education* and *active participation*. Here is a brief recap of the lessons we have drawn regarding these themes:

- *The power of positive emotions.* Many of the principles across the different themes centre on a common issue, that of the learners feeling comfortable, confident and safe to approach their language learning without any fear of making mistakes or being ridiculed, and being surrounded by relationships of trust and respect. Emotions create the foundations on which engagement is built and they also emerge from the processes of being engaged: if learners are engaged and enjoying working on a task, this will generate positive emotions with positive expectations for the next and future language task encounters. Success does breed success. As teachers, we need to be sensitive to the feelings generated by the L2 and its learning, most notably emotions associated with enjoyment, curiosity and interest on the positive side and anxiety, embarrassment, boredom and risk on the negative. As a field, we know relatively little about how best to harness the emotions that have featured prominently in this book (for early exceptions, see Arnold 1999), but recent advances in emotion research (e.g. Dewaele 2018) as well as in establishing a link between positive psychology and SLA (MacIntyre, Gregersen and Mercer 2016) indicate that this situation is in the process of change.
- *Empowering learners as partners in their education.* The importance of autonomy for engagement is well established, and we saw repeatedly how impactful for engagement it can be when learners are empowered to make decisions and express their voice through democratic participation in all aspects of their education and learning process. Treating learners as partners in their own learning means teachers and institutions showing respect and trust to the learners, and also giving them the power and opportunities to take responsibility and direct their own learning within the bounds of the contextual constraints. Engagement is about action and so learners benefit when they are directing that action in ways that are authentic, meaningful and purposeful. We also saw that any genuine learner empowerment has a relational basis, as learner-led tasks frequently require collaboration and cooperation with others and trustful, positive rapport with the teacher-facilitator.

- *Active participation.* Finally, the most important dimension of engagement is active participation by the learner. There are no two ways about it: engagement is about action. Having said that, it has also been stressed repeatedly that being engaged is not the same as being busy – genuine student engagement is purposeful, meaningful and leads to learning. Yet, the truth remains that teaching with engagement in mind means teaching with learner action and participation in mind. Learning can never be a spectator sport.

REFLECTION TASK

Think of your classroom and your upcoming classes. Which of the above three themes are most relevant to keep in mind in your lesson design? Are there any particular actions that lend themselves to be tried out in relation to this selected theme?

Final Words

We know that it is highly unlikely to ever achieve 100% high engagement from ALL learners at any one time. The best we can realistically aim for is what Schlechty (2011: 32) explains as 'most students are engaged most of the time'. The fact that some will just be complying but not deeply engaged and some others will be fully off task or even engaging in rebellious behaviour is part of the daily challenges of being a (language) teacher. We hope, however, that this book has shown that the level of student engagement in a class is not a mysterious phenomenon that is attributable to coincidence or factors completely outside our control. L2 lessons and tasks *can* be designed to be more engaging, following some relatively straightforward principles. In addition, it is worth remembering and drawing hope from the fact that the learners themselves do not like to be bored or passive; they would usually prefer to be engaged. So, our job is to engage learners in their learning by designing language learning experiences that provide learners with the opportunity and encouragement to engage. Our hope is that this book can help you to do just that.

References

Abbott, A. L. (2017). Fostering student interest development: An engagement intervention. *Middle School Journal*, 48(3), 34–45. doi.org/10.1080/00940771.2017.1297666

Ainley, M. (2012). Students' interest and engagement in classroom activities. In S. L. Christenson, A. L. Reschly & C. Wylie (eds.), *Handbook of Research on Student Engagement* (283–302). New York, NY: Springer Science + Business Media.

Ainley, M. & Hidi, S. E. (2014). Interest and enjoyment. In R. Pekrun & L. Linnenbrink-Garcia (eds.), *International Handbook of Emotions in Education* (205–227). New York, NY: Routledge.

Ajzen, I. (1988). *Attitudes, Personality, and Behavior*. Chicago, IL: Dorsey Press.

Ajzen, I. (2002). Perceived behavioral control, self-efficacy, locus of control, and the theory of planned behavior. *Journal of Applied Social Psychology*, 32(4), 665–683. doi.org/10.1111/j.1559-1816.2002.tb00236.x

Allen, D. E., Donham, R. S. & Bernhardt, S. A. (2011). Problem-based learning. *New Directions for Teaching and Learning*, 2011(128), 21–29. doi.org/10.1002/tl.465

Alter, A. (2017). *Irresistible: The Rise of Addictive Technology and the Business of Keeping us Hooked*. New York, NY: Penguin Press.

Amabile, T. & Kramer, S. (2011). *The Progress Principle: Using Small Wins to Ignite Joy, Engagement, and Creativity at Work*. Boston, MA: Harvard Business Review Press.

Amador, J. A., Miles, L. & Peters, C. B. (2006). *The Practice of Problem-Based Learning: A Guide to Implementing PBL in the College Classroom*. Bolton, MA: Anker.

Antonetti, J. V. & Garver, J. R. (2015). *17,000 Classroom Visits Can't Be Wrong: Strategies that Engage Students, Promote Active Learning, and Boost Achievement*. Alexandria, VA: ASCD.

Arnold, J. (ed.) (1999). *Affect in Language Learning*. Cambridge: Cambridge University Press.

Arzubiaga, A., Rueda, R. & Monzó, L. (2002). Family matters related to the reading engagement of Latino children. *Journal of Latinos and Education*, 1(4), 231–243. doi.org/10.1207/S1532771XJLE0104_3

Assor, A., Kaplan, H. & Roth, G. (2002). Choice is good, but relevance is excellent: Autonomy-enhancing and suppressing teacher behaviours predicting students' engagement in schoolwork. *British Journal of Educational Psychology*, 72(2), 261–278. doi.org/10.1348/000709902158883

Au, W. (2007). High-stakes testing and curricular control: A qualitative metasynthesis. *Educational Researcher*, 36(5), 258–267. doi.org/10.3102/0013189X07306523

Bahman, S. & Maffini, H. (2008). *Developing Children's Emotional Intelligence*. London: Bloomsbury.

Bajorek, Z., Gulliford, J. & Taskila, T. (2014). *Healthy teachers, higher marks? Establishing a link between teacher health and wellbeing, and student outcomes*. London: The Work Foundation. Retrieved from: https://www.educationsupportpartnership.org.uk/sites/default/files/resources/healthy_teachers_higher_marks_report_0.pdf [Accessed 13th August 2019]

Bandura, A. (1977). Self-efficacy: Toward a unifying theory of behavioral change. *Psychological Review*, 84(2), 191–215. doi.org/10.1037/0033-295X.84.2.191

Bandura, A. (1997). *Self-Efficacy: The Exercise of Control*. New York, NY: W.H. Freeman.

Bandura, A. & Schunk, D. H. (1981). Cultivating competence, self-efficacy, and intrinsic interest through proximal self-motivation. *Journal of Personality and Social Psychology*, 41(3), 586–598. doi.org/10.1037/0022-3514.41.3.586

Barber, D. & Foord, D. (2014). *From English Teacher to Learner Coach [Kindle Edition]*. The Round.

Barkley, E. F. (2010). *Student Engagement Techniques: A Handbook for College Faculty*. San Francisco, CA: Jossey-Bass.

Baumeister, R. F. & Leary, M. R. (1995). The need to belong: Desire for interpersonal attachments as a fundamental human motivation. *Psychological Bulletin*, 117(3), 497–529. doi.org/10.1037//0033-2909.117.3.497

Baumeister, R. F. & Tierney, J. (2011). *Willpower: Rediscovering the Greatest Human Strength*. New York, NY: Penguin Books.

Beere, J. & Broughton, T. (2013). *The Perfect Teacher Coach* [*Kindle Edition*]. Carmarthen: Independent Thinking Press.

Benson, P. (2001). *Teaching and Researching Autonomy in Language Learning*. Harlow: Pearson Education.

Benson, P. & Reinders, H. (eds.). (2011). *Beyond the Language Classroom*. Basingstoke: Palgrave Macmillan.

Bentley-Davies, C. (2010). *How to be an Amazing Teacher*. Glasgow: Crown House Publishing.

Berger, W. (2014). *The Book of Beautiful Questions: The Powerful Questions that Will Help You Decide, Create, Connect, and Lead*. New York, NY: Bloomsbury.

Berns, G. S., McClure, S. M., Pagnoni, G. & Montague, P. R. (2001). Predictability modulates human brain response to reward. *The Journal of Neuroscience*, 21(8), 2793–2798. doi.org/10.1523/JNEUROSCI.21-08-02793.2001

Birch, B. M. (2009). *The English Language Teacher in Global Civil Society*. New York, NY: Routledge.

Bjork, E. L. & Bjork, R. (2011). Making things hard on yourself, but in a good way: Creating desirable difficulties to enhance learning. In M. A. Gernsbacher, R. W. Pew, L. M. Hough & J. R. Pomerantz (eds.), *Psychology and the Real World: Essays Illustrating Fundamental Contributions to Society* (56–64). New York, NY: Worth Publishers.

Blackwell, L. S., Trzesniewski, K. H. & Dweck, C. S. (2007). Implicit theories of intelligence predict achievement across an adolescent transition: A longitudinal study and an intervention. *Child Development*, 78(1), 246–263. doi.org/10.1111/j.1467-8624.2007.00995.x

Bloom, B. S. (ed.). (1956). *Taxonomy of Educational Objectives: Handbook 1, Cognitive Domain*. New York, NY: David McKay Co Inc.

Blumenfeld, P. C., Soloway, E., Marx, R. W., Krajcik, J. S., Guzdial, M. & Palincsar, A. (1991). Motivating project-based learning: Sustaining the doing, supporting the learning. *Educational Psychologist*, 26(3–4), 369–398. doi.org/10.1080/00461520.1991.9653139

Bonwell, C. C. & Eison, J. A. (1991). *Active Learning: Creating Excitement in the Classroom* (No. ASHE–ERIC Higher Education Report No. 1). Washington, DC: The George Washington University, School of Education and Human Development.

Boo, Z., Dörnyei, Z. & Ryan, S. (2015). L2 motivation research 2005–2014: Understanding a publication surge and a changing landscape. *System*, 55, 145–157. doi.org/10.1016/j.system.2015.10.006

Bowlby, J. (1969). *Attachment and Loss, Vol. 1: Attachment*. New York, NY: Basic Books.

Bown, J. (2009). Self-regulatory strategies and agency in self-instructed language learning: A situated view. *The Modern Language Journal*, 93(4), 570–583. doi.org/10.1111/j.1540-4781.2009.00965.x

Brandes, D. & Ginnis, P. (1986). *A Guide to Student-Centred Learning* (Reprint). Oxford: Blackwell.

Bryk, A. S. & Schneider, B. (2002). *Trust in Schools: A Core Resource for Improvement*. New York, NY: Russell Sage Foundation.

Buchanan, S., Harlan, M. A., Bruce, C. S. & Edwards, S. L. (2016). Inquiry based learning models, information literacy, and student engagement: A literature review. *School Libraries Worldwide*, 22(2), 23–39. Retrieved from: https://eprints.qut.edu.au/102823/ [Accessed 13th August 2019]

Cacioppo, J. T. & Petty, R. E. (1982). The need for cognition. *Journal of Personality and Social Psychology*, 42(1), 116–131. doi.org/10.1037/0022-3514.42.1.116

Campbell, N. & Schumm Fauster, J. (2013). Learner-centred feedback on writing: Feedback as dialogue. In M. Reitbauer, N. Campbell, S. Mercer, J. Schumm Fauster & R. Vaupetitsch (eds.), *Feedback Matters: Current Feedback Practices in the EFL Classroom,* (55–68). Frankfurt: Peter Lang.

Carriere, J. S. A., Cheyne, J. A. & Smilek, D. (2008). Everyday attention lapses and memory failures: The affective consequences of mindlessness. *Consciousness and Cognition*, 17(3), 835–847. doi.org/10.1016/j.concog.2007.04.008

Castles, J. (2004). Persistence and the adult learner. *Active Learning in Higher Education,* 5(2), 166-179. doi.org/10.1177/1469787404043813

Cavanagh, S. R. (2016). *The Spark of Learning: Energizing the College Classroom with the Science of Emotion.* Morgantown, WV: West Virginia University Press.

Cayanus, J. L., Martin, M. M. & Goodboy, A. K. (2009). The relation between teacher self-disclosure and student motives to communicate. *Communication Research Reports*, 26(2), 105–113. doi.org/10.1080/08824090902861523

Cemalcilar, Z. (2010). Schools as socialisation contexts: Understanding the impact of school climate factors on students' sense of school belonging. *Applied Psychology*, 59(2), 243–272. doi.org/10.1111/j.1464-0597.2009.00389.x

Charney, R. (2015). *Teaching Children to Care: Classroom Management for Ethical and Academic Growth, K–8* (Rev. ed). Greenfield, MA: Northeast Foundation for Children.

Chen, A., Ennis, C. D., Martin, R. & Sun. H. (2005). Situational interest: A curriculum component enhancing motivation to learn. *Research Quarterly for Exercise and Sport,* 76(1), 1–28. Retrieved from: https://www.researchgate.net/publication/296294352_Situational_interest_A_curriculum_component_enhancing_motivation_to_learn [Accessed 13th August 2019]

Christenson, S. L., Reschly, A. L. & Wylie, C. (eds.). (2012). *Handbook of Research on Student Engagement*. New York, NY: Springer Science + Business Media.

Claxton, G., Chambers, M., Powell, G. & Lucas, B. (2011). *The Learning Powered School: Pioneering 21st Century Education*. Bristol: TLO Limited.

Cleary, T. J. & Zimmerman, B. J. (2012). A cyclical self-regulatory account of student engagement: Theoretical foundations and applications. In S. L. Christenson, A. L. Reschly & C. Wylie (eds.), *Handbook of Research on Student Engagement* (237–257). New York, NY: Springer Science + Business Media.

Cohen, A. D. (2011). *Strategies in Learning and Using a Second Language* (2nd ed). Harlow: Pearson.

Cohen, A. D. & Macaro, E. (eds.). (2007). *Language Learner Strategies: Thirty Years of Research and Practice*. Oxford: Oxford University Press.

Cohen, E. G. & Lotan, R. (2014). *Designing Groupwork: Strategies for the Heterogeneous Classroom* (3rd ed). New York, NY: Teachers College Press.

Cooper, B. (2011). *Empathy in Education: Engagement, Values and Achievement*. New York, NY: Continuum.

Cowley, S. (2009). *Teaching Skills for Dummies*. Chichester: John Wiley.

Cowley, S. (2013). *The Seven R's of Great Group Work*. Bristol: Sue Cowley Books.

Cowley, S. (2018). *The Ultimate Guide to Differentiation: Achieving Excellence for All*. London: Bloomsbury.

Cox, J. (n.d.). All about differentiated instruction with menus. *Teach Hub*. Retrieved from: http://www.teachhub.com/classroom-management-differentiated-instruction-menus [Accessed 7th February, 2019].

Coyle, D. (2018). *The Culture Code: The Secrets of Highly Successful Groups*. New York, NY: Bantam Books.

Crehan, L. (2016). *Cleverlands*. London: Unbound.

Csikszentmihalyi, M. (2002). *Flow: The Classic Work on How to Achieve Happiness* (Rev. ed). London: Rider.

Daschmann, E. C., Goetz, T. & Stupnisky, R. H. (2014). Exploring the antecedents of boredom: Do teachers know why students are bored? *Teaching and Teacher Education*, 39, 22–30. doi.org/10.1016/j.tate.2013.11.009

Davenport, T. H. & Beck, J. C. (2001). The attention economy. *Ubiquity*, 2001 (May). Retrieved from: https://ubiquity.acm.org/article.cfm?id=376626 [Accessed 13th August 2019]

Davies, J. (2014). *Riveted: The Science of Why Jokes Make us Laugh, Movies Make us Cry, and Religion Makes us Feel One with the Universe*. New York, NY: Palgrave Macmillan.

Davis, H. A., Summers, J. J. & Miller, L. M. (2012). *An Interpersonal Approach to Classroom Management: Strategies for Improving Student Engagement*. Thousand Oaks, CA: Corwin Press.

Day, C. & Gu, Q. (2009). Teacher emotions: Well being and effectiveness. In P. A. Schutz & M. Zemblyas (eds.), *Advances in Teacher Emotion Research* (15–31). New York, NY: Springer Science + Business Media.

Deci, E. L. & Flaste, R. (1995). *Why we do what we do: The Dynamics of Personal Autonomy*. New York, NY: Putnam's Sons.

Deci, E. L., Koestner, R. & Ryan, R. M. (2001). Extrinsic rewards and intrinsic motivation in education: Reconsidered once again. *Review of Educational Research*, 71(1), 1–27. doi.org/10.3102/00346543071001001

Deci, E. L. & Ryan, R. M. (1985). *Intrinsic Motivation and Self-Determination in Human Behavior*. New York, NY: Plenum Press.

Deci, E. L. & Ryan, R. M. (eds.). (2002). *Handbook of Self-Determination Research*. Rochester, NY: University of Rochester Press.

Deci, E. L., Schwartz, A. J., Sheinman, L. & Ryan, R. M. (1981). An instrument to assess adults' orientations toward control versus autonomy with children: Reflections on intrinsic motivation and perceived competence. *Journal of Educational Psychology*, 73(5), 642–650. doi.org/10.1037/0022-0663.73.5.642

Denton, P. (2007). *The Power of our Words: Teacher Language that Helps Children Learn*. Turners Falls, MA: Northeast Foundation for Children.

DeSteno, D. (2018). *Emotional Success: The Motivational Power of Gratitude, Compassion and Pride*. London: Bluebird.

Dewaele, J.-M. (2018). Special issue: Emotions in second language acquisition. *Studies in Second Language Learning and Teaching*, 8(1). Retrieved from: https://pressto.amu.edu.pl/index.php/ssllt/issue/view/847 [Accessed 13th August 2019]

Dewaele, J.-M. & MacIntyre, P. D. (2016). Foreign language enjoyment and foreign language classroom anxiety: The right and left feet of the language learner. In P. D. MacIntyre, T. Gregersen & S. Mercer (eds.), *Positive Psychology in SLA* (215–236). Bristol: Multilingual Matters.

Dewey, J. (1922). *Democracy and Education: An Introduction to the Philosophy of Education*. New York, NY: The MacMillan Company.

Dickey, M. D. (2005). Engaging by design: How engagement strategies in popular computer and video games can inform instructional design. *Educational Technology Research and Development*, 53(2), 67–83. doi.org/10.1007/BF02504866

Dirksen, J. (2016). *Design for How People Learn* (2nd ed). San Francisco, CA: New Riders.

Dörnyei, Z. (2001). *Motivational Strategies in the Language Classroom*. Cambridge: Cambridge University Press.

Dörnyei, Z. (2009). Individual differences: Interplay of learner characteristics and learning environment. *Language Learning*, 59(s1), 230–248. doi.org/10.1111/j.1467-9922.2009.00542.x

Dörnyei, Z., Csizér, K. & Németh, N. (2006). *Motivation, Language Attitudes and Globalisation: a Hungarian Perspective*. Clevedon: Multilingual Matters.

Dörnyei, Z., Henry, A. & Muir, C. (2016). *Motivational Currents in Language Learning: Frameworks for Focused Interventions*. New York, NY: Routledge.

Dörnyei, Z. & Kubanyiova, M. (2014). *Motivating Learners, Motivating Teachers: Building Vision in Language Education*. Cambridge: Cambridge University Press.

Dörnyei, Z., MacIntyre, P. D. & Henry, A. (eds.). (2015). *Motivational Dynamics in Language Learning*. Bristol: Multilingual Matters.

Dörnyei, Z. & Muir, C. (2019). Creating a motivating classroom environment. In X. A. Gao (ed.), *Second Handbook of English Language Teaching* (719–736). Cham: Springer.

Dörnyei, Z. & Murphey, T. (2003). *Group Dynamics in the Language Classroom*. Cambridge: Cambridge University Press.

Dörnyei, Z. & Ryan, S. (2015). *The Psychology of the Language Learner Revisited*. New York, NY: Routledge.

Dörnyei, Z. & Ushioda, E. (eds.). (2011). *Teaching and Researching Motivation* (2nd ed). Harlow: Pearson.

Dotterer, A. M., McHale, S. M. & Crouter, A. C. (2007). Implications of out-of-school activities for school engagement in African American adolescents. *Journal of Youth and Adolescence*, 36(4), 391–401. doi.org/10.1007/s10964-006-9161-3

Downey, M. (2014). *Effective Modern Coaching: The Principles and Art of Successful Business Coaching*. London: LID Publishing Ltd.

Dresel, M. & Hall, N. (2013). Motivation. In N. C. Hall & T. Goetz (eds.), *Emotion, Motivation, and Self-Regulation: A Handbook for Teachers* (57–122). Bingley: Emerald.

Duckworth, A. (2016). *Grit: The Power of Passion and Perseverance*. New York, NY: Scribner.

Dweck, C. S. (2006). *Mindset: The New Psychology of Success*. New York, NY: Ballantine Books.

Edmondson, A. C. (2019). *The Fearless Organization: Creating Psychological Safety in the Workplace for Learning, Innovation, and Growth*. Hoboken, NJ: John Wiley & Sons.

Egan, K. (2005). *An Imaginative Approach to Teaching*. San Francisco, CA: Jossey-Bass.

Ehrman, M. E. & Dörnyei, Z. (1998). *Interpersonal Dynamics in Second Language Education: The Visible and Invisible Classroom*. Thousand Oaks, CA: SAGE Publications.

Eidswick, J. (2010). Interest and prior knowledge in second language reading comprehension. *JALT Journal*, 32(2), 149–168. Retrieved from: https://jalt-publications.org/jj/articles/116-article-interest-and-prior-knowledge-second-language-reading-comprehension [Accessed 14th August 2019]

Erling, E. J. (ed.). (2017). *English Across the Fracture Lines: The Contribution and Relevance of English to Security, Stability and Peace*. London: British Council.

Evans, K. R. & Lester, J. N. (2013). Restorative justice in education: What we know so far. *Middle School Journal,* 44(5), 57–63. doi.org/10.1080/00940771.2013.11461873

Fan, W. & Williams, C. M. (2010). The effects of parental involvement on students' academic self-efficacy, engagement and intrinsic motivation. *Educational Psychology*, 30(1), 53–74. doi.org/10.1080/01443410903353302

Fan, X. & Chen, M. (2001). Parental involvement and students' academic achievement: A meta-analysis. *Educational Psychology Review*, 13(1), 1–22. doi.org/10.1023/A:1009048817385

Farmer, T. W., McAuliffe Lines, M. & Hamm, J. V. (2011). Revealing the invisible hand: The role of teachers in children's peer experiences. *Journal of Applied Developmental Psychology*, 32(5), 247–256. doi.org/10.1016/j.appdev.2011.04.006

Feldman, A. F. & Matjasko, J. L. (2005). The role of school-based extracurricular activities in adolescent development: A comprehensive review and future directions. *Review of Educational Research*, 75(2), 159–210. doi.org/10.3102/00346543075002159

Fenker, D. & Schütze, H. (2008, December). Learning by surprise. *Scientific American*. Retrieved from: https://www.scientificamerican.com/article/learning-by-surprise/ [Accessed 13th August 2019]

Finn, J. D. & Zimmer, K. S. (2012). Student engagement: What is it? Why does it matter? In S. L. Christenson, A. L. Reschly & C. Wylie (eds.), *Handbook of Research on Student Engagement* (97–131). New York, NY: Springer Science + Business Media.

Fisher, A. V., Godwin, K. E. & Seltman, H. (2014). Visual environment, attention allocation, and learning in young children: When too much of a good thing may be bad. *Psychological Science*, 25(7), 1362–1370. doi.org/10.1177/0956797614533801

Flavell, J. H. (1979). Metacognition and cognitive monitoring: A new area of cognitive-developmental inquiry. *American Psychologist*, 34(10), 906–911. doi.org/10.1037/0003-066X.34.10.906

Flynn, C. J. & Harris, J. (2016) Motivational diversity among adult minority language learners: Are current theoretical constructs adequate? *Journal of Multilingual and Multicultural Development,* 37(4), 371–384. doi.org/10.1080/01434632.2015.1072204

Fontana, D. (1988). *Psychology for Teachers* (2nd ed). London: Macmillan Education UK.

Forsyth, D. R. (2019). *Group Dynamics* (7th ed). Boston, MA: Cengage.

Frank, C. & Rinvolucri, M. (1991). *Grammar in Action Again: Awareness Activities for Language Learning* (2nd ed). London: Prentice Hall UK.

Fredricks, J. A. (2014). *Eight Myths of Student Disengagement: Creating Classrooms of Deep Learning*. Thousand Oaks, CA: Corwin Press.

Fredricks, J. A., Blumenfeld, P. C. & Paris, A. H. (2004). School engagement: Potential of the concept, state of the evidence. *Review of Educational Research*, 74(1), 59–109. doi.org/10.3102/00346543074001059

Frenzel, A. & Stephens, E. (2013). Emotions. In N. C. Hall & T. Goetz (eds.), *Emotion, Motivation, and Self-Regulation: A Handbook for Teachers* (1–56). Bingley: Emerald.

Fronius, T., Persson, H., Guckenburg, S., Hurley, N. & Petrosino, A. (2016). *Restorative Justice in U.S. Schools: A Research Review*. San Francisco, CA: WestEd.

Fuller, B. Jr. & Marler, L. E. (2009). Change driven by nature: A meta-analytic review of the proactive personality literature. *Journal of Vocational Behavior*, 75(3), 329–345. doi.org/10.1016/j.jvb.2009.05.008

Furrer, C. J., Skinner, E. A. & Pitzer, J. R. (2014). The influence of teacher and peer relationships on students' classroom engagement and everyday motivational resilience. *National Society for the Study of Education*, 113(1), 101–123. Retrieved from: https://www.researchgate.net/publication/248702173_The_Influence_of_Teacher_and_Peer_Relationships_on_Students%27_Classroom_Engagement_and_Everyday_Resilience [Accessed 13th August 2019]

Gagné, R. M., Briggs, L. J. & Wager, W. W. (1974). *Principles of Instructional Design*. New York, NY: Holt, Rinehart & Winston.

Gallup, Inc. (2015). *Gallup Student Poll: Engaged Today — Ready for Tomorrow*. Retrieved from: www.gallup.com/file/services/189863/GSP_2015KeyFindings.pdf [Accessed 13th August 2019]

Gao, X. (2010). *Strategic Language Learning: The Roles of Agency and Context*. Buffalo, NY: Multilingual Matters.

Garrett, J. J. (2011). *The Elements of User Experience: User-Centered Design for the Web and Beyond* (2nd ed). Berkeley, CA: New Riders.

Genesee, F. & Hamayan, E. (2016). *CLIL in Context: Practical Guidance for Educators*. Cambridge: Cambridge University Press.

Gershon, M. (2016). *How to Develop Growth Mindsets in the Classroom*. CreateSpace Independent Publishing Platform.

Gillies, R. M. (2002). The residual effects of cooperative-learning experiences: A two-year follow-up. *The Journal of Educational Research*, 96(1), 15–20. doi.org/10.1080/00220670209598787

Gkonou, C. & Mercer, S. (2017). *Understanding Emotional and Social Intelligence Among English Language Teachers*. London: British Council.

Gollwitzer, P. M. & Oettingen, G. (2012). Goal Pursuit. In R. M. Ryan (ed.), *The Oxford Handbook of Human Motivation*. Oxford: Oxford University Press.

Gonzalez-DeHass, A. R., Willems, P. P. & Holbein, M. F. D. (2005). Examining the relationship between parental involvement and student motivation. *Educational Psychology Review*, 17(2), 99–123. doi.org/10.1007/s10648-005-3949-7

Goodall, J. & Montgomery, C. (2014). Parental involvement to parental engagement: A continuum. *Educational Review*, 66(4), 399–410. doi.org/10.1080/00131911.2013.781576

Gordon, M. (2009). *Roots of Empathy: Changing the World Child by Child.* New York, NY: The Experiment.

Graesser, A. C., Singer, M. & Trabasso, T. (1994). Constructing inferences during narrative text comprehension. *Psychological Review*, 101(3), 371–395. doi.org/10.1037/0033-295X.101.3.371

Gregersen, T. & MacIntyre, P. D. (2014). *Capitalizing on Language Learners' Individuality: From Premise to Practice*. Bristol: Multilingual Matters.

Griffiths, C. (2013). *The Strategy Factor in Successful Language Learning.* Bristol: Multilingual Matters.

Guilford, J. P. (1967). *The Nature of Human Intelligence.* New York, NY: McGraw-Hill.

Guskey, T. R. (2010). Lessons of mastery learning. *Educational Leadership.* Retrieved from: http://www.ascd.org/publications/educational-leadership/oct10/vol68/num02/Lessons-of-Mastery-Learning.aspx [Accessed 13th August 2019]

Hadfield, J. (1992). *Classroom Dynamics*. Oxford: Oxford University Press.

Haidt, J. (2006). *The Happiness Hypothesis: Finding Modern Truth in Ancient Wisdom.* New York, NY: Basic Books.

Harp, S. F. & Mayer, R. E. (1998). How seductive details do their damage: A theory of cognitive interest in science learning. *Journal of Educational Psychology*, 90(3), 414–434. doi.org/10.1037/0022-0663.90.3.414

Harris, B. & Bradshaw, L. (2018). *Battling Boredom Part 2: Even More Strategies to Spark Student Engagement*. New York, NY: Routledge.

Hart, S. & Hodson, V. K. (2004). *The Compassionate Classroom: Relationship-Based Teaching and Learning*. Encinitas, CA: Puddle Dancer Press.

Hattie, J. (2003). Teachers make a difference: What is the research evidence? Paper presented at the *Building Teacher Quality: What Does the Research Tell Us? ACER Research Conference*, Melbourne, Australia. Retrieved from: http://research.acer.edu.au/research_conference_2003/4/ [Accessed 13th August 2019]

Hattie, J. (2009). *Visible Learning: A Synthesis of over 800 Meta-Analyses Relating to Achievement*. London: Routledge.

Hattie, J. & Timperley, H. (2007). The power of feedback. *Review of Educational Research*, 77(1), 81–112. doi.org/10.3102/003465430298487

Hattie, J. & Yates, G. (2014). *Visible Learning and the Science of How We Learn.* London: Routledge.

Hattie, J. & Zierer, K. (2018). *10 Mindframes for Visible Learning: Teaching for Success.* London: Routledge.

Haynes, T. L., Perry, R. P., Stupnisky, R. H. & Daniels, L. M. (2009). A review of attributional retraining treatments: Fostering engagement and persistence in vulnerable college students. In J.C. Smart (ed.), *Higher Education: Handbook of Theory and Research Vol. 24* (227–272). Dordrecht: Springer.

Hazan, C. & Shaver, P. R. (1994). Attachment as an organizational framework for research on close relationships. *Psychological Inquiry,* 5(1), 1–22. doi.org/10.1207/s15327965pli0501_1

Henry, A., Sundqvist, P. & Thorsen, C. (2019). *Motivational Practice: Insights from the Classroom.* Lund, Sweden: Studentliteratur.

Heron, J. (1999). *The Complete Facilitator's Handbook.* London: Kogan Page.

Hersey, P., Blanchard, K. H. & Johnson, D. E. (2008). *Management of Organizational Behavior: Leading Human Resources* (9th ed). Upper Saddle River, NJ: Pearson Prentice Hall.

Hidi, S. (2001). Interest, reading, and learning: Theoretical and practical considerations. *Educational Psychology Review*, 13(3), 191–209. doi.org/10.1023/A:1016667621114

High Quality Project Based Learning. (n.d.). *The HQPBL Framework.* Retrieved from: hqpbl.org/ [Accessed 7th February 2019]

Hill, N. E. & Tyson, D. F. (2009). Parental involvement in middle school: A meta-analytic assessment of the strategies that promote achievement. *Developmental Psychology*, 45(3), 740–763. doi.org/10.1037/a0015362

Hobbes, T. (1985) *Leviathan.* London: Penguin Books.

Hoskins, B., Janmaat, J. G. & Villalba, E. (2012). Learning citizenship through social participation outside and inside school: An international, multilevel study of young people's learning of citizenship. *British Educational Research Journal*, 38(3), 419–446. doi.org/10.1080/01411926.2010.550271

Howe, D. (2013). *Empathy: What It Is and Why It Matters.* Basingstoke: Palgrave Macmillan.

Hüttner, J., Dalton-Puffer, C. & Smit, U. (2013). The power of beliefs: Lay theories and their influence on the implementation of CLIL programmes. *International Journal of Bilingual Education and Bilingualism*, 16(3), 267–284. doi.org/10.1080/13670050.2013.777385

Hyland, K. & Hyland, F. (eds.) (2006). *Feedback in Second Language Writing: Contexts and Issues.* Cambridge: Cambridge University Press.

Immordino-Yang, M. H. & Damasio, A. (2007). We feel, therefore we learn: The relevance of affective and social neuroscience to education. *Mind, Brain, and Education*, 1(1), 3–10. doi.org/10.1111/j.1751-228X.2007.00004.x

Jang, H., Reeve, J. & Deci, E. L. (2010). Engaging students in learning activities: It is not autonomy support or structure but autonomy support and structure. *Journal of Educational Psychology*, 102(3), 588–600. doi.org/10.1037/a0019682

Jeynes, W. H. (2007). The relationship between parental involvement and urban secondary school student academic achievement: A meta-analysis. *Urban Education*, 42(1), 82–110. doi.org/10.1177/0042085906293818

Johnson, D., W. & Johnson, F. P. (2017). *Joining Together: Group Theory and Group Skills* (12th ed). New York: Pearson.

Juliani, A. J. (2015). *Inquiry and Innovation in the Classroom: Using 20% Time, Genius Hour, and PBL to Drive Student Success*. New York, NY: Routledge.

Juvonen, J., Espinoza, G. & Knifsend, C. (2012). The role of peer relationships in student academic and extracurricular engagement. In S. L. Christenson, A. L. Reschly & C. Wylie (eds.), *Handbook of Research on Student Engagement* (387–401). New York, NY: Springer Science + Business Media.

Kalaja, P., Alanen, R., Palviainen, Å. & Dufva, H. (2011). From milk cartons to English roommates: Context and agency in L2 learning beyond the classroom. In P. Benson & H. Reinders (eds.), *Beyond the Language Classroom* (47–58). Basingstoke: Palgrave Macmillan.

Kapp, K. M. (2012). *The Gamification of Learning and Instruction: Game-Based Methods and Strategies for Training and Education*. San Francisco, CA: Pfeiffer.

Kato, S. & Mynard, J. (2016). *Reflective Dialogue: Advising in Language Learning*. New York, NY: Routledge.

Keller, J. M. (1983). Motivational design of instruction. In C. Reigeluth (ed.), *Instructional-design Theories and Models: An Overview of Their Current Status* (383–434). Hillsdale, NJ: Erlbaum.

Keller, J. M. (2010). *Motivational Design for Learning and Performance: The ARCS Model Approach*. New York, NY: Springer Science + Business Media.

Kessels, U., Heyder, A., Latsch, M. & Hannover, B. (2014). How gender differences in academic engagement relate to students' gender identity. *Educational Research*, 56(2), 220–229. doi.org/10.1080/00131881.2014.898916

King, H. & King, W. (2018). *The Wild Card: 7 Steps to an Educator's Creative Breakthrough*. San Francisco, CA: Dave Burgess Consulting, Inc.

Klusmann, U., Kunter, M., Trautwein, U., Lüdtke, O. & Baumert, J. (2008). Teachers' occupational well-being and quality of instruction: The important role of self-regulatory patterns. *Journal of Educational Psychology*, 100(3), 702–715. doi.org/10.1037/0022-0663.100.3.702

Knight, J. (2016). *Better Conversations: Coaching Ourselves and Each Other to be More Credible, Caring, and Connected.* Thousand Oaks, CA: Corwin Press.

Knogler, M. (2017). Situational interest: A proposal to enhance conceptual clarity. In P. A. O'Keefe & J. M. Harackiewicz (eds.), *The Science of Interest* (109–124). Cham: Springer.

Kohn, A. (1999). *Punished by Rewards: The Trouble with Gold Stars, Incentive Plans, A's, Praise, and Other Bribes*. Boston, MA: Houghton Mifflin Co.

Kohn, A. (2006). *Beyond Discipline: From Compliance to Community.* Alexandria, VA: ASCD.

Kohn, A. (2013). The roots of grades-and-tests. In J. Bower & P. L. Thomas (eds.), *De-testing and De-grading schools: Authentic Alternatives to Accountability and Standardization* (1–4). New York, NY: Peter Lang.

Kort-Butler, L. A. & Hagewen, K. J. (2011). School-based extracurricular activity involvement and adolescent self-esteem: A growth-curve analysis. *Journal of Youth and Adolescence*, 40(5), 568–581. doi.org/10.1007/s10964-010-9551-4

Kouzes, J. M. & Posner, B. Z. (2004). The five practices of exemplary leadership. In J. M. Kouzes & B. Z. Posner (eds.), *Christian Reflections on the Leadership Challenge* (7–38). San Francisco, CA: Jossey-Bass.

Kraft, T. L. & Pressman, S. D. (2012). Grin and bear it: The influence of manipulated facial expression on the stress response. *Psychological Science,* 23(11), 1372–1378. doi.org/10.1177/0956797612445312

Ladd, G. W., Herald-Brown, S. L. & Kochel, K. (2009). Peers and motivation. In K. R. Wenzel & A. Wigfield (eds.), *Educational Psychology Handbook Series. Handbook of Motivation at School* (323–348). New York, NY: Routledge, Taylor & Francis Group.

Lannutti, P. & Strauman, E. (2006). Classroom communication: The influence of instructor self-disclosure on student evaluations. *Communication Quarterly*, 54(1), 89–99. doi.org/10.1080/01463370500270496

Lanvers, U., Doughty, H. & Thompson, A. S. (2018). Brexit as linguistic symptom of Britain retreating into its shell? Brexit-induced politicization of language learning. *The Modern Language Journal,* 102(4), 775–796. doi.org/10.1111/modl.12515

Larmer, J., Mergendoller, J. R. & Boss, S. (2015). *Setting the Standard for Project-Based Learning: A Proven Approach to Rigorous Classroom Instruction*. Alexandria, VA: ASCD.

Larsen-Freeman, D. (2012). Complex, dynamic systems: A new transdisciplinary theme for applied linguistics? *Language Teaching,* 45(2), 202–214. doi.org/10.1017/S0261444811000061

Larson, R. W. & Richards, M. H. (1991). Boredom in the middle school years: Blaming schools versus blaming students. *American Journal of Education*, 99(4), 418–443. doi.org/10.1086/443992

Lasagabaster, D. (2011). English achievement and student motivation in CLIL and EFL settings. *Innovation in Language Learning and Teaching*, 5(1), 3–18. doi.org/10.1080/17501229.2010.519030

Lee, J. (2002). Racial and ethnic achievement gap trends: Reversing the progress toward equity? *Educational Researcher*, 31(1), 3–12. doi.org/10.3102/0013189X031001003

Lemov, D. (2015). *Teach Like a Champion 2.0: 62 Techniques that put Students on the Path to College* (2nd ed). San Francisco, CA: Jossey-Bass.

Leslie, I. (2014). *Curious: The Desire to Know and Why your Future Depends on it*. New York, NY: Basic Books.

Lewin, K. (1947). Frontiers in group dynamics: Concept, method and reality in social science; social equilibria and social change. *Human Relations*, 1(1), 5–41. doi.org/10.1177/001872674700100103

Lewin, K., Lippitt, R. & White, R. K. (1939). Patterns of aggressive behavior in experimentally created 'social climates'. *The Journal of Social Psychology*, 10(2), 269–299. doi.org/10.1080/00224545.1939.9713366

Linley, A. (2008). *Average to A+: Realising Strengths in Yourself and Others*. Coventry: CAPP Press.

Linnenbrink, E. A. & Pintrich, P. R. (2003). The role of self-efficacy beliefs in student engagement and learning in the classroom. *Reading & Writing Quarterly*, 19(2), 119–137. doi.org/10.1080/10573560308223

Livio, M. (2017). *Why?: What Makes Us Curious*. New York, NY: Simon & Schuster.

Loewenstein, G. (1994). The psychology of curiosity: A review and reinterpretation. *Psychological Bulletin*, 116(1), 75–98. doi.org/10.1037/0033-2909.116.1.75

Lucas, B. & Claxton, G. (2010). *New Kinds of Smart: How the Science of Learnable Intelligence is Changing Education*. Maidenhead: Open University Press.

Luiselli, J. K., Putnam, R. F., Handler, M. W. & Feinberg, A. B. (2005). Whole-school positive behaviour support: Effects on student discipline problems and academic performance. *Educational Psychology*, 25(2–3), 183–198. doi.org/10.1080/0144341042000301265

Luna, T. & Renninger, L. (2015). *Surprise: Embrace the Unpredictable and Engineer the Unexpected*. New York, NY: Perigee Trade.

Lynch, A. D., Lerner, R. M. & Leventhal, T. (2013). Adolescent academic achievement and school engagement: An examination of the role of school-wide peer culture. *Journal of Youth and Adolescence*, 42(1), 6–19. doi.org/10.1007/s10964-012-9833-0

MacIntyre, P. D., Gregersen, T. & Mercer, S. (eds.). (2016). *Positive Psychology in SLA*. Bristol: Multilingual Matters.

Macklem, G. L. (2015). *Boredom in the Classroom: Addressing Student Motivation, Self-Regulation, and Engagement in Learning*. Cham: Springer.

Maley, A. (2011). Squaring the circle - reconciling materials as constraint with materials as empowerment. In B. Tomlinson (ed.), *Materials Development in Language Teaching* (2nd ed) (379–402). Cambridge: Cambridge University Press.

Mann, S. (2016). *The Science of Boredom: The Upside (and Downside) of Downtime*. London: Robinson.

Marzano, R. J., Marzano, J. S. & Pickering, D. (2003). *Classroom Management that Works: Research-Based Strategies for Every Teacher*. Alexandria, VA: ASCD.

McAdams, D. P. (1993). *The Stories We Live By: Personal Myths and the Making of the Self*. New York, NY: The Guildford Press.

McCombs, B. L. & Miller, L. (2007). *Learner-Centered Classroom Practices and Assessments: Maximizing Student Motivation, Learning, and Achievement*. Thousand Oaks, CA: Corwin Press.

McCombs, B. L. & Whisler, J. S. (1997). *The Learner-Centered Classroom and School: Strategies for Increasing Student Motivation and Achievement*. San Francisco, CA: Jossey-Bass.

Mccrea, P. (2017). *Memorable Teaching*. CreateSpace.

McDonough, J., Shaw, C. & Masuhara, H. (2013). *Materials and Methods in ELT: A Teacher's Guide*. Chichester: John Wiley & Sons.

McDrury, J. & Alterio, M. (2003). *Learning Through Storytelling in Higher Education: Using Reflection and Experience to Improve Learning*. London: Kogan Page.

McGrath, I. (2006). Teachers' and learners' images for coursebooks. *ELT Journal*, 60(2), 171–180. doi.org/10.1093/elt/cci104

McKay, S. L. & Rubdy, R. (2009). The social and sociolinguistic contexts of language learning and teaching. In M. H. Long & C. J. Doughty (eds.), *The Handbook of Language Teaching* (7–25). Oxford: Wiley-Blackwell.

McLaughlin, C. & Clarke, B. (2010). Relational matters: A review of the impact of school experience on mental health in early adolescence. *Educational and Child Psychology*, 27(1), 91–103.

McLoughlin, C. & Lee, M. J. W. (2010). Personalised and self-regulated learning in the Web 2.0 era: International exemplars of innovative pedagogy using social software. *Australasian Journal of Educational Technology*, 26(1), 28–43. doi.org/10.14742/ajet.1100

Mercer, S. (2005). Vocabulary strategy work for advanced learners of English. *English Teaching Forum*, 43(2), 24–35. Retrieved from: https://americanenglish.state.gov/resources/english-teaching-forum-2005-volume-43-number-2 [Accessed 16th November 2019]

Mercer, S. (2011). *Towards an Understanding of Language Learner Self-Concept*. Dordrecht: Springer Science + Business Media.

Mercer, S. (2012). Dispelling the myth of the natural-born linguist. *ELT Journal*, 66(1), 22–29. doi.org/10.1093/elt/ccr022

Mercer, S. (2013). Working with language learner histories from three perspectives: Teachers, learners and researchers. *Studies in Second Language Learning and Teaching*, 3(2), 161–185. doi.org/10.14746/ssllt.2013.3.2.2

Mercer, S., Ryan, S. & Williams, M. (eds.). (2012). *Psychology for Language Learning*. London: Palgrave Macmillan UK.

Mercer, S. & Schumm, J. (2009). Learner-generated criteria for evaluating writing. In R. Vaupetitsch, N. Campbell, S. Mercer, M. Reitbauer & J. Schumm (eds.), *The Materials Generator: Developing Innovative Materials for Advanced Language Production* (31–36). Frankfurt: Peter Lang.

Merrell, K. W. & Gueldner, B. A. (2010). *Social and Emotional Learning in the Classroom: Promoting Mental Health and Academic Success*. New York, NY: The Guildford Press.

Mifsud, M. (2011). *The Relationship of Teachers' and Students' Motivation in ELT in Malta: A Mixed Methods Study*. PhD. University of Nottingham. Retrieved from: http://eprints.nottingham.ac.uk/12983/1/555348.pdf [Accessed 13th August 2019]

Mischel, W. (2014). *The Marshmallow Test: Understanding Self-Control and How to Master It*. New York, NY: Little, Brown and Company.

Mo, Y. & Singh, K. (2008). Parents' relationships and involvement: Effects on students' school engagement and performance. *RMLE Online*, 31(10), 1–11. doi.org/10.1080/19404476.2008.11462053

Mora, R. (2011). 'School is so boring': High-stakes testing and boredom at an urban middle school. *PennGSE Perspectives on Urban Education*, 9(1), 1–9. Retrieved from: https://www.urbanedjournal.org/archive/volume-9-issue-1-fall-2011/school-so-boring-high-stakes-testing-and-boredom-urban-middle-sch [Accessed August 14th 2019]

Mueller, C. M. & Dweck, C. S. (1998). Praise for intelligence can undermine children's motivation and performance. *Journal of Personality and Social Psychology*, 75(1), 33–52. doi.org/10.1037/0022-3514.75.1.33

Muir, C. (in press). *Sustained Motivation in the Language Classroom: Inspiring Strong Motivational Currents Through Projects.* Bristol: Multilingual Matters.

Murphey, T. & Arao, H. (2001). Reported belief changes through near peer role modeling. *TESL-EJ* 5(3), 1–15. Retrieved from: http://www.tesl-ej.org/wordpress/issues/volume5/ej19/ej19a1/ [Accessed 16th November 2019]

Murray, G. (ed.). (2014). *Social Dimensions of Autonomy in Language Learning*. London: Palgrave Macmillan UK.

NAIS. (2017). *NAIS Report on the 2016 High School Survey of Student Engagement*. Washington, DC: NAIS. Retrieved from: https://www.fcis.org/uploaded/Data_Reports/2016-HSSSE_Final_1.pdf [Accessed 13th August 2019]

Nakamura, S. (2016). *Willingness to Communicate in L2 Writing: An Exploratory Study of Japanese EFL learners' Writing Development*. Presented at the Psychology for Language Learning II (PLLT), Jyväskylä, Finland.

Nassaji, H. & Kartchava, E. (eds.) (2017). *Corrective Feedback in Second Language Teaching and Learning: Research, Theory, Applications, Implications*. New York, NY: Routledge.

Nicol, D. (2010). From monologue to dialogue: Improving written feedback processes in mass higher education. *Assessment & Evaluation in Higher Education*, 35(5), 501–517. doi.org/10.1080/02602931003786559

Nunan, D. (1988). *The Learner-Centred Curriculum*. Cambridge: Cambridge University Press.

Nunan, D. (2004). *Task-Based Language Teaching*. Cambridge: Cambridge University Press.

Nunan, D. (2014). Plenary presentation. *International Conference on Japanese Language Education*.

Nunan, D. & Richards, J. C. (eds.). (2015). *Language Learning Beyond the Classroom*. New York, NY: Routledge.

Ofsted (2013). *Redhill Academy School Report*. Retrieved from: https://files.api.ofsted.gov.uk/v1/file/2206915 [Accessed 13th August 2019]

Olsen, R. E. W.-B. & Kagan, S. (1992). About cooperative learning. In C. Kessler (ed.), *Cooperative Language Learning: A Teacher's Resource Book* (1–30). Englewood Cliffs, NJ: Prentice Hall Regents.

Ortega, L., Lyubansky, M., Nettles, S. & Espelage, D. L. (2016). Outcomes of a restorative circles program in a high school setting. *Psychology of Violence*, 6(3), 459–468. doi.org/10.1037/vio0000048

Orthner, D. K., Jones-Sanpei, H., Akos, P. & Rose, R. A. (2013). Improving middle school student engagement through career-relevant instruction in the core curriculum. *The Journal of Educational Research*, 106(1), 27–38. doi.org/10.1080/00220671.2012.658454

Osterman, K. F. (2000). Students' need for belonging in the school community. *Review of Educational Research*, 70(3), 323–367. doi.org/10.3102/00346543070003323

Oxford, R. L. (2011). Strategies for learning a second or foreign language. *Language Teaching*, 44(02), 167–180. doi.org/10.1017/S0261444810000492

Oxford, R. L. (2017). *Teaching and Researching Language Learning Strategies: Self-Regulation in Context* (2nd ed). London: Routledge.

Park, J.-H. & Choi, H. J. (2009). Factors influencing adult learners' decision to drop out or persist in online learning. *Journal of Educational Technology & Society*, 12(4), 207–217. Retrieved from: https://www.learntechlib.org/p/74987/ [Accessed 13th August 2019]

Park, S. & Lim, J. (2007). Promoting positive emotion in multimedia learning using visual illustrations. *Journal of Educational Multimedia and Hypermedia*, 16(2), 141–162. Retrieved from: https://www.learntechlib.org/primary/p/21781/ [Accessed 13th August 2019]

Parker, S. K. & Wu, C. (2014). Leading for proactivity: How leaders cultivate staff who make things happen. In D. Day (ed.), *The Oxford Handbook of Leadership and Organizations* (380–406). New York, NY: Oxford University Press.

Patrick, H., Knee, C. R., Canevello, A. & Lonsbary, C. (2007). The role of need fulfillment in relationship functioning and well-being: A self-determination theory perspective. *Journal of Personality and Social Psychology*, 92(3), 434–457. doi.org/10.1037/0022-3514.92.3.434

Pekrun, R., Goetz, T., Daniels, L. M., Stupnisky, R. H. & Perry, R. P. (2010). Boredom in achievement settings: Exploring control–value antecedents and performance outcomes of a neglected emotion. *Journal of Educational Psychology*, 102(3), 531–549. doi.org/10.1037/a0019243

Pekrun, R., Goetz, T., Titz, W. & Perry, R. (2002). Academic emotions in students' self-regulated learning and achievement: A program of qualitative and quantitative research. *Educational Psychologist*, 37(2), 91–105. doi.org/10.1207/S15326985EP3702_4

Pennycook, A. (2017). *The Cultural Politics of English as an International Language.* Abingdon: Routledge.

Petty, G. (2014). *Teaching Today: A Practical Guide* (5th Ed). Oxford: Oxford University Press.

Pham, T. H. N. (2019). *The impact of English-for-teaching training in Vietnam.* Presented at IATEFL 2019, Liverpool.

Philp, J. & Duchesne, S. (2016). Exploring engagement in tasks in the language classroom. *Annual Review of Applied Linguistics,* 36, 50–72. doi.org/10.1017/S0267190515000094

Pintrich, P. R. & De Groot, E. V. (1990). Motivational and self-regulated learning components of classroom academic performance. *Journal of Educational Psychology*, 82(1), 33–40. doi.org/10.1037/0022-0663.82.1.33

Pomerantz, E. M., Grolnick, W. S. & Price, C. E. (2007) The role of parents in how children approach achievement. In A. J. Elliot & C. S. Dweck (eds.), *Handbook of Competence and Motivation* (259–278). New York, NY: The Guilford Press.

Posey, A. (2019). *Engage the Brain: How to Design for Learning that Taps into the Power of Emotion*. Alexandria, VA: ASCD.

Puchta, H. & Williams, M. (2011). *Teaching Young Learners to Think.* Innsbruck: Helbling Languages.

Quigley, A. (2016). *The Confident Teacher: Developing Successful Habits of Mind, Body and Pedagogy.* Abingdon: Routledge.

Quint Oga-Baldwin, W. L. & Nakata, Y. (2017). Engagement, gender and motivation: A predictive model for Japanese young language learners. *System,* 65, 151–163. doi.org/10.1016/j.system.2017.01.011

Raffini, J. P. (1996). *150 Ways to Increase Intrinsic Motivation in the Classroom.* Boston, MA: Allyn and Bacon.

Ratey, J. J. & Hagerman, E. (2009). *Spark! The Revolutionary New Science of Exercise and the Brain.* London: Quercus.

Redhill Academy (n.d.) *The Redhill Academy Pledge System.* Retrieved from: https://www.theredhillacademy.org.uk/mod/resource/view.php?id=13781 [Accessed 13th August 2019]

Reeve, J. (2006). Teachers as facilitators: What autonomy-supportive teachers do and why their students benefit. *The Elementary School Journal,* 106(3), 225–236. doi.org/10.1086/501484

Reeve, J. (2012). A self-determination theory perspective on student engagement. In S. L. Christenson, A. L. Reschly & C. Wylie (eds.), *Handbook of Research on Student Engagement* (149–172). New York, NY: Springer Science + Business Media.

Reeve, J. & Tseng, C.-M. (2011). Agency as a fourth aspect of students' engagement during learning activities. *Contemporary Educational Psychology,* 36(4), 257–267. doi.org/10.1016/j.cedpsych.2011.05.002

Renninger, K. A. & Hidi, S. (2016). *The Power of Interest for Motivation and Engagement.* New York, NY: Routledge.

Ricci, M. C. (2017). *Mindsets in the Classroom: Building a Culture of Success and Student Achievement in Schools* (Updated Ed). Waco, TX: Prufrock Press.

Rigby, S. & Ryan, R. M. (2011). *Glued to Games: How Video Games Draw us in and Hold us Spellbound.* Santa Barbara, CA: Praeger.

Ripley, A. (2013). *The Smartest Kids in the World: And How They Got That Way.* New York, NY: Simon & Schuster.

Robinson, K. (2013). How to escape education's Death Valley. *TED.* Retrieved from: https://www.ted.com/talks/ken_robinson_how_to_escape_education_s_death_valley?language=en [Accessed 13th August 2019]

Roffey, S. (2011). *Changing Behaviour in Schools: Promoting Positive Relationships and Wellbeing.* London: SAGE.

Rogers, B. (2007). *Behaviour Management: A Whole-School Approach* (2nd ed). London: Paul Chapman.

Rogers, C. R. (1983). *Freedom to Learn for the 80's* (2nd Rev. ed). Columbus, OH: C.E. Merrill Pub. Co.

Rothwell, J. (2011). Bodies and language: Process drama and intercultural language learning in a beginner language classroom. *Research in Drama Education: The Journal of Applied Theatre and Performance*, 16(4), 575–594. doi.org/10.1080/13569783.2011.617106

Rubie-Davies, C. (2015). *Becoming a High Expectation Teacher: Raising the Bar*. Abingdon: Routledge.

Russell, V. & Riley, T. (2011). Personalising learning in secondary schools: Gifted education leading the way. *APEX*, 16(1), 1–9. doi.org/10.21307/apex-2011-005

Ryan, R. M. & Deci, E. L. (2000). Self-determination theory and the facilitation of intrinsic motivation, social development, and well-being. *American Psychologist*, 55(1), 68–78. doi.org/10.1037//0003-066X.55.1.68

Ryan, R. M. & Deci, E. L. (2017). *Self-Determination Theory: Basic Psychological Needs in Motivation, Development, and Wellness*. New York, NY: Guilford Press.

Sahlberg, P. (2015). *Finnish Lessons 2.0*. New York, NY: Teachers College Press.

Schlechty, P. C. (2011). *Engaging Students: The Next Level of Working on the Work*. San Francisco, CA: Jossey-Bass.

Schmuck, R. A. & Schmuck, P. A. (2001). *Group Processes in the Classroom* (8th ed). Boston, MA: McGraw Hill.

Schommer, M. (1990). Effects of beliefs about the nature of knowledge on comprehension. *Journal of Educational Psychology*, 82(3), 498–504. doi.org/10.1037/0022-0663.82.3.498

Schraw, G., Flowerday, T. & Lehman, S. (2001). Increasing situational interest in the classroom. *Educational Psychology Review*, 13(3), 211–224. doi.org/10.1023/A:1016619705184

Scrivener, J. (2012). *Classroom Management Techniques*. Cambridge: Cambridge University Press.

Sheldon, L. (2012). *The Multiplayer Classroom: Designing Coursework as a Game*. Boston, MA: Course Technology / Cengage Learning.

Shernoff, D. J. (2013). *Optimal Learning Environments to Promote Student Engagement*. New York, NY: Springer Science + Business Media.

Shernoff, D. J., Csikszentmihalyi, M., Schneider, B. & Shernoff, E. S. (2003). Student engagement in high school classrooms from the perspective of flow theory. *School Psychology Quarterly,* 18(2), 158–176. doi.org/10.1521/scpq.18.2.158.21860

Shindler, J. (2010). *Transformative Classroom Management: Positive Strategies to Engage All Students and Promote a Psychology of Success*. San Francisco, CA: Jossey-Bass.

Shrum, J. L. (1984). Wait-time and student performance level in second language classrooms. *The Journal of Classroom Interaction*, 20(1), 29–35.

Retrieved from: https://www.jstor.org/stable/43997866 [Accessed 13th August 2019]

Shrum, J. L. (1985). Wait-time and the use of target or native languages. *Foreign Language Annals*, 18(4), 305–314. doi.org/10.1111/j.1944-9720.1985.tb01808.x

Silvia, P. J. (2017). Curiosity. In P. A. O'Keefe & J. M. Harackiewicz (eds.), *The Science of Interest* (97–107). Cham: Springer.

Simons, D. J. & Chabris, C. F. (1999). Gorillas in our midst: Sustained inattentional blindness for dynamic events. *Perception*, 28(9), 1059–1074. doi.org/10.1068/p281059

Sinatra, G. M., Heddy, B. C. & Lombardi, D. (2015). The challenges of defining and measuring student engagement in science. *Educational Psychologist*, 50(1), 1–13. doi.org/10.1080/00461520.2014.1002924

Skinner, E. A. & Belmont, M. J. (1993). Motivation in the classroom: Reciprocal effects of teacher behavior and student engagement across the school year. *Journal of Educational Psychology*, 85(4), 571–581. doi.org/10.1037/0022-0663.85.4.571

Skinner, E., Furrer, C., Marchand, G. & Kindermann, T. (2008). Engagement and disaffection in the classroom: Part of a larger motivational dynamic? *Journal of Educational Psychology*, 100(4), 765–781. doi.org/10.1037/a0012840

Smith, M. (2018). *The Emotional Learner: Understanding Emotions, Learners and Achievement*. Abingdon: Routledge.

Smith, L. & King, J. (2017). A dynamic systems approach to wait time in the second language classroom. *System*, 68, 1–14. doi.org/10.1016/j.system.2017.05.005

Snyder, B. & Alperer-Tatli, S. (2007). Classroom practice: Learner engagement. In J. Egbert & E. Hanson-Smith (eds.), *CALL Environments*, (349–361). Alexandria, VA: TESOL.

Stambor, Z. (2006). *How Laughing Leads to Learning*. American Psychological Association. Retrieved from: https://www.apa.org/monitor/jun06/learning [Accessed 13th August 2019]

Steinwidder, S. (2016). EFL learners' post-sojourn perceptions of the effects of study abroad. *Comparative and International Education / Éducation Comparée et Internationale*, 45(2). Retrieved from: ir.lib.uwo.ca/cie-eci/vol45/iss2/5 [Accessed 13th August 2019]

Stepp-Greany, J. (2002). Student perceptions on language learning in a technological environment: Implications for the new millennium. *Language Learning & Technology*, 6(1), 165–180. dx.doi.org/10125/25148

Stroud, R. (2017). The impact of task performance scoring and tacking on second language engagement. *System*, 69, 121–132. doi.org/10.1016/j.system.2017.07.002

Subotnik, R. F., Olszewski-Kubilius, P. & Worrell, F. C. (2012). A proposed direction forward for gifted education based on psychological science. *Gifted Child Quarterly*, 56(4), 176–188. doi.org/10.1177/0016986212456079

Summerhill School (n.d.) Summerhill School homepage. Retrieved from: http://www.summerhillschool.co.uk/ [Accessed 13th August 2019]

Svalberg, A. M.-L. (2009). Engagement with language: Interrogating a construct. *Language Awareness,* 18(3–4), 242–258. doi.org/10.1080/09658410903197264

Svalberg, A. M.-L. (2018). Researching language engagement: Current trends and future directions. *Language Awareness,* 27(1–2), 21–39. doi.org/10.1080/09658416.2017.1406490

Talbot, K. & Mercer, S. (2018). Exploring university ESL/EFL teachers' emotional well-being and emotional regulation in the United States, Japan and Austria. *Chinese Journal of Applied Linguistics*, 41(4), 410–432. doi.org/10.1515/cjal-2018-0031

Thalheimer, W. (2004). Bells, whistles, neon, and purple prose: When interesting words, sounds, and visuals hurt learning and performance—a review of the seductive-augmentation research. *Work-Learning.* Retrieved from: https://www.worklearning.com/wp-content/uploads/2017/10/Review_Seductive_Augmentations_2009.pdf [Accessed 13th August 2019]

Tin, T. B. (2016). *Stimulating Student Interest in Language Learning: Theory, Research and Practice*. London: Palgrave Macmillan UK.

Tinsley, T. & Board, K. (2017). *Languages for the Future*. London: British Council.

Tobin, K. (1987). The role of wait time in higher cognitive level learning. *Review of Educational Research,* 57(1), 69–95. doi.org/10.3102/00346543057001069

Tomlinson, B. (2012). Materials development for language learning and teaching. *Language Teaching,* 45(2), 143–179. doi.org/10.1017/S0261444811000528

Tomlinson, C. A. (2011). One to grow on / Respecting students. *Educational Leadership,* 69(1), 94–95. Retrieved from: http://www.ascd.org/publications/educational-leadership/sept11/vol69/num01/Respecting-Students.aspx [Accessed 13th August 2019]

Toward, G., Henley, C. & Cope, A. (2015). *The Art of Being a Brilliant Teacher*. Carmarthen: Crown House Publishing.

Tschannen-Moran, M. (2014). *Trust Matters: Leadership for Successful Schools* (2nd ed). San Francisco, CA: Jossey-Bass.

Tsou, W., Wang, W. & Tzeng, Y. (2006). Applying a multimedia storytelling website in foreign language learning. *Computers & Education,* 47(1), 17–28. doi.org/10.1016/j.compedu.2004.08.013

Tyler, S. W., Hertel, P. T., McCallum, M. C. & Ellis, H. C. (1979). Cognitive effort and memory. *Journal of Experimental Psychology: Human Learning & Memory*, 5(6), 607–617. doi.org/10.1037/0278-7393.5.6.607

UNHCR, (n.d.). *Letters of Love*. Retrieved from: www.unhcr.org/withrefugees/send-message-refugee-children-letters-love/ [Accessed 7th February 2019]

VanDeWeghe, R. (2009). *Engaged Learning*. Thousand Oaks, CA: Corwin Press.

Verspoor, M., de Bot, K. & Lowie, W. (eds.). (2011). *A Dynamic Approach to Second Language Development: Methods and Techniques*. Amsterdam: John Benjamins Publishing.

Vygotsky, L. S. (1978). *Mind in Society: The Development of Higher Psychological Processes*. Cambridge, MA: Harvard University Press.

Wallace, I. & Kirkman, L. (2014). *Talk-Less Teaching: Practice, Participation and Progress*. Carmarthen: Crown House Publishing.

Walsh, J. A. & Sattes, B. D. (2011). *Thinking Through Quality Questioning: Deepening Student Engagement*. Thousand Oaks, CA: Corwin Press.

Wang, S. & Vasquez, C. (2012). Web 2.0 and second language learning: What does the research tell us? *CALICO Journal*, 29(3), 412–430. doi.org/10.11139/cj.29.3.412-430

Wang, Z., Zhang, J., Thomas, C. L., Yu, J. & Spitzmueller, C. (2017). Explaining benefits of employee proactive personality: The role of engagement, team proactivity composition and perceived organizational support. *Journal of Vocational Behavior*, 101, 90–103. doi.org/10.1016/j.jvb.2017.04.002

Wanzer, M. B., Frymier, A. B. & Irwin, J. (2010). An explanation of the relationship between instructor humor and student learning: Instructional humor processing theory. *Communication Education*, 59(1), 1–18. doi.org/10.1080/03634520903367238

Weiner, B. (1992). *Human Motivation: Metaphors, Theories, and Research.* Thousand Oaks, CA: SAGE.

Weinstein, R. (2002). *Reaching Higher: The Power of Expectations in Schooling*. Cambridge, MA: Harvard University Press.

Wentzel, K. R. (1997). Student motivation in middle school: The role of perceived pedagogical caring. *Journal of Educational Psychology*, 89(3), 411–419. doi.org/10.1037/0022-0663.89.3.411

Wentzel, K. R. (2009). Students' relationships with teachers as motivational contexts. In K. R. Wentzel & A. Wigfield (eds.), *Handbook of Motivation at School* (301–322). New York, NY: Routledge.

White, K. R. (1982). The relation between socioeconomic status and academic achievement. *Psychological Bulletin*, 91(3), 461–481. doi.org/10.1037/0033-2909.91.3.461

Whitmore, J. (2017). *Coaching for Performance: The Principles and Practice of Coaching and Leadership* (5th ed). London: Nicholas Brealey Publishing.

Wigfield, A. & Eccles, J. S. (2000). Expectancy-value theory of achievement motivation. *Contemporary Educational Psychology,* 25(1), 68–81. doi.org/10.1006/ceps.1999.1015

Wilden, S. (2017). *Mobile Learning.* Oxford: Oxford University Press.

Williams, M., Burden, R. & Lanvers, U. (2002). 'French is the language of love and stuff': Student perceptions of issues related to motivation in learning a foreign language. *British Educational Research Journal,* 28(4), 503-528. doi.org/10.1080/0141192022000005805

Williams, M., Mercer, S. & Ryan, S. (2015). *Exploring Psychology in Language Learning and Teaching.* Oxford: Oxford University Press.

Williams, M., Puchta, H. & Mercer, S. (in press). *Psychology in Practice.* Innsbruck: Helbling.

Willis, D. & Willis, J. R. (2007). *Doing Task-Based Teaching.* Oxford: Oxford University Press.

Wilson, G. L. (2002). *Groups in Context: Leadership and Participation in Small Groups.* Boston, MA: McGraw-Hill.

Winsborough, D. (2017). *Fusion: The Psychology of Teams.* Tulsa, OK: Hogan Press.

Wright, A. (2008). *Storytelling with Children* (2nd ed). Oxford: Oxford University Press.

Wright, T. (2005). *Classroom Management in Language Education.* Basingstoke: Palgrave Macmillan.

Xenikou, A. & Furnham, A. (2013). *Group Dynamics and Organizational Culture: Effective Work Groups and Organizations.* Basingstoke: Palgrave Macmillan.

Zahran, K. A. H. (2005). *Contact, Acculturation and Fluency: The Case of International Students in the University of Nottingham.* PhD. University of Nottingham.

Zimmerman, B. J. & Cleary, T. J. (2009). Motives to self-regulate learning: A social cognitive account. In K. R. Wentzel & A. Wigfield (eds.), *Handbook of Motivation at School* (247–264). Abingdon: Routledge.

Zimmerman, B. J. & Dibenedetto, M. K. (2008). Mastery learning and assessment: Implications for students and teachers in an era of high-stakes testing. *Psychology in the Schools*, 45(3), 206–216. doi.org/10.1002/pits.20291

Index